D1346025

The History of Reading, Volume 1

Other publications by Palgrave Macmillan in association with the Institute of English Studies

Brycchan Carey et al. (eds.), *Discourses of Slavery and Abolition: Britain and Its Colonies, 1760–1838*

Gail Marshall and Adrian Poole (eds.) *Victorian Shakespeare*, Vol. 1: *Theatre, Drama and Performance*, Vol. 2: *Literature and Culture*

Andrew Nash (ed.), *The Culture of Collected Editions*

Jerome McGann, *Radiant Textuality: Literary Study after the World Wide Web*

Elizabeth James (ed.), *Macmillan: A Publishing Tradition*

Elizabeth Maslen, *Political and Social Issues in British Women's Fiction, 1928–1968*

Angelique Richardson and Chris Willis (eds.), *The New Woman in Fiction and Fact: Fin-de-Siècle Feminisms*

Warren Chernaik, Martin Swales and Robert Vilain (eds.), *The Art of Detective Fiction*

Rebecca D'Monte and Nicole Pohl (eds.), *Female Communities 1600–1800*

Isobel Armstrong and Virginia Blain (eds.), *Women's Poetry in the Enlightenment: The Making of a Canon, 1730–1820*

Isobel Armstrong and Virginia Blain (eds.), *Women's Poetry, Late Romantic to Late Victorian: Gender and Genre, 1830–1900*

Warren Chernaik and Martin Dzelzainis (eds.), *Marvell and Liberty* (July 1999)

Andy Leak and George Paizis (eds.), *The Holocaust and the Text: Speaking the Unspeakable*

Warwick Gould and Thomas F. Staley (eds.), *Writing the Lives of Writers*

Ian Willison, Warwick Gould and Warren Chernaik (eds.), *Modernist Writers and the Marketplace* (1996)

John Spiers (ed.), *George Gissing and the City: Cultural Crisis and the Making of Books in Late Victorian England*

Mary Hammond and Shafquat Towheed (eds.), *Publishing in the First World War* (2007)

Mary Hammond and Robert Fraser (eds.), *Books without Borders, Volume 1: The Cross-National Dimension in Print Culture* (2008), *Books without Borders, Volume 2: Perspectives from South Asia* (2008)

Gina Potts and Lisa Shahriari (eds.), *Virginia Woolf's Bloomsbury, Volume 1: Aesthetic Theory and Literary Practice* (2010), *Virginia Woolf's Bloomsbury, Volume 2: International Influence and Politics* (2010)

Robert J. Balfour (ed.), *Culture, Capital and Representation* (2010)

John Spiers (ed.), *The Culture of the Publisher's Series, Volume 1: Authors, Publishers and the Shaping of Taste* (2011), *The Culture of the Publisher's Series, Volume 2:* (2011)

Shafquat Towheed and W. R. Owens (eds.), *The History of Reading, Volume 1: International Perspectives, c.1500–1990*. Katie Halsey and W. R. Owens (eds.), *The History of Reading, Volume 2: Evidence from the British Isles, c.1750–1950*. Rosalind Crone and Shafquat Towheed (eds.), *The History of Reading, Volume 3: Methods, Strategies, Tactics*

The History of Reading, Volume 1

International Perspectives, *c*.1500–1990

Edited by

Shafquat Towheed
The Open University

and

W. R. Owens
The Open University

Foreword by

Simon Eliot

In association with the Institute of English Studies, School of Advanced Study, University of London

Selection and editorial matter © Shafquat Towheed and W.R.Owens 2011
Individual chapters © contributors 2011

Foreword © Simon Eliot 2011

First published 2011 by
PALGRAVE MACMILLAN

Palgrave Macmillan in the UK is an imprint of Macmillan Publishers Limited,
registered in England, company number 785998, of Houndmills, Basingstoke,
Hampshire RG21 6XS.

Palgrave Macmillan in the US is a division of St Martin's Press LLC,
175 Fifth Avenue, New York, NY 10010.

Palgrave Macmillan is the global academic imprint of the above companies
and has companies and representatives throughout the world.

Palgrave® and Macmillan® are registered trademarks in the United States,
the United Kingdom, Europe and other countries.

ISBN 978–0–230–24751–2   hardback

This book is printed on paper suitable for recycling and made from fully
managed and sustained forest sources. Logging, pulping and manufacturing
processes are expected to conform to the environmental regulations of the
country of origin.

A catalogue record for this book is available from the British Library.

Library of Congress Cataloging-in-Publication Data

The history of reading. Volume 1, International perspectives,
c.1500–1990/edited by Shafquat Towheed & W.R. Owens.
  p. cm.
Includes index.
"In association with the Institute of English Studies, School of
Advanced Study, University of London."
ISBN 978–0–230–24751–2 (alk. paper)
 1. Books and reading–History.   I. Towheed, Shafquat, 1973–
II. Owens, W.R.   III. Title: International perspectives, c.1500–1990.
Z1003.H588 2011
028'.9—dc22   2011013868

10   9   8   7   6   5   4   3   2   1
20 19 18 17 16 15 14 13 12 11

Printed and bound in Great Britain by
CPI Antony Rowe, Chippenham and Eastbourne

To Sydney Shep, a pioneer in more than one field

Contents

List of Figures

List of Tables

Foreword

Simon Eliot

> People say that life is the thing, but I prefer reading.
> (Logan Pearsall Smith, 1865–1946)

> To pass her time 'twixt reading and Bohea,
> To muse, and spill her solitary tea,
> Or o'er cold coffee trifle with the spoon,
> Count the slow clock, and dine exact at noon.
> (Alexander Pope, 1688–1744)

> Laudant illa sed ista legunt.
> (They praise those works, but read these.)
> (Martial, *c*.AD 40–104)

Little that is commonplace registers in history. Until relatively recently history has been a record of the exceptional, of change, of difference, or of contrast. To reverse the cliché, it's always been about the elephant in the room, and never about how the room was furnished or its other, less striking occupants. Essential commonplaces such as eating, casual conversations in the street, and the street itself, fudge into a fuzzy background against which sharp change or notable differences are brought into focus. In most history the ordinary is at best out of focus or, more commonly, invisible. The quotidian is never quoted, the ordinary is frequently ignored, and 'the same old, same old' is worn out before it is ever recorded.

In most literate societies, reading is usually this sort of prosaic activity. Most of us do it most of the time. It is not necessarily a matter of settling down to spend a few hours with *On the Origin of Species* or catching up with the latest vogue novel, it is more often a matter of reading a cornflakes packet for want of anything better, or reading a 'use by' date on something dubious from the fridge, or a timetable, or a free newspaper, or an email, or an advertisement, or a street name, or a menu, or the instructions on a bottle of aspirin.

However, the reading that we tend to remember, and the reading that much more frequently gets recorded, is of the exceptional sort: the book, the chapter, perhaps even just the sentence, which strikes home, which affects us in some profound way, which sometimes even transforms us. One should never underestimate the power of reading to surprise with joy, shock with facts or reason, or force us to see things from a disturbingly different point of view, and doing so commonly against our will and inclination. Samuel Johnson's experience, while he was an undergraduate at Oxford, of taking up Law's *Serious Call to a Holy Life* on the assumption that he might laugh at it, only to find Law 'an overmatch for me' is an example of such unexpected and sometimes unwelcome power. Reading, as so many other human experiences do, often relies for its impact on the law of unintended consequences.

Now, there is a natural and understandable tendency of those, particularly in literary studies, to prioritize this exceptional form of reading. After all, what is the use of studying something if it does not have a huge potential power to change and to convert? To study something that merely entertained, or diverted, or allowed escape or, worst of all, simply passed the time, is somehow demeaning. What we want are roads to Damascus: the flash, the crash, the conversion.

But if most, or even a significant minority, of reading experiences were of this transformational sort, we as readers would soon be exhausted by it, like Mr Brooke in George Eliot's *Middlemarch*, endlessly buffeted from one set of opinions to the next as he read one pamphlet and then another.

There is, of course, a middle type of reading between the entirely functional and the disconcertingly transcendental. This consists of reading for entertainment (escapist or otherwise), for instruction and information – and for confirmation. The first two are self-explanatory, but the third may need some unpacking. Although we are occasionally subject, often accidentally, to a reading experience that is transformational, we do spend a lot of our reading time trying to avoid such experiences. For instance, we usually choose for our newspaper one that tends to parallel our own views, and we naturally gravitate to other texts that are disposed to assure us that our opinions are the correct ones, and to provide us with further examples to back up our own prejudices. To provide the 'And I am right, and you are right' reassurance is one of the necessary and comforting functions of reading. Much of the content of even the most modern forms of communication, the text and the tweet, are devoted to variations on the theme of 'I'm OK, and you're OK'. It was ever thus: many of the clay tablets exchanged between Assyrian monarchs and their civil servants performed a similar function.

We must not forget that the act of reading or, at least, the act of appearing to read, is also an invaluable social tool. For those wishing to promote themselves as studious, for those wanting to avoid social contact or (even worse) eye contact, for those wishing to create space around themselves in a crowded place, reading is a godsend. How many of us, in dining alone in a restaurant, have taken a book or a newspaper not merely for entertainment, but in order to indicate that we are certainly not sad and lonely people?

Finally, there is the history of implied reading; that is, of reading we have not done but either implicitly or explicitly claimed to have done. The unread books borrowed from libraries, the un-perused books on our tables and bookshelves, all those monuments to our good intentions. Or, equally common, the books we bluff about, the allusion to a text that we hope will impress without being picked up by someone who has actually read the book to which we have casually referred. That this is both not new and all too human is attested by the quotation from Martial at the beginning of this foreword.

The history of reading is as much about the reader as it is about what is read. It is about the cocktail of motives and circumstances that leads us to select one text rather than another, and about the texture of our personalities and the nature of our predicament that determine how we react to that text. In our various attempts to recreate the humanity of the world we have lost, the study of the reading experiences of those in earlier centuries is an important and worthwhile endeavour. The essays that follow are part of a heroic project to explore one of the most significant of the intellectual experiences that we share with the past.

Acknowledgements

The editors would like to thank the Arts and Humanities Research Council for funding The Reading Experience Database, 1450–1945 (RED) project, established at The Open University in collaboration with the Institute of English Studies, University of London. Among the outcomes of the RED project was an international conference, 'Evidence of Reading, Reading the Evidence', held at the Institute of English Studies in July 2008, from which many of the essays in these three volumes emerged. Thanks are also due to Adam Mathew Digital, The Bibliographical Society, the British Academy, *History Today*, The Open University, and the Royal Historical Society, who provided additional financial support for the conference, and to all the colleagues at the Institute of English Studies and The Open University who helped with its organization, in particular Dr Karen Attar (Rare Books Librarian, Senate House Library), curator of the accompanying exhibition. Permission to reproduce 'At a Book' by Marie Konstantinova Bashkirtseva (1860–84) (oil on canvas, Kharkov Art Museum, Kharkov, Ukraine), on the cover of this volume was kindly granted by courtesy of Bridgeman Education. We would also like to thank the following for permission to quote or reproduce material in individual chapters: National Library of Scotland (Chapter 1); Opole University Library, Poland (Chapter 6); South Canterbury Museum, Wellington, New Zealand (Chapter 10). Every effort has been made to trace all copyright holders, but if any have been inadvertently overlooked, the publisher will be pleased to make the necessary arrangements at the first opportunity.

Notes on Contributors

Richard Bell is Assistant Professor of History at the University of Maryland, College Park, USA. He is the author of *We Shall Be No More: Suicide and Power in the Early United States* (2011) as well as several articles examining the cultural politics of suicide in early America.

Ian Desai is a Postdoctoral Associate and Lecturer in South Asian Studies and History at Yale University, USA. His doctoral dissertation at Oxford was entitled 'Producing the Mahatma: Communication, Community and Political Theatre behind the Gandhi Phenomenon, 1893–1942'. His current work examines how Gandhi and his colleagues collected and utilized books.

Archie L. Dick is a full Professor in the Department of Information Science at the University of Pretoria, South Africa. His monograph, *The Philosophy, Politics, and Economics of Information* was published in 2002. His book on South Africa's hidden book and reading cultures will appear in 2011.

Ilona Dobosiewicz is Professor of English Literature at Opole University, Poland. She is the author of *Female Relationships in Jane Austen's Novels* (1997) and *Ambivalent Feminism: Marriage and Women's Social Roles in George Eliot's Works* (2003). She co-edits the series *Readings in English and American Literature and Culture*, published by Opole University.

Lawrence (Lou) Duggan is a librarian and researcher at Saint Mary's University in Halifax, Nova Scotia, Canada. His historical research centres on the study of print culture as experienced by Victorian era scientists. He is currently investigating the private library, publications and archival papers of Alexander Graham Bell.

Simon Eliot is Professor of the History of the Book at the Institute of English Studies, School of Advanced Study, University of London. He has published on quantitative book history, publishing history, the history of lighting, and library history. He is general editor of the new multi-volume *History of Oxford University Press*.

John Ford is *maître de conférences* in English and Head of Department of Languages and Literature at Champollion University in Albi, France.

He has authored several publications on the Middle English and Anglo-Norman verse romances, including *Anglo-Norman Amys e Amilioun* (2004), an edition of the text in MS Karlsruhe 345.

Barbara Hochman is Associate Professor of Literature at Ben Gurion University in Israel. She has written widely on nineteenth- and twentieth-century American fiction and reading habits. Her book, *'Uncle Tom's Cabin' and the Reading Revolution: Race, Literacy, Childhood, and Fiction 1852–1911* was published in 2011.

Isabelle Lehuu is Professor of History at the Université du Québec à Montréal, Canada. She is the author of *Carnival on the Page: Popular Print Media in Antebellum America* (2000), and editor of *Blanches et Noires: Histoire(s) des Américaines au XIXe siècle* (2010).

Susann Liebich is a doctoral candidate in history at Victoria University of Wellington, New Zealand. She is currently working on a trans-local study of middle-class reading culture in New Zealand and the British World, *c*.1890–1930. Her previous research focused on bookselling in colonial Wellington and on the paperback revolution in post-1945 West Germany.

Bertrum H. MacDonald is Professor of Information Management, Dalhousie University, Halifax, Nova Scotia, Canada. His research focuses on the communication of scientific information from the nineteenth century to the present. He is currently leading an interdisciplinary team investigating the use and influence of marine environmental information published as grey literature.

Kate McDowell is an Assistant Professor at the Graduate School of Library and Information Science at the University of Illinois, Urbana-Champaign, USA, and a faculty affiliate of the Center for Children's Books. Her articles have appeared in *Library Quarterly*, *Book History* and *Children and Libraries*.

W. R. Owens is Professor of English Literature at The Open University. He has published widely on John Bunyan and Daniel Defoe, and is Director of The Reading Experience Database, 1450–1945 (RED) project. His most recent publication is an edition of the AV text of *The Gospels* for Oxford World's Classics (2011).

Liliana Piasecka is Professor of Second Language Acquisition and Methodology of Teaching English as a Foreign Language at Opole University, Poland. She is the author of many articles and two books: *Ways with Words: Strategies of Lexical Acquisition* (2001), and *Psycholinguistic and Socio-cultural Perspectives on Native and Foreign Language Reading* (2008).

Shafquat Towheed is Lecturer in English at The Open University and Co-Investigator on The Reading Experience Database, 1450–1945 (RED) project. He is co-editor (with Rosalind Crone and Katie Halsey) of *The History of Reading: A Reader* (2010), and co-editor (with Rosalind Crone) of *The History of Reading, Vol. 3: Methods, Strategies, Tactics* (2011).

Jeffrey T. Zalar is a historian of modern Germany and Central Europe. His publications address nationalism, confessional conflict and intellectual culture. He teaches at the University of Wisconsin-Whitewater, USA.

Introduction

Shafquat Towheed and W. R. Owens

Perhaps it is best to open the first of three volumes on the history of reading with an imaginary example, albeit a cautionary one. Let us consider the case of a particular reader, already past middle age and perhaps approaching retirement, with an ordinary education and standard level of literacy, i.e. proficient enough to read a 500-page novel without too much difficulty. Let us call this reader X. Reader X regularly consumes fiction, some religious reading and the daily newspaper, as well as the odd magazine. Reading takes place largely in leisure time (evenings at home or while commuting) and away from the world of work; reader X's practice is elastic, and expands or contracts based on the amount of leisure time available. Reader X reads carefully but quickly, but usually does not scribble any marginalia or comments in owned books, nor does reader X keep a reading diary or commonplace book. Reader X is happy and willing to discuss recent reading with friends and family members, but lacks the articulacy or confidence to express this in a written or reflexive practice. Apart from the turned corners of pages, the creases in the spines of paperbacks, and the marks of ownership (a simple name and date in the inside cover, or the occasional bit of underlining), there is almost no recoverable textual evidence of reader X's engagement with owned books.

Of course, as a proportion of reader X's reading material consists of newspapers which are bought, assiduously read and immediately recycled, or of library books which are borrowed and returned, information about reading habits might be reconstructed through circulation and purchasing records, although reader X's actual responses to reading are unavailable to us. Recently, reader X has learned to use the Internet, and has started to read additional, mainly foreign, newspapers online. Again, there is information here that might be usefully gathered and

1

gleaned through web statistics programmes, or by examining reader X's computer, even though we have no way of gauging reader X's agreement, disagreement or indifference to material read on the Internet. Reader X is a proficient and heterogeneous reader, gathering reading matter from a range of sources, and reading across a variety of genres and formats, while leaving very little in the form of a material or recoverable trace of reading practices. As historians of reading, what do we do with reader X? How do we reconstruct such fugitive reading practices, and narrate such a reader's real enough engagement with textual matter? How do we account for this kind of reader in social and cultural histories about reading nations, communities or groups? How do we record this epitome of the common reader for posterity?

The probable answer lies in identifying and collectively recovering as much data of reading engagement and experiences as possible, using a wide range of approaches: library circulation records, marks of ownership, web statistics, perhaps even a direct interview of remembered and current reading through oral history. Much of reader X's actual reading and response may be occluded from us, but there is still recoverable data about some forms of engagement with textual matter that we can identify, quantify and interpret. This methodological process can of course be extrapolated across communities of readers. A single reader can tell us little beyond their own possibly idiosyncratic habits, but the collective record of thousands of readers in a given historical period or geographical location can tells us a great deal about broader trends in reading practices. The putative reader described above is a hypothetical one, but we must remember that the world is peopled with billions of readers, in many cases just like reader X, and that the history of reading is faced with the problem of identification, recovery, data gathering, classification and interpretation. If the challenge of finding enough recoverable evidence is considerable in research in contemporary reading, it is doubly so in earlier and more remote historical periods. Historians of reading are limited by what has survived (often accidentally) through the centuries: evidence-based studies are invariably histories of reading based on extant evidence.

Theorists of reading such as Stanley Fish, Wolfgang Iser, Judith Fetterley, Mikhail Bakhtin, Hans Robert Jauss, Michel de Certeau and Rolf Engelsing have proposed a range of models for readers that are not necessarily mutually exclusive. There can be intensive or extensive readers, implied or intended readers, continuous or discontinuous readers, dialogic readers and intertextual readers, sympathetically absorbed or critically resistant readers. Readers may read against the grain of intended meaning, or as Michel de Certeau has observed, they might selectively pick what they want from a text, when they want it. In the history of reading, theory has until recently been in the vanguard, and theoretical models have by and large preceded evidence-based practice. These theoretical models, though compelling, are not substantively supported by a body of evidence of actual reading practice. Was there in fact a shift from intensive to extensive reading? Did the move from the scroll to the codex promote discontinuous over continuous reading, or did the change in format have no bearing on how people read? Was there a *Leserevolution*, a reading revolution, in the Romantic period in Europe? If there is to be any way of testing, validating or modifying the numerous hypotheses proposed by theorists, or of supporting or contesting these theoretical models, it must involve the production and analysis of a large body of material evidence of how readers through history actually read. This is the considerable intellectual challenge that so many historians of reading are currently addressing in their work.

The twelve chapters in this volume (like the contributions in the other two volumes of *The History of Reading*) directly address the central question of finding the evidence of readers' responses, but they collectively do so from a chronological sweep that covers five centuries, and a geographical compass that takes in eight nations on five continents. The researchers in this volume use both macroanalytical (library surveys and publishing figures) and microanalytical (diaries and correspondence of individual readers) perspectives in their enquiry, and gather and interpret both qualitative (e.g. oral history and entries in reading diaries) and quantitative (e.g. library circulation figures) data. While the research methodology may often be similar in studies of different countries and historical periods (e.g. library circulation records in South Carolina and Polish Silesia respectively, or institutional records in India and South Africa), the socioeconomic and political contexts for these studies are widely divergent and geographically specific. The multiple local and international perspectives that these chapters bring to bear in their evidence-based investigations reminds us again of the complex negotiations of meaning that readers bring to texts, meanings that are often socially, culturally or historically located.

In the world of manuscript production before the printing press, and in the centuries before mass literacy, the relationship between reading and listening, between the oral and the aural, and between text and the spoken word was much more evident than it is today. Some of the most important scholarship in the history of reading in the last few decades has brought to the fore this particularly complex relationship between orality and text in the era before the widespread availability of print. Paul Saenger has demonstrated the close relationship between the rise of monastic silent reading and the development of spaces between words in medieval scribal manuscript production, while Armando Petrucci has argued that the shift from a largely monastic to an increasingly secular (and often solitary) engagement with books gave rise to new intensive humanist reading practices.

This and the other two volumes of *The History of Reading* are explicitly concerned with the relationship between readers and texts in the post-Gutenberg, print dominated world, a transformative epoch famously described by Lucien Febvre and Henri Martin in their landmark 1958 work, *L'Apparition du livre* ('The Coming of the Book'), and developed further by Elizabeth Eisenstein in *The Printing Press as an Agent of Change* (1979). The selection of chapters in all three volumes is shaped in no small part due to the radical transformation of readers' engagement with texts caused by the rise of this technology.

Despite the print revolution sweeping late fifteenth-century Europe, some particular pre-print patterns in the reading and consumption of texts continued for decades if not centuries after Gutenberg's first mastery of metal movable type. The first two chapters in Part 1 ('Readers in the Medieval and Early Modern World') examine the evidence for reading in two British-based studies, and demonstrate that pre-print oral and aural practices continued to shape readers' engagement with texts before and after the rise of the printing press. John Ford's 'Speaking of Reading and Reading the Evidence: Allusions to Literacy in the Oral Tradition of the Middle English Verse Romances' (Chapter 1) is concerned with the evidence of a transition from orality to literacy as manifested in extant verse romances of the thirteenth and fourteenth centuries. These romances retain many of the structural devices of oral-formulaic composition, including, for example, the heavy use of stock phrases and repetitive epithets which served an important mnemonic function in the memorization of these tales for oral recitation. Ford argues that the manuscript versions of tales which were originally designed to be heard also include many references to reading and writing, and that these references are themselves couched in the formulaic structures and techniques more characteristic of the oral tradition. The evidence he brings forward indicates that in this transitional period 'literacy is informed by orality', and that an essentially oral form of composition and narrative remained popular even with literacy on the rise. In the presentation of the manuscripts, however, it is clear that solitary reading was becoming a more widespread practice. Whereas in the earlier manuscripts the text was written across the page like prose, indicating that they were meant to be heard, in manuscripts of a later date the text is laid out with line-breaks and other devices indicating that they were meant to be read. By the time of Chaucer, poets were composing and circulating their work in written form, with no further need of mnemonic aids. Innovation, not repetition, was to be the mark of literature meant to be read rather than heard.

While medieval romances were popular amongst the courtly elite, the Bible was by far the most widely read book in the early modern period; however, it is by no means clear how readers engaged with this very large and complex text. Many of the early Renaissance Bibles, in particular the Geneva Bible of 1560, included an extensive apparatus of support to help readers find their way through the text, including summaries of books and chapters, detailed marginal annotations, subject headers at the top of pages, maps, genealogies, historical tables and translations of Hebrew names. This apparatus was dropped from the Authorized, or King James, Version of the Bible published in 1611, and perhaps in response to this other publications began to appear offering assistance to Bible readers. These included commentaries, paraphrases, abridgments and concordances of various kinds. Of particular interest are the manuals or guide books which gave advice on how the Bible should be read and which often included a calendar setting out how the whole Bible could be read in a continuous sequence over the course of one year. This Protestant emphasis on sequential reading has been taken to represent an important break with the Roman Catholic tradition of 'discontinuous' reading of the Bible, and its subordination to the structure of the liturgical year, but in an influential article Peter Stallybrass has argued that no such break took place, and that the Bible continued to be read by Protestants in a non-linear way, with readings both private and public arranged to coincide with the liturgy of the Prayer Book of the Church of England. However, as W. R. Owens demonstrates in 'Modes of Bible Reading in Early Modern England' (Chapter 2), there is much evidence to show not only that continuous, linear reading practices were frequently and strongly recommended by Protestant writers, but that this was in fact one of the most important ways in which many people read the Bible in early modern England.

If Bible reading was an everyday practice in early modern England, Enlightenment and Romantic readers on both sides of the Atlantic increasingly turned to fiction (and often, the most sensational type of fiction) to satisfy their burgeoning appetite for new reading matter. Part 2 ('Readers in the Enlightenment and Romantic World') neatly juxtaposes two American studies of reading in this period. In 'Weeping for Werther: Suicide, Sympathy and the Reading Revolution in Early America' (Chapter 3), Richard Bell examines one of the most extraordinary episodes in the history of reading: the furore in America about the supposedly malign influence of Wolfgang von Goethe's best-selling novel *The Sorrows of Young Werther* (1774) and the swathe of 'suicide novels' that followed its appearance. The widespread popularity of these novels with impressionable young readers led many commentators to believe that they were leading to an epidemic of suicide. This belief was given credence by widely-publicized cases where copies of *Werther* were left at the scene of suicides, and led to an onslaught of criticism. Whether as a result of the dire warnings of critics, or for other reasons, the taste for these novels slackened off, and the fashion for them disappeared as quickly as it had sprung up. However, anxieties about the impact of novel reading on apparently susceptible readers (especially women and juveniles) kept reappearing in almost all novel-reading societies throughout the century and beyond.

Isabelle Lehuu's 'Reconstructing Reading Vogues in the Old South: Borrowings from the Charleston Library Society, 1811–1817' (Chapter 4) takes a directly quantitative methodological approach to recovering the evidence of a Romantic period reading community by scrutinizing records of library borrowings. Her example is the Charleston Library Society in South Carolina, which was founded in 1748 and is the third oldest library in the United States. Her chapter focuses on what was borrowed by library users in the early nineteenth century, between July 1811 and February 1817, using the surviving ledgers of transactions which recorded the names of borrowers, titles of books and date and length of charges. Interpreting these apparently inert records enables us to chart the reading tastes of the past, allowing us to follow the interests of individual readers as well as larger patterns. They allow us to identify which genres and titles were most popular, and among which groups of readers. Lehuu's study of this particular source suggests that 'reading vogues in the Old South were marked by Anglophilia', and that gothic novels and historical romances written by British women novelists were among the most widely consumed reading material in this period. Despite the differences of climate, location and social structure (Charleston was in slave-owning South Carolina), the reading habits of the clientele of Charleston Library Society were not hugely different from that of a upper-middle-class provincial library in Britain: often, both groups showed similar preferences for books. This affinity across borders through novel reading is something we see reciprocated in another study in this volume, Barbara Hochman's chapter on *Uncle Tom's Cabin*.

It was the nineteenth century that saw the rise of the first mass literate societies and this was often accompanied by a growing sense of national, religious, professional or community consciousness. The four chapters in Part 3 ('Readers in the Nineteenth-Century World') narrate particular cultural trends that are discernible for historians of reading. One of the most popular and widely-published novels of the nineteenth century was Harriet Beecher Stowe's abolitionist polemic, *Uncle Tom's Cabin* (1852). Over 300,000 copies were sold in its first year of publication in book form, and it was widely believed that its effect on readers contributed directly to the abolition of slavery. Barbara Hochman's 'Devouring *Uncle Tom's Cabin*: Antebellum "Common" Readers' (Chapter 6) studies the responses of American readers in both the free and slave owning states, and their accounts of the powerful emotional effect reading the novel had on them. As she shows, the idea of 'devouring' that so often characterized accounts of reading *Uncle Tom's Cabin* was not at all the kind of reading that was recommended at the time, including by Harriet Beecher Stowe herself. These readers were violating the 'protocols' of reading of which Stowe approved, going well beyond the sympathy and reflection she regarded as appropriate, and giving themselves up to their appetites ('devouring') and their selfish needs ('indulging themselves'). This intensity of absorption in a novel greatly worried nineteenth-century cultural commentators, but, as Hochman argues, Stowe's novel drew readers into identifying with 'racial otherness' in a way that no previous text had ever managed to do. It challenged not only assumptions about slavery, but assumptions about how fiction should be read. While Hochman's chapter focuses on American readers' responses, Stowe's novel was also an international bestseller, with dozens of translations and foreign editions in the decade after first publication. The appetite for the novel shaped a transnational reading community with a common emotional and political affinity: the abolition of slavery in the United States.

In 'Reading in Polish and National Identity in Nineteenth-Century Silesia' (Chapter 7), Ilona Dobosiewicz and Liliana Piasecka investigate the intimate relationship between reading and the formation of national consciousness. Poland was partitioned three times between 1772 and 1795, as a result of which the country was divided between German (Prussian), Austrian and Tsarist Russian rule. Despite attempts to eradicate a sense of Polish national identity, and even the language itself, Poles in the German-controlled region of Silesia managed to retain their sense of Polishness, in part through the avid reading of books in Polish, not only by canonical authors, but by popular Silesian writers who aimed their works at this local readership. As Dobosiewicz and Piasecka argue here, the act of reading in Polish and about Polish subjects was one of the most important means of maintaining a sense of belonging to a common Polish culture bisected by artificial political borders. They trace the mechanisms by which the readership of Polish books was promoted, through the establishment of popular lending libraries affiliated with schools, parish churches and local cultural associations, and discuss some of the more popular texts read by Silesians in the nineteenth century. At a time when Poland had no political existence as a nation state, the act of reading in Polish had a particular charge: it was not only a marker of collective identity, but a forceful articulation of national sentiment.

While Dobosiewicz and Piasecka uncover the close relationship between reading and national identity, Jeffrey T. Zalar in 'Reading in an Age of Censorship: The Case of Catholic Germany, 1800–1914' (Chapter 8) unpicks the often thorny relationship between sectarian identity, the teachings of the Catholic Church and the preferences of readers. Zalar challenges a deeply entrenched historical account of the reading practices of millions of Catholic Germans through the nineteenth century and up to the First World War. According to this account, the reading material of Catholics in this period was almost entirely dictated by their clergy, who operated a powerful system of oversight and permitted the faithful to read only approved religious texts. In an effort to test the strength of the evidence for this account of lay acquiescence under an authoritarian clerical domination, Zalar carried out research in diocesan and parish archives across the Rhineland and Westphalia to uncover a vast array of evidence about the actual reading habits of German Catholics. This evidence includes information from letters giving details about access to forbidden literature; accounts by priests of the reading behaviour of parishioners; data on the use made by Catholics of lending institutions; details of ownership of books at home; and reports of surveillance of reading and intellectual activities reported to diocesan authorities. While there is certainly much evidence of consumption by Catholics of great quantities of religious literature, there is also a great deal of evidence that ordinary Catholics avidly read a variety of forbidden material, in defiance of the threats of bishops and priests. According to Zalar, the laity greatly resented clerical attempts to constrain their choice of reading matter, and indeed his conclusion is that far from acquiescing in clerical control of their reading, Catholic readers everywhere read secular and Protestant literature with impunity. These two chapters cogently demonstrate that while readers in *Mitteleuropa* in the nineteenth-century may have shared a common, post-Enlightenment, post-*Werther* cultural heritage, they had considerable autonomy, and different sets of contingencies that shaped their engagements with texts. Polish Catholics in Silesia and their German co-religionists in the Rhineland and Westphalia differed considerably in their reading practices, despite their shared religious background.

The great scientific and technological developments of the nineteenth century (railways, steam ships, mechanized printing, etc.) massively increased the availability and circulation of reading material. For the first time in human history, geographically and culturally dispersed populations could become members of a self-selecting professional community through reading and the exchange of ideas. Nowhere was this more evident than in the development of professional scientific bodies in the latter half of the century. Scientists were themselves avid and voracious readers, and not just of professional material. With the exception of studies of famous scientists such as Charles Darwin (who left extensive records of his reading), or the psychologist Sir Henry Head (see Stephen Jacyna's chapter in *The History of Reading, Vol. 2*), relatively little work has been done on the reading habits and practices of scientists. In 'Reading Science: Evidence from the Career of Edwin Gilpin, Mining Engineer' (Chapter 7), Lawrence J. Duggan and Bertrum H. MacDonald trace the reading activity of Edwin Gilpin (1850–1907), a prominent mining engineer in late nineteenth-century Nova Scotia, Canada. They bring to bear a diverse body of evidence, including the nature of his education; the contents of his extensive personal library of books and journals; marginalia in books that he owned; citations in his publications; records from a diary and other personal documents; and information from his extensive national and international correspondence. Their study of Gilpin illustrates the extent of the reading activity of a typical scientist of this period, and emphasizes the importance of reading in the circulation and communication of scientific information. Duggan and MacDonald convincingly demonstrate the extent to which the development of a modern scientific community unconstrained by political or geographical borders was dependent upon a particular type of engaged and reflective reading practice – perhaps the very opposite of the 'devouring' of novels that had so alarmed earlier commentators.

Finally, the four chapters in Part 4 ('Readers in the Twentieth-Century World') bring together complementary studies from countries on four different continents and with widely disparate political circumstances: the

USA at a time of increasing enfranchisement; New Zealand during the Dominion period; India under British colonial rule; and apartheid era South Africa. Books and the ideas that they carry have the ability to circulate across astonishing distances, and infiltrate even the tightest systems of control and surveillance. More importantly, these four case studies highlight the autonomy and preferences of individual readers, even when their access to reading matter is controlled by availability, political regimes or the guiding influence of parents and educationalists.

Often, the very institutions that mediate our access to reading matter preserve the evidence of individual readers' choices and responses. A rich source of evidence about the reading of children (a group often overlooked in academic studies of reading) is to be found in data collected by librarians. In 'Understanding Children as Readers: Librarians' Anecdotes and Surveys in the United States from 1890 to 1930' (Chapter 9), Kate McDowell focuses on surveys published in library journals in which the responses of children to questions about their reading and use of libraries was recorded. No fewer than thirty-six such surveys were carried out in this period, and these not only provide statistical information of various kinds, but are replete with anecdotes in the verbatim words of children themselves. McDowell gives an account of the nature of the questions asked in these surveys, and what these reveal about the values and assumptions of the librarians, but she also analyses in depth the responses of children, who not only identified the books they liked or disliked, but gave often extraordinarily detailed reasons for their choices of reading matter, and their experience of using libraries. Despite the inequality of power between adult librarians and child readers, McDowell demonstrates how children's voices and individual reading preferences can be recovered from the historical archive.

If McDowell mines institutional archives to recover the voices of a group of readers, Susann Liebich in 'Letters to a Daughter: An Archive of Middle-Class Reading in New Zealand, *c.*1872–1932' (Chapter 10) provides a richly textured account of the reading career of an individual reader, Fred Barkas, who in 1881, at the age of twenty-seven, emigrated from the north of England to New Zealand, where he spent the rest of his life. Reading was an extraordinarily important part of Barkas's life, and he kept extensive notes of his reactions to books. Typically, he read middle-brow and classic literature, particularly novels, but also a great deal of non-fiction, including history, biography and political (especially Socialist) writing. Many of his books came from the Timaru Public Library, and he formed a close relationship with the head librarian there. He was also an active member of a reading group, which met to discuss books. A large collection of his private letters, diaries and notebooks is now held in the National Library of New Zealand. This extensive archive enables Liebich to trace the extent to which Barkas's reading was shaped by his own personal circumstances and predilections, and the extent to which it may be seen as representative of a wider social group in a particular place and time. What is perhaps most interesting in Liebich's analysis of Barkas's reading is the extent to which association and affinity is shaped through the experience of reading, and not through physical distance or geographical location (all the more pertinent considering New Zealand's distance from many of the sources of published books in this period). For Barkas, domesticity and conviviality is constructed both through the experience of reading, and by relating an account of this reading back to his family in England.

In 'Books Behind Bars: Mahatma Gandhi's Community of Captive Readers' (Chapter 11), Ian Desai explores the extensive programme of reading undertaken by Mahatma Gandhi during the four years or so that he spent in colonial prisons in South Africa and India during the first part of the twentieth century. This reading was not a purely individual or private affair, but widened out to become a collective engagement with books and ideas among a community of readers who were able to transform the experience of imprisonment into an opportunity to equip themselves to carry on more effectively their resistance to imperialism. Examining book requests, borrowing records, marginalia and correspondence, Desai shows how Gandhi learned to mine books for the knowledge he needed, but also how reading enabled him to cope with the psychological pressures of imprisonment. The same was true of many of Gandhi's colleagues, especially his close associate Mahadev Desai, who likewise read extensively in prison, and was able to have books sent to him by friends in India and elsewhere. When they were forbidden overtly political books, Gandhi and his colleagues studied social and religious writings, which informed the development of their broader political programme. Interestingly, Desai and Gandhi's collective and collaborative reading practice was shared with others in the Indian National Congress circle, and this practice that was forged under the exacting conditions of incarceration was productively utilized in the wider political struggle against British colonial rule.

Perhaps no other liberation struggle in recent history has been as reader-centred and bookish as the lengthy campaign for freedom and democracy in twentieth-century South Africa. An extraordinary number of memoirs have been published in recent years by anti-apartheid activists imprisoned during the liberation war, and many have touched on the central importance of reading. Despite the draconian regime of censorship and restricted access to reading material, South Africa's apartheid era prisons, like the prisons of British colonial India, were concentrated centres of reading, with political prisoners keeping detailed and often reflective accounts of how reading shaped their moral and political thinking. What has until recently been overlooked is the extent to which many of these accounts of reading that took place in apartheid era prisons are remembered reading, and need to be balanced by the wide range of material evidence produced by the very structures of surveillance designed to control the inmates. In 'Remembering Reading: Memory, Books, and Reading in South Africa's Apartheid Prisons, 1956–60' (Chapter 12), Archie L. Dick scrutinizes the reading of political prisoners. Based on a study of sources ranging from government and institutional records, prison diaries and letters, autobiographies, and interviews with former prisoners, Dick focuses on the nature of the evidence for reading, and how this evidence is to be interpreted, given that much of it takes the form of *memories* of reading. He discusses in turn state memory, institutional memory and reader's memory. As he shows, a large body of evidence for reading is to be found in official state documents such as trial records, police notebooks and prison library reports. Institutional records, such as official enquiries, educational reading lists and legal documents are also a rich source of evidence. Finally, the experiences of individual readers are recorded in autobiographies and biographies, prison diaries, library borrowing registers, visual material, films and documentaries, and interviews. Although each of these categories of evidence has its own problems, and needs to be interpreted, Dick summarizes the reading practices of these political prisoners as 'survivalist', 'substitutive', and 'subversive'. He argues that the evidence of reading provides an important insight into the nature of the liberation struggle in South Africa.

The task of recovering the evidence of reading of actual readers through history is an enormous one, and one that is never likely to be completed. However, the twelve chapters in this book, and the studies in the other two volumes of *The History of Reading* compellingly demonstrate that the evidence of readers in the past and the present can be recovered, assessed and interpreted productively. The cumulative labour of scholarship in this area is now beginning to provide complex answers to the suppositions made by theorists in the history of reading, and this in turn is prompting new questions. Far from being dispirited by the prospect of not being able to fully capture the experiences of our putative reader X, we should take heart from the fact that readers throughout history are not invisible, and their traces of reading have not been completely erased.

Part 1
Readers in the Medieval and Early Modern World

1

Speaking of Reading and Reading the Evidence: Allusions to Literacy in the Oral Tradition of the Middle English Verse Romances

John Ford

Most modern readers from literate societies have little difficulty in equating verse with literacy. The very presentation of poetry on the page – with line breaks, stanza divisions, the occasional caesura – shows poetry to be informed by visualization of language as much as by any quality of sound. The traditional fourteen-line sonnet of Shakespeare, Donne, Milton or Spenser, with each line ending after its tenth syllable, provides such a tidy little box that Thomas Foster advises students: 'if it's square, it's a sonnet'.[1] Some modern sonneteers have even provided spacing or indentation to delineate their quatrains, sextets or couplets. While the bases of such poetic compositions founded on rhyme, rhythm, metre, assonance and alliteration do indeed exploit the oral qualities of a language, their final form is almost always arranged in such a way that the visual presentation serves an important function in allowing the *reader* to perceive the oral/aural elements manipulated by the poet. Poetry is also meant to be read, and this visualization is an essentially literate means of digesting the poem.

Many modern poets have even abandoned the formal oral constraints, turning instead to 'free verse'. Here, the oral/aural aspects of poetry have given way entirely to literacy. While the visual conventions of poetry with line breaks and even stanza division (initially contrived to highlight the oral quality by permitting the reader – as opposed to the listener – to ascertain them) are usually maintained, it is now more often the visual presentation that gives the poem effect, as opposed to the manipulation of a language's sound. Some poets have gone so far in this direction that their works can only be appreciated visually, and are unreadable in the sense that they cannot be recited or even pronounced; e.e. cummings's 'r-p-o-p-h-e-s-s-a-g-r' is an example, as is his 'a leaf falls on loneliness'.[2] In such examples we see poetry at its most literate stage: it cannot be fully appreciated by a non-literate audience; it can hardly be enunciated by a literate one.

However, even when verse constraints are retained, the resulting product usually has an affected quality that is intended to move the reader (or listener) in a way that natural speech would not. Poetry is therefore conceived of as being a highly unnatural form of discourse – 'No one would ever speak that way', one thinks – and so even if legible and recite-able, poetry is usually far from anything that one would think of as 'orality'. It is more often than not meant to be read. This is even true of free verse compositions, replete with poetic diction and the conceits, turns of phrase, metaphors and allusions that make the word play admirable despite (or because of) the fact that it is somewhat artificial. Orality, however, is usually considered to be the reproduction of actual speech-ways, often through the use of non-standard language and spelling.[3] It is an attempt, in other words, to write what people might say, but knowing that normally 'no one would ever *write* that way'.

This was not always the case. Preliterate societies do not have recourse to the written word for recording their thoughts and histories. However, lack of writing does not mean that they do not have elaborately preserved thoughts and histories, only that they are stored in another form. By far the most straightforward form is oral recitation.

But how does one remember long, complex, detailed histories without an *aide-mémoire*? A very simple mnemonic device is the use of verse. Albert Lord's *The Singer of Tales* (1960) concentrated on the theory of oral-formulaic composition and drew on the works of Milman Parry.[4] Analyses of performances and interviews with illiterate Serbo-Croatian 'histrions' – able to recite hours-long verse histories – demonstrated how the use of verse-formulae was indispensable to the fluid maintenance of a recital. A tale might not be identical at each retelling – in fact each new recitation would to some extent be a new composition – but the essential gist would remain the same, and the narrative readily identifiable as a slight variation in the telling of the same tale. Lord then successfully applied this Oral-Formulaic Hypothesis to the Homeric epics, a proposition that had first met with a great deal of criticism when proposed in the 1920s by Parry, because it seemed to attack the integrity of the fount of the Western canon. The *Iliad* and the *Odyssey* were believed to have existed in a fixed written form that had been meticulously enumerated and analysed for about two millennia.

Lord convincingly showed that the employment of such oral formulae, manipulated repeatedly by a succession of *rhapsodes* over decades or centuries, could account for the numerous repetitive epithets, such as 'red-haired king' for Menelaus, or 'swift-footed' for Achilles, that lent continuity to various tellings. Furthermore, reliance on such (often inter-changeable) formulae from different versions of various tales with diverse origins from various times also explained the appearance of archaisms and expressions from different dialects and periods of the Greek language side-by-side in the same 'definitive' version, 'irregularities' that had even troubled ancient Alexandrian scholars. What had always been taken as the wellspring of Western literature (the word 'literature' itself implying writing) clearly seemed to be no more than the transcription of one par-ticular version of an oft improvised, ad-libbed, ever evolving history. By being preserved in a concrete written form, this evolution was effectively 'stopped'. Henceforward, to tell the tale correctly, it must be read.

Lord also notes how these characteristics were also true of medieval French and English 'epic' poetry.[5] It is beyond reasonable doubt that the apocryphal version of the *Chanson de Roland* chanted by Taillefer at the Battle of Hastings would not have been word-for-word the same as the version that exists in the famous Oxford manuscript, considered to be 'the original', but written some 90 to 100 years later by Turold. Likewise, the famous Old English *Hymn to the Creation* by Caedmon, reported by Bede to have been a miraculous spontaneous act after which the illiterate herdsman could compose verse at will, abounds with heroic epithets and poetic formulae. Here, for example, with the most obvious examples in bold, is an edited version of the Northumbrian text as found in the Moore manuscript:

> Nu scylun hergan   **hefaenricaes Uard,**
> metudæs maecti   end his modgidanc,
> uerc Uuldurfadur   sue he uundra gihuaes,
> **eci Dryctin**   or astelidæ.
> He aerist scop   aelda barnum
> heben til hrofe,   haleg scepen.
> Tha middungeard   **monocynnaes Uard,**
> **eci Dryctin** aefter   tiadæ;
> firum foldu,   Frea allmectig.[6]

> [Now (we) must praise   (the) **heaven-kingdom's guardian,**
> (the) Creator's power(s)   and his mind's intent,
> (the) work of the Glory-Father   as he, of each of wonders,
> **Eternal lord**   in the beginning established.
> He first created   for the sons of men
> Heaven as (a) roof,   holy Creator.

> Then middle-earth **mankind's guardian,**
> **Eternal lord,**   afterwards fashioned;
> (for) men of the earth,   God almighty.]

Though modern editions apply conventional editorial procedures to highlight the hemistiches divided by a caesura, it is clear that the medieval composers did not thus conceive of their poems. For example, the above printed text version of Caedmon's hymn and the following opening lines to *Beowulf* are typical examples of the modern edition:

> Hwæt! We Gardena   in geardagum,
> þeodcyninga,   þrym gefrunon,
> hu ða æþelingas   ellen fremedon . . .

$$(1-3)^7$$

> [Lo! We of the Spear-Danes   in days of yore,
> Of the kings of a people,   heard (about their) glory,
> How the princes   deeds of valour accomplished . . .]

The original manuscript versions, however, are rather different, as can be seen in Figure 1.1 and Figure 1.2:

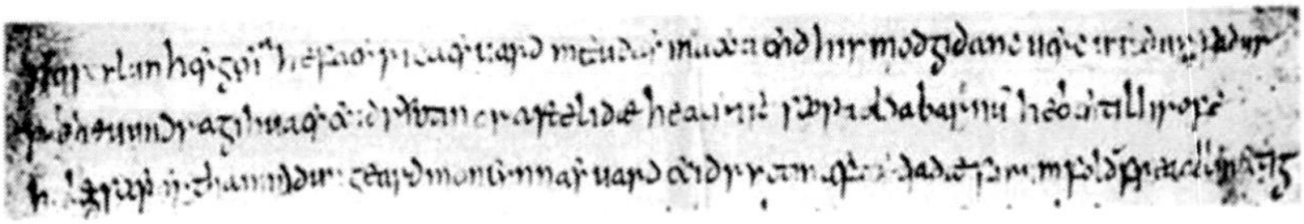

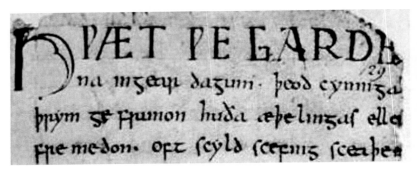

Figure 1.1 Caedmon's *Hymn to the Creation*, from the Moore MS *c*.750 (Cambridge University Library Kk. 5. 16)[8]

Figure 1.2 *Beowulf*, from the Nowell MS *c*.1000 (Cotton Vitellius A.XV)[9]

One sees here that the transcribers were not overly concerned about marking the verse visually, but wrote it directly across the page like prose. Despite the argument that parchment was expensive and utilization of as much of its surface as possible was an economic necessity, it is nevertheless equally evident that there did not seem to be much of a need to distinguish verse from prose by its visual representation. One can conclude that though the transcriber was evidently literate, the focus was on the preservation of an essentially oral composition. It was the preservation of sound and not its appearance that was important. It was meant to be heard more than to be read.

Verse was equated with orality, and indeed perhaps even more so than prose in respect to narration. Where today we have paragraphs, punctuation, chapter headings and other devices to divide and regulate a narrative, preliterate cultures tended to depend on aural/oral arrangements to lend structure to a composition. The earliest preserved examples of literature in most cultures are indeed in verse, usually written transcriptions that fossilize in a fixed form poetic works that had evolved and been created and recreated orally over decades or centuries. In this respect, at least initially, verse was seen as more reflective of orality than prose.

In the slow transition from pre-literate to literate cultures, it would be natural that *writers* of tales, composing with stylus in hand, would retain the characteristics of the earlier, established and accepted pre-literate 'literature' that had been composed and circulated orally. Indeed, as with the *Iliad* or the *Odyssey*, many of these written compositions were simply transcriptions of tales that had already circulated orally. It is therefore not surprising that the rhymes, repetitions and epithets – which were accepted as the mark of a good story – were expected and carried over into the written form.

While today we might find such features clumsy, tedious and highly 'unnatural', a pre-literate audience, or one in a period of transition from pre-literate to literate, would be vexed more by their curious absence than their reassuring presence. As Brewer notes, 'No poet could stand up in his pulpit before the audience, as medieval poets did, if he was not prepared to use a poetic language with which his audience was reasonable familiar, and which it could be expected to understand and even to like.'[10] Even after the act of writing fixed some of the stories (as Homer did with the *Iliad* and the *Odyssey*), it is certain that they continued to be recited before an audience more often than read individually. Later, as literacy became commonplace and writers began to compose their own stories, these expected and accepted features were naturally retained because they were already well established hallmarks of narrative. The audience expected them. With an eye (or perhaps an ear) to this, writers would likewise compose their written work in the same way as an oral composer. The oral element was thus imbedded in the literate tradition using a medium that was meant to be read.

We can see an example of this in the extant Middle English verse romances composed from the thirteenth to the fourteenth century, which exist in written form replete with formulae and stock phrases. The definition of formula used here takes into account prototype theory, which accounts for the fuzziness of formula creation and variation:[11]

1. one or more lexical units which are coextensive with a complete phrase;
2. arrangement in a metrically useful structure;
3. imparting a given meaning;
4. repeatable due to a lack of particularizing force.

By using such definitions, many turns of phrase that might be excluded as formulae by overly stringent definition easily come to light. Casual readers of verse romances will readily recognize such formulae; newcomers might well see the repetitive quality of the word selections. Here, for example, are the opening lines of *Amis and Amiloun* (c.1330) with twenty identifiable formulae underlined.

> For Goddes love in Trinyté
> Al that ben hend herkenith to me,
> I pray yow, par amoure,
> What sumtyme fel beyond the see
> Of two Barons of grete bounté
> And men of grete honoure;
> Her faders were barons hende,
> Lordinges com of grete kynde
> And pris men in toun and toure;
> To here of these children two
> How they were in wele and woo,
> Ywys, it is grete doloure.[12]

Of these formulae, eight are repeated two or more times in the text itself (half-lines 1a, 5a, 5b, 7b, 9a/b, 10b, 11a, 12a). Three occur only one other time in the text but are also found in other romances (2b, 3a, 11b). Eight others that are not repeated in the text are, however, found in other romances (1b, 2a, 3b, 4b, 8a, 10a, 12b, 6b).[13] There remains one which, despite conforming to the proposed definition of a formula, appears to be relatively rare (8b). The fact that it is difficult to find elsewhere does not necessarily mean that it is a unique occurrence, but even if it were, its integrity as a formula should not be doubted. It is not the repetition itself, but the *repeatability* that makes a phrase formulaic. In any case, this unique occurrence appears to be simply a variation on the formulaic structure of (5b) 'of great bounty' and (6b) 'of great honour'. Likewise, these seem to be variations of the common formula, 'of great renown', frequently found in other verse romances, and found three times in *Amis and Amiloun*.

According to their own testimony – and in line with the definition of a formula based on prototype theory – such alteration is characteristic of the process used by the Yugoslav histrions and presumably the same as that employed by griots in West Africa today. It is akin to the process employed by illiterate English scops, Scandinavian skalds and Celtic bards, all of whom recited (or composed) orally in the minstrel tradition. All of these traditions seem to be related to that of the rhapsodes of ancient Greece (fifth to fourth century BCE), professional performers of epic poetry, and particularly to that of Homer, thus supporting Lord and Parry's hypothesis.

The name 'rhapsode' itself comes from 'rhapsoidein', meaning 'to stitch songs together', and this is exactly what the rhapsodes, scops, bards, histrions and griots did and do. They draw on a fund of existent formulae, each of which has little particularizing force in and of itself, but sew them together in improvisational recitations, tailoring them as necessary to fit constraints of rhyme or metre, ultimately producing coherent ideas. The process can be used either to recount an existing tale – in which case the recital is essentially an impromptu composition of a new version of recognizably the same tale – or for the composition of new tales. This technique of composing (or recomposing) a tale is indeed very much part of the oral tradition.

In *Amis and Amiloun*, however, we find the technique being employed in the creation of a 'literate' composition designed to be read as much as recited. No less than 61 per cent of the text of *Amis and Amiloun* consists of formulae.[14] That these are related to the oral tradition is clear in the manner in which the formulae are manipulated and 'sewn together' to provide a coherent narrative. The oral tradition is also apparent in the structure of the verse romances as a whole.[15] They tend to begin with an exhortative opening that names the audience and calls it to listen, make use of direct address and frequent repetition of plot and invocations to regulate the narrative, and usually end with a prayer that calls on a blessing for the audience, the poet and/or the protagonists.[16] Such elements not only aid the storyteller in keeping his narrative in mind, they are also useful for allowing the audience to absorb the material more easily aurally when they do not have visual cues to regulate the narrative.

Here, however, they enter a text whose presentation shows that it is to be seen as much as heard: in other words, it is to be read. As the above stanza demonstrates, the intended audience is named and called to listen (lines 2–3). Further along, reference is made to hearing (lines 10–12). Since, however, the formulae themselves have their origins in the oral tradition, it is not surprising that they make reference to hearing or listening. Other such formulae employed by the author include the injunction: 'Herkeneth and ye mow here' (24). Elsewhere we find reference to the act of composition and recital itself:

> The childrenis names, as y yow hyght,
> In ryme y wol rekene ryght
> And tel in my talking.
>
> (37–9)

More interesting, for our purposes, are the references to reading and writing. For example, in the third stanza, we read:

> In Lumbardy, y understond,
> Whilom bifel in that lond,
> **In romance as we reede**,
> Two barouns hend wonyd in lond.
>
> (25–8)

Other references to reading include the following:

> In gest as so we rede (144);
> In boke as so we rede (447);
> In gest to rede it is gret rewthe (1546);
> Thus in gest rede we (1729);
> In romaunce as we rede (2448).

What is perhaps most interesting here is that these references to reading are couched in formulaic structures typical of the oral tradition. Susan Wittig notes 'the poet's ability to vary the acoustical patterns of a twelve-line stanza by altering elements of the line and yet without altering the felt formulaic meaning of the whole phrase':[17]

al thus in
{ romaunce
  boke
  geste }
{ as we say
  as we tell
  as it is told
  as (so) we rede
  as ye may here
  rede we
  to rede is grete rewthe }

She calls this a 'substitution system', but it is essentially a typical aspect of oral-formulaic composition. Here, however, this tool of the oral tradition has been appropriated by a literate one, for despite the largely oral structure and use of formulae, the references to books and reading make it clear that these narratives are written by and for a literate society. Orality has been adapted to literacy.

Even *King Horn*, arguably the earliest Middle English verse romance (thirteenth century), twice refers to writing and written documents:

> A writ he dude devise;
> Athulf hit dude write.
>
> (938–9)

> He dude writes sende
> Into Yrlonde.
>
> (1011–12)

Nevertheless, it opens in a traditionally oral fashion with a call to the audience to listen:

> Alle beon he blithe
> That to my song lythe!
> A sang ich schal you singe.
>
> (1–3)

Another well known romance, *Athelston* (fourteenth century), actually 'relies on deceit practised through letter writing' for its plot, and 'its four main protagonists meet in their youth while serving as letter carrying messengers'.[18] Letters are mentioned eleven times in the romance (ll. 14, 187,

193, 203, 206, 224, 300, 303, 363, 366, 715). There are numerous other references to reading and writing, and while the romance does begin with an exhortative opening to listen to the tale, the compositor also claims that there is a written source: 'In book iwreten we fynde' (21). It seems this claim was probably just as spurious as Geoffrey of Monmouth's claim to an ancient British book as the source of his *Historium regum britanniae*. While a high degree of literacy is implied in its telling, it is nevertheless structured and composed like an oral composition.

Many other tales do have antecedents and, despite claims to be original, many are simply reworkings of pre-existing tales. *Sir Launfal* (late fourteenth century), for example, closes by saying:

> Thomas Chestre made thys tale
> Of the noble knyght Syr Launfale,
> Good of chyvalrye.
>
> (1039–41)

But, as pointed out in the TEAMS introduction to the text:

> When Thomas Chestre composed his version of the narrative, he drew on three earlier texts, two of which survive. The immediate and primary source for Chestre is the 538-line Middle English *Sir Landevale*, which is an adaptation from Marie de France. It has been preserved in a number of manuscripts and early printed books. Verbal echoes of *Sir Landevale* are pronounced in Chestre's text; in fact, Chestre borrowed whole lines from it. The Old French lay of *Graelent* forms the other known source for *Sir Launfal*. This anonymous text, or some version of it, appears to be the source for four passages in *Sir Launfal*.[19]

His borrowings demonstrate a degree of literacy in at least two languages. Nevertheless, where Chestre shows his skills in composing original verses, especially in portions of translation, he continues to employ the oral formulae that are the hallmark of oral composition. Literacy is informed by orality.

Lai le Fresne is another of Marie de France's twelfth-century lays that was translated into English in the fourteenth century as *Lay Le Freine*. Here again, the author/compositor/translator uses oral-formulaic constructions, referring to both the oral and written traditions:

> We **redeth** oft and findeth **ywrite** –
> And this clerkes wele it wite –

Layes that ben in harping
Ben yfounde of ferli thing.
Sum bethe of wer and sum of wo,
And sum of joie and mirthe also,
And sum of trecherie and of gile,
Of old aventours that fel while;
And sum of bourdes and ribaudy,
And mani ther beth of fairy.
Of al thinges that men **seth**,
Mest o love for sothe thai beth.
In Breteyne bi hold time
This layes were wrought, **so seith this rime.**
When kinges might our yhere
Of ani mervailes that ther were,
Thai token an harp in gle and game,
And maked a lay and gaf it name.
Now of this aventours that weren yfalle,
Y can tel sum ac nought alle.
Ac herkneth lordinges, sothe to sain,
Ichil you telle Lay le Frayn.

(1–22)

This oral structure in a written form actually became the basis for the prologue of another tale, *Sir Orfeo* (late fourteenth century). In fact, the beginning of that work is word-for-word the same as its source, and astonishingly, even the orthography is closely followed. The first substantial variation only comes at the end of line 13 ('In Breteyne this layes were wrought'), requiring a subsequent change in the following line for the sake or rhyme ('First y-founde and forth y-brought'). Two additional lines are then added ('Of aventours that fel bi dayes,/ Wherof Bretouns maked her layes'). The next noteworthy change comes in the ending of line 23 (equivalent to line 21 of *Lay Le Freine*), where the original 'sothe to sain' – which rhymes with 'Lay le Frayn' in the following line – is changed to 'that ben trewe' to rhyme with the name of the work presented in the next line, 'Sir Orfewe'. However, even in these variations the substitutions are formulae typical of the oral tradition.

Such reference to writing, not to mention direct copying, shows that these romances were indeed the products of a literate society, but structurally they retain the hallmarks of oral-formulaic composition: the method of freely borrowing from earlier sources is highly characteristic of oral composition. While this work would be considered shameless plagiarism today, from the point of view of the 'author', this would not be any sort of theft of intellectual property; it would simply be the appropriation and knitting together of pre-existing formulae which he has tailored to meet the needs of his particular story. In the tradition of an essentially oral culture it would presumably be admirable to be able to reproduce so accurately a pre-existing string of formulae. Only with the rise of literacy does such a practice become blameworthy.

At this point in the transition from orality to literacy, it seems that such free borrowing was still very much an accepted part of the creative process. Thus we see that the compositors of the Middle English verse romances, composing 'literately', were nevertheless indebted to an earlier oral tradition for their methods. German Minnesänger, Provençal troubadours and French trouvères presumably used the same techniques for their literate creations.

Even though it is certain that oral recitation continued to be popular – no doubt accounting for the continued popularity of the form and structure to please audiences that still had to digest the tales orally – the raconteur no longer need to rely on memory to keep his narrative together; he or she could now rely on a written support. Nevertheless, the written versions retain the use of oral-formulaic formulae and repetition long after the mnemonic function which necessitated their employment in pre-literate cultures had become obsolete. All of this indicates that for at least a few centuries an essentially oral form of composition and narrative enjoyed popularity, even when composed by and intended for a literate society.

There is, however, evidence that more solitary reading began to become popular at this time. Many of the romances alluded to in this paper (for example *Amis and Amiloun*, *Sir Degaré*, *Lay le Frein*) appear in the celebrated Auchinleck Manuscript (NLS Adv MS 19.2.1). Produced in London in the early fourteenth century, the manuscript (see Figure 1.3) is evidently a presentation copy, indicating that it was intended to be seen as much as heard. Though far from being the most elaborately decorated manuscript, its illustrations were still pleasing enough to induce mutilation of the manuscript at a later date in order to procure the drawings. Furthermore, we see in what remains (as we do in almost all the manuscript copies, even the most mundane) line-breaks, capitalization and a sort of punctuation that is absent in the manuscripts of Caedmon's *Hymn* and *Beowulf*. While the punctuation employed is somewhat different from that which would be used today, it is clear that its use, as well as the *mise-en-page* employed throughout the manuscript, show that visualization of the verse was as important as its aural quality.

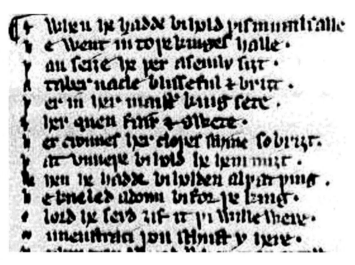

Figure 1.3 Lines 410–420 of *Sir Orfeo* from the Auchinleck Manuscript *c.*1340 (National Library of Scotland Adv. MS 19.2.1. f. 302ra)[20]

The stories that were being told were beginning to be read as much as simply heard. Writing was no longer just a means of preserving 'oral literature', but it was coming to be appreciated in and of itself.

Around this time two important developments were coming about in England. First, English was beginning to assert itself as a language worthy of literature after centuries of domination by French. Second, the verse romance and its characteristic oral form were falling out of fashion. While verse itself was still valued, there seemed to be a new appreciation for novelty and innovation, which had previously been eschewed. This can clearly be seen in the works of Geoffrey Chaucer, who arguably gave English back her *lettres de noblesse*. *The Canterbury Tales* is almost entirely composed in verse and was intended to be recited. His verses, though making use of plenty of formulae, are not filled to the brim with the trite clichés so common of the verse romances on which he occasionally relied for his stories. He even derides this type of poetry; when the fictional pilgrim 'Chaucer' is called upon to tell a tale, he responds:

> For oother tale certes kan I noon,
> But of a rym I lerned longe agoon.

> (708–09)[21]

In the one tale he ascribes to 'himself', Chaucer intends to tell a tale of the 'old-fashioned' sort. He duly begins in the style expected of the verse romances, using common formulae to address the intended audience and announcing that his tale will be *told*:

> Listeth, lordes, in good entent,
> And I wol telle verrayment
> Of myrthe and of solas.
>
> (1–3)

Using the same formula we have seen in line 4b of *Amis and Amiloun*, Chaucer says that Sir Thopas:

> Yboren was in fer contree,
> In Flaudres, **al beyond the see**.
>
> (718–19)

Other typical formulae include: 'Ful many a mayde, bright in bour' (742), or 'And so it bifel upon a day, / For sothe, as I yow telle may' (748–9). The brief tale is full of the stock phrases frequently encountered in the verse romances, but rarely utilized elsewhere in Chaucer's verse. Its employment here is not admiring emulation, but ironic mockery. This becomes plainly evident about two hundred lines later when the Host cries out: 'Namoore of this, for Goddes dignitee . . . Thy drasty rymyng is nat worth a toord!' (919–30). When Chaucer (satirically) protests that it is the best he can do, the host suggests that he tell something in prose – and there follows the prose *Tale of Melibee*.

It seems highly probable that novelty in verse (such as one more frequently finds in Chaucer) and in prose itself (as the *Tale of Melibee* and the *Parson's Tale*) was gaining acceptance precisely because compositors and their audiences were more literate. They no longer needed the repetition of formulaic stock phrases to serve as mnemonic aids to hold a story together. They could compose and record them in writing, using reading rather than memory to recall them. Since the formulae were no longer actually necessary, their frequent employment was no longer a reassurance as it had been, but was becoming increasingly annoying as it would be for a modern audience. Rather than holding a story together, they began to be seen as unnecessary filler that distracted from the meat of the story. They could ultimately be done away with. Good poetry would be novel, and not all literature need be in verse. Prose, which had long been acceptable for scientific, religious or didactic treatises, was finally becoming acceptable for narration, or fiction, of an essentially ludic nature.

Evidence of this can be seen in the proliferation of prose literature in English that began to emerge at this time. Two striking examples would be Mandeville's *Travels* (fourteenth century) or the *Gesta Romanorum* (1440), widely popular with over 165 manuscripts whose *exempla* would later serve as source material for Shakespeare.[22] In the fifteenth century, the romances themselves would be recast in prose by Sir Thomas Malory, who whiled away his time in prison compiling and writing his celebrated *Le Morte D'Arthur*. One reason for the wide popularity of Malory's work is that it was soon printed by Caxton. It thus not only became more widely available and more affordable, but in a rather circular effect, the increase in literacy afforded by printing no doubt led to a greater appreciation for prose literature of this kind. In subsequent centuries, it was Malory's prose version, not the verse romance originals, that most often formed the basis for reformulation of Arthuriana (as in works by Tennyson and White among others). This was how largely literate audiences were now beginning to prefer literature.

In his book, *From Memory to Written Record*, M. T. Clanchy wrote that: 'Literacy is unique among technologies in penetrating and structuring the intellect itself, which makes it hard for scholars, whose own skills are shaped by literacy, to reconstruct the mental changes which it brings about.'[23] This is true not only for scholars, but for anyone who grows up with a more or less literate mentality. I would hold that one aspect where we most often have trouble appreciating the pre-literate or illiterate mentality is in the appreciation of verse. Today, it is conceived of as being a highly 'literate' form of writing – associated with cultivation, education and indeed, writing. It is intended to be read. And it is undeniable that modern poetry from literate societies is deeply informed by literate culture and literature – so much so that the oral/aural qualities that originally engendered its formation and creation are hidden or even eclipsed. Often it even does away with the employment of verse that was the defining characteristic of poetry. But the fact remains that verse poetry is ultimately oral in origins. This oral aspect can be seen in the Middle English verse romances, which became popular with the revival of English as a language fitting for literary creation. In this period of transition from a largely oral society to an essentially literate one, the old forms of oral composition initially played an important role in the creation and elaboration of the popular genre. Ironically, it also appears that the subsequent rise of literacy in the linguistic culture that had led to their creation, and in which they played a part, ultimately led to their decline. But even in what remains, the poetry and literature that we can still read today, vestiges of orality are ever present.

Notes and references

1. Thomas C. Foster, *How to Read Literature Like a Professor* (New York: Harper-Collins, 2003), pp. 22–3.
2. See e.e. cummings, *Complete Poems*, ed. George James Firmage (New York and London: Granada, 1981).
3. See John Ford, 'In romance as we read and as we hear in Geste: written orality in the Medieval "short story": the Verse Romances of the 13th and 14th centuries', *Journal of the Short Story in English*, 47 (2006), 29–48 (p. 30).
4. Albert B. Lord, *The Singer of Tales* (Cambridge, MA: Harvard University Press, 1960).
5. Ibid., Chapter 10, 'Some notes on medieval epic'.
6. From CUL MS Kk. 5.16, as found in *Sweet's Anglo-Saxon Reader*, ed. Dorothy Whitelock (Oxford: Clarendon Press, 1967), p. 181.
7. From the University of Georgetown's website: 'Labyrinth: resources for medieval studies', http://labyrinth.georgetown.edu/, 21 December 2008.
8. The image presented has been declared to be in the public domain in the United States, Canada and the European Union. Image source and declaration can be found at the following site: http://en.wikipedia.org/wiki/File:Caedmon%27s_Hymn_Moore_mine01.gif (accessed 21 December 2008).
9. This is a public domain image from Kip Wheeler's homepage at Carson-Wheeler College. Wheeler states: 'This image is public domain'; http://web.cn.edu/kwheeler/images/Beowulfpage.jpeg (accessed 21 December 2008).
10. D. S. Brewer, 'The relationship of Chaucer to the English and European traditions', in *Chaucer and the Chaucerians*, ed. D. S. Brewer (London: Nelson, 1966), p. 1.
11. John Ford, 'Towards a new understanding of formulae: prototypes and the mental template', *Neuphilologische Mitteilungen*, 103 (2002), 205–26 (p. 225).
12. See appendix to John Ford, 'From poésie to poetry: remaniement and medieval techniques of french-to-english translation of verse romance' (unpublished doctoral thesis, University of Glasgow, 2000).
13. For example 1b, *Athelston* 420; 2a, *Athelston* 7; 3b, *Launfal* 106; 4b, *Havelok* 1377; 8a, *Degaré* 581; 10a, *Degaré* 841; 12b, *Launfal* 393; 6b, *Degaré* 802. References to lines in text other than *Amis and Amiloun* are from texts provided by the TEAMS Middle English Text Series, http://www.lib.rochester.edu/camelot/teams/tmsmenu.htm
14. Ford, 'from Poésie to poetry', p. 322.
15. Ford, 'In romance as we read', pp. 29–48 (p. 38).
16. Ibid., pp. 29–48 (p. 42).
17. Susan Wittig, *Stylistics and Narrative Structures in the Middle English Romance* (Austin: University of Texas Press, 1978), p. 30.
18. Ford, 'In romance as we read', pp. 38–9.

19. Introduction to *Sir Launfal*, TEAMS, http://www.lib.rochester.edu/camelot/teams/launint.htm, 10 July 2008.
20. Image used by permission of Dr Iain G. Brown, Principal Curator of the Manuscripts Division of the National Library of Scotland on 15 July 2008.
21. This and all further quotations from Chaucer taken from *The Riverside Chaucer*, ed. L. D. Benton (Oxford: Oxford University Press, 1987).
22. Thomas Garbaty, *Medieval English Literature* (Lexington, MA: D. C. Heath, 1984), p. 813.
23. M. T. Clanchy, *From Memory to Written Record* (1979; Oxford: Blackwell, 1993), p. 185.

2
Modes of Bible Reading in Early Modern England

W. R. Owens

In an article entitled 'Books and scrolls: navigating the Bible' (2002), Peter Stallybrass argues that what he calls 'discontinuous reading' has been central to Christianity ever since it adopted the codex in preference to the scroll. He points to the ways in which Renaissance bibles were designed to facilitate easy reference backwards and forwards within the text by being divided into chapters and furnished with finding aids such as tables of contents, running heads, consistent pagination and indexes, arguing that 'navigational aids' such as these encouraged discontinuous reading practices. Stallybrass indeed regards the habit of sequential reading, or reading forward through a book in a continuous fashion, as a 'radically reactionary' practice, describing it as 'scroll reading', a practice which has only come to seem natural to us because of the influence of the novel, where 'the teleological drive' to keep turning the pages discourages dipping about or turning back in the text.[1]

Stallybrass admits that there may seem to be something counterintuitive about his argument, since, at first glance, the Christian Bible would appear to be structured in such a way as to assume a continuous method of reading. It begins with Genesis, an account of the beginning of things, and ends with Revelation, an account of how things will end, and so it would seem logical to read it sequentially. As an example of a reader who apparently does just this, Stallybrass quotes from the opening of the autobiography of Lady Grace Mildmay, begun in 1617, where she says that she has found by experience that the best way to read the Bible is to begin reading every day and continue 'until we have gone through the whole book of God from the first of Genesis unto the last of the Revelation and then begin again and so over and over without weariness'.[2] Stallybrass comments that 'This would appear at first sight to be a recommendation to read the bible as we would read a novel', the only difference being the idea of immediately starting reading all over again. The thrust of his article, however, is to argue that the 'navigational aids' included in Renaissance bibles 'showed one how to read the bible other than as a continuous narrative', and in his view the presence of such aids would have made it difficult for Lady Mildmay to read in the linear way she seems to describe here. He takes as his central example a copy of the 1580 quarto edition of the Geneva Bible now in the Folger Shakespeare Library. This is a compilation volume, including not only the text of the Bible itself, but the Book of Common Prayer, and a set of two concordances which, Stallybrass says, 'suggest nonlinear readings of the text, in which one can detach a word from its narrative context and/or reattach a word to other seemingly disconnected passages in which the same word occurs'. His conclusion is that this bible 'suggests a wide range of ways to read the scriptures, *none* of them continuous' (his emphasis), and he returns to Lady Mildmay to show that we would be mistaken in thinking on the basis of the earlier quotation that she was 'extolling a reading of the bible as continuous narrative'.[3] In fact, as becomes evident later on in her autobiography, in referring to reading right through 'the whole book of God' she meant reading it in a sequence of chapters taken from various parts of the sacred book:

> every day . . . I did read a chapter in the books of Moses, another in one of the Prophets, one chapter in the Gospels and another in the Epistles to the end of the Revelation and the whole Psalms appointed for the day, ending and beginning again and so proceeded in that course. Wherein I found that as the water pierceth the hard stone by often dropping thereupon, so the continual exercise in the word of God made a deep impression in my stony heart . . .[4]

Stallybrass describes these daily readings as 'discontinuous', and says that it was 'the collation of widely separated passages [in the Bible] that worked the magic of making "a deep impression" . . . upon Lady Grace's "stony heart"'. Such collative reading practices, he says, are based on the long history within Christianity of 'the creation of systematic methods of discontinuous reading'.[5]

Stallybrass's article is a fascinating and provocative one, and it has certainly had an influence on subsequent scholarship.[6] Nevertheless, there are a number of problems in accepting his account of how the Bible was read, in particular its argument that Protestant denominations shared with Roman Catholicism 'an emphasis upon techniques of discontinuous reading', and that non-sequential reading practices remained central 'to nearly all Christians in early modern England'.[7] Stallybrass is, in part, responding to an earlier article by Patrick Collinson, in which Collinson had argued that one of the ways in which Protestantism had broken with Catholicism was the new stress it placed on reading the Bible in continuous fashion. In support of his argument, Collinson quoted a famous passage from John Foxe, describing some weavers in the Suffolk town of Hadleigh in the reign of Henry VIII:

> a great number of that parish became exceeding well learned in the holy scriptures, as well women as men: so that a man might have found among them many that had often read the whole Bible through, and that could have said a great part of Saint Paul's epistles by heart, and very well and readily have given a godly learned sentence in any matter of controversy.[8]

Even when due allowance is made for Foxe's polemical purposes in recounting it, this passage tells us much about Protestant Bible reading practices in the sixteenth century, including the remarkable fact that many ordinary men and women had 'often read the whole Bible through'. Writing in the later seventeenth century, Thomas Hobbes thought that such widespread reading of the Bible had been a prime cause of the breakdown in authority that had led to the Civil Wars:

> after the Bible was translated into *English*, every Man, nay every Boy and Wench, that could read *English*, thought they spoke with God Almighty, and understood what he said, when by a certain number of Chapters a day, they had read the Scriptures once or twice over, the Reverence and Obedience due to the Reformed Church here, and to the Bishops and Pastors therein, was cast off, and every Man became a Judge of Religion, and an Interpreter of the Scriptures to himself.[9]

As I shall demonstrate, there is a great deal of evidence to support Collinson's argument that repeated, sequential reading of the Bible was a practice frequently and strongly recommended by Protestant writers, and was indeed one of the main ways in which people read the Bible in early modern England.

In a prologue written by Archbishop Cranmer and included in the second and subsequent editions of the Great Bible from 1540 onwards, he made it clear that individuals had a duty to undertake serious and sustained reading of the Bible. Responding to an imagined reader of 'simple witte and capacyte' who finds it hard to understand the sacred text, Cranmer gives the following advice:

> take [the Bible] into thyne hands, reade the hole storye, and that thou understandest kepe it well in memorye: that thou understandest not, reade it agayne, and agayne: if thou can neither so come by it, counsaylle with some other that is better learned. . . . And I doubte not, but God seinge thy diligence and redynesse . . . will hym selfe vouchsaffe with his holy spyrete to illuminate thee, and to open unto thee that which was locked from thee.[10]

Bible reading by Protestants in the early modern period was regarded as a strenuous and intensive activity characterized by repetition and memorization. The point I want to focus on, however, is Cranmer's concern that the Bible be read *as a whole*. In the Preface to his 1549 Book of Common Prayer he launches an attack on the Catholic practice of dividing up public Bible readings in a non-sequential fashion to fit the requirements of the liturgical year.[11] According to Cranmer, the early Church Fathers had ordained that 'all the whole Bible (or the greatest parte thereof) should be read over once in the yeare', but in subsequent Catholic practice this injunction had been 'altered, broken, and neglected'. Non-scriptural material and activities had been included in the liturgy, with the result that books of the Bible 'were onely begon, and never read thorow'. Cranmer's Protestant Prayer Book included a calendar in which 'the readyng of holy scripture is so set furthe, that all thynges shall bee doen in ordre, without breakyng one piece therof from another'. His arrangement was designed to ensure that the Psalter should be read through once a month, that the Old Testament (all except some passages deemed to be less edifying, but including most of the Apocrypha) should be read through over the course of a year, and that the New Testament (with the exception of most of the book of Revelation) should be read through three times a year. Any other readings or responses which would 'breake the continuall course of the readyng of the scripture' were to be omitted as far as possible.[12]

Cranmer's intention is clearly that the Old Testament, the Gospels and the Epistles should each be read through in church in a sequential order. There will be some exceptions to this broadly sequential ordering; specific readings are stipulated for days of particular liturgical importance, such as Christmas day, even though such readings break the normally linear sequence. Stallybrass stresses the 'innumerable exceptions' that disrupt the attempt to produce a sequential reading structure,[13] but as Alison A. Chapman has argued, what is much more striking than the exceptions is the extent to which 'despite the frequent interruptions, Cranmer constructed his lectionary calendar so as to linearize the Scripture reading whenever feasible'.[14]

Cranmer's insistence on the importance of sequential reading of the Bible was shared by other Protestant reformers. Calvin argued for a return to the practice of the early church, in which 'the Books of Scripture were expounded to the people in one uninterrupted series'.[15] The *Book of Discipline* (1560) of the Scottish Church similarly required that 'the Scripturis be red in ordour': skipping from place to place in the Bible is, it says, 'not so proffitabill to edifie the Churche, as the continewall following of ane text'.[16] The English Presbyterian *Directory for the Publick Worship of God* prepared by the Westminster Assembly and passed into law by Parliament in March 1645 as a replacement for the Prayer Book, enjoined that 'all the Canonicall Books be read over in order, that the people may be better acquainted with the whole body of the Scriptures: And ordinarily, where the Reading in either Testament endeth on one Lord's day, it is to begin the next.'[17]

Clearly English (and Scottish) Protestants regarded sequential reading of the Bible as important in public worship. There were debates about the matter, and later in the seventeenth century nonconformist opponents of the Church of England often complained that the order of worship laid down in the Book of Common Prayer did not go far enough in the direction of preserving sequential reading of the Bible. Right into the eighteenth century we find Anglican writers having to defend the Prayer Book on this point. Thomas Bisse, for example, argues that its inclusion of readings from the Old and the New Testaments at each service was a way of demonstrating the unity of the Bible, the 'harmony and consent' between the two Testaments. The faith of hearers will be better established, he says, because by this mode of Bible reading they are 'gradually led from a darker revelation to a clearer view, and prepared by the veils of the Law to bear the light breaking forth in the Gospel'. Bisse even argues that the Anglican order of reading Scripture is superior to that laid down by the early Church Fathers: 'for whereas they so ordered it, that all the whole Bible (or the greatest part of it) should be read over once every year; in our Church the Old Testament is read once, but the New thrice every year'.[18]

As far as public reading of the Bible is concerned, the evidence seems incontrovertible that early modern Protestants were strongly of the view that it should not be read in a disconnected, piecemeal fashion. Nor should it be the prerogative of church authorities to select and arrange readings according to ecclesiastical requirements without regard to sequential ordering. Instead, the Bible was to be regarded as a unified work, whose contents had been arranged in a canonical order, and which was to be read through in sequence as far as possible.

The same emphasis was a feature of the books of instruction on private and family reading of the Bible that appeared in great numbers in the sixteenth and seventeenth centuries.[19] The earliest such set of directions for Bible reading to have been published in England seems to have been a translation in 1579 of a work by the Flemish Lutheran theologian Andreas Hyperius, *The Course of Christianitie: or, As Touching the Dayly Reading and Meditation of the Holy Scriptures*. This included a chart with a page for each month of the year divided into the number of days in that month, showing how to read each of the two Testaments over the course of one year in a broadly sequential manner. Each day's reading would include a chapter or two from the Old Testament, together with a Psalm, and a chapter from the New Testament. Within this tripartite reading structure the Old Testament is begun at Genesis and read through to Malachi, but omitting Job, Proverbs, Ecclesiastes and Song of Solomon, which were to be read at the end of the sequence. The New Testament was to be read through in strict sequence and the Psalms likewise. The instructions are set out in tabular form, so that readers can 'fasten them to the wals in their studie, Parlour, privie chamber, shoppe, chappel, Oratory, and wheresoever they list [find] themselves'.[20]

Another early example of the 'directions for Bible reading' genre was Edward Vaughan's *Ten Introductions: How to Read, and in Reading, how to Understand; and in Understanding, how to Beare in Mind all the Bookes, Chapters, and Verses, contained in the Holie Bible* (1594). Vaughan repeatedly emphasizes the value of getting to know the Bible as a whole. Readers should learn the names of all the books 'as they are in order, from *Genesis* to the *Revelation*', and they should 'go over these books old and new, by some proportion dayly, either morning or evening'.[21] He offers a brief synopsis of each book, and even goes so far as to reduce the entire Bible to a set of ten 'stories', which he sets out in diagrammatic form. The authors of *A Garden of Spirituall Flowers* (1609) also included 'rules' for reading the Bible in a regular sequence. 'In reading of the Scriptures, reade not heere and there a Chapter (except upon some good occasion) but the Bible in order throughout, and that as oft as thou canst, that so by little and little thou maiest bee acquainted with the whole course and historie of the Bible.' These rules applied not only to individual reading, but to family reading as well: 'one Chapter in the Morning, another at Meales, another in the Evening before Prayer: beginning at the beginning of the Bible, and continuing to the end'.[22]

Similar advice was included in one of the most popular devotional works published in the seventeenth century, Lewis Bayly's *The Practice of Pietie* (1612). In a chapter setting out '*Briefe directions how to read the Holy Scriptures, once every yeare over, with ease, profit, and reverence*', Bayly recommended reading three chapters a day (morning, midday, and in the evening) so that the canonical books of the Bible can be read through in one year. As he explains, 'The reading of the Bible in *order*, will helpe thee the better to understand both the *Historie* and *scope* of the holy *Scripture*.' The reader is enjoined to 'apply these thinges to thine own heart, and read not these Chapters, as matters of *Historicall* discourse; but as if they were so many *Letters* or *Epistles* sent downe from God out of *Heaven* unto thee'.[23]

Perhaps the most widely used of these books of advice on Bible reading was Nicholas Byfield's *Directions for the Private Reading of the Scriptures* (1617). Like Vaughan, Byfield includes an outline of each book, chapter by chapter, but he also includes a tabular calendar setting out which chapters are to be read each day, so that the entire Bible can be read over the course of one year, starting, on 25 March,[24] with Genesis, and ending up with Revelation the following January, reserving Psalms to be read over in order at the end, from the 23 of January to the 28 of February. The reading programme recommended here is by no means a mechanical one, but one undertaken in a highly active and engaged fashion. Byfield offers detailed and practical advice on how the reader should collect and record passages that seem of particular significance:

> First make thee a little paper booke of a sheete or two of paper . . . then write upon the toppe of every leafe the title for that that thou wouldest observe in reading. . . . In reading observe onely such places as stare thee in the face, that are so evident, thy heart cannot looke of them. . . . In noting the places, set downe under each title only the booke, Chapter, and verse, and not the words, for that will tire thee in the end. . . . Now when thou hast done thy quarters taske, or thy yeeres taske, then thou maist write out the choicest things, as thou thinkest good.[25]

Many more examples of books of advice on how to read the whole Bible through in a year might be cited. In a table appended to *A Way to the Tree of Life* (1647), John White set out a programme beginning on 1 January, with two or three chapters from the Old Testament and one from the New being read each day up to the middle of September, by which time the New Testament had been completed; thereafter, until the end of December, readings were from the Old Testament only.[26] A similar cycle of reading was recommended by Walter Holmes, in a brief pamphlet published in 1649. His table began on 25 March, with an average of about four chapters being read each day. The Old Testament would have been completed by December, and the New Testament by the following March, when the cycle would begin again.[27]

These tables were designed to help readers put into practice what was almost universal advice: to read the whole Bible right through. Occasionally authors of books of instruction would recommend that before embarking on the whole Bible readers should become familiar with some of the 'easier' books:

> I would advise that in our reading we begin first with the easiest and plainest Bookes, as the History of Christ, set downe by the Evangelists, and the Booke of *Genesis*: Then to reade the Epistles, first, the short-est, as the Epistles to the *Philippians*, *Colossians*, the first and second to the *Thessalonians*; then the Epistles to the *Galatians*, and to the *Romans*, which last Epistle is called of some, The Key of the Bible: And when we have tryed our selves in these, then to begin the Bible, and to read it thorow.[28]

More often, though, there was no such preliminary 'tasting' or lead-in period. Instead, as William Burkitt put it, 'that we may read it with the greater Profit, resolve we to read the Bible through and in Order; which may be done once a Year, but reading about three Chapters every Day, two out of the Old Testament, and one out of the New'.[29] John Tickell, while accepting that different kinds of Bible reading might be appropriate for different purposes and occasions nevertheless strongly advised reading the Bible 'in order', so as to gain a 'generall knowledge of the Scripture'.[30] To help readers, Tickell provided a summary account of each book of the Bible. The famous preacher Daniel Burgess stressed that the Bible should not be read like other books, 'that is, by leaps, and with skipping over many Parts, to the few good ones worth our time', but should be read in its entirety and in order: '*All of it*; for there is nothing but what has been, or is now, or will one day or other be of use to you. And, in Order; which is such a Servant and Friend to Memory, that one wou'd think it should easily command Practice.'[31]

These books of instruction and advice show conclusively that sequential reading of the whole Bible was the approved and recommended method for private and family reading, but did ordinary readers follow the advice that they should read the Bible in sequence? There is plenty of evidence to suggest that many did, such as Anne Clifford, who kept a diary between 1616 and 1619. She notes in March 1619 that she had just finished a complete reading of a Bible which had belonged to her mother: 'I began to read it the 1st of Feb^ry so as I read all over the whole Bible in less than two months.' Sequential reading was her normal practice because earlier in her diary, in 1617, she records how her husband's chaplain read the Bible with her each day, and that this was being done sequentially, at the rate of three books a month. On 8 March they 'made an end of Exodus', on 13 March 'an end of Leviticus' and on 27 March 'an end of reading Deuteronomy'. At that point, unfortunately, her husband stopped his chaplain reading with her.[32] Another good example is that of the Church of England clergyman Isaac Archer. In the diary he kept from 1641 to 1700, covering almost the whole of his adult life, Archer records that as an undergraduate at Cambridge he was 'diligent in reading the scriptures every day', and had 'read them once through in a yeare for the 3 first yeares according to Mr. Bifield's directions'.[33] Here is explicit evidence of reading behaviour being influenced by the advice given in books of instruction such as Byfield's.

Funeral sermons provide further evidence of Bible reading practices. In a collection entitled *Threnoikos: The House of Mourning*, published in a number of editions in the middle of the seventeenth century, we read of an unnamed young woman who had died in childbirth that she had 'read over the Bible seven times in the seven years that she was married'. In the same collection we are told of a John Moulson that 'He read three chapters in the old Testament, and three in the New every day', and of a 'Mistris I. R.' that she was noted especially for her 'private diligently reading the Word, not contenting her self with a cursory reading it over by task (as some do) but she had a Paper-book by her, and in reading would note down particular points . . . and that in such a manner, as if so be they had been the Common places of some young Divine'.[34] In a funeral sermon commemorating the life of Katherine Brettergh (1602) and much reprinted in the seventeenth century, it is reported that 'she [did] accustome her selfe to read every day eight chapters in the bible: and would not suffer any occasion to hinder her in that *taske*'.[35] The reference to eight chapters a day strongly suggests a sequential programme of reading. Similarly, in the life of Mary Gunter appended to the sermon preached at her funeral, her diligence in Bible reading is singled out for special mention:

she would every yeare read over the whole Bible in an ordinary course, which course she constantly observed for the space of fifteene

yeares together, beginning her taske upon her birth day, and reading every day so many Chapters as to bring it about just with the
yeare. . . . By her great industry in the Scriptures, she had gotten by
heart many select Chapters, and speciall *Psalmes*; and of every Booke
of the Scripture one choyse verse: all which she weekly repeated in
an order which she propounded to her selfe.[36]

Gunter's record of fifteen complete readings was outdone by an Exeter
merchant named Ignatius Jordan, who 'did not onely read the Bible
above twenty times over, but he read it with special observation (as
appeareth by the *Asterisks*, and marks in the Bible which he used) making particular application to himself'.[37]

These may be exceptional cases, but the evidence as a whole suggests
that sequential, linear reading was one of the most important modes of
Bible reading in the early modern period. Quite what the implications
of this may have been is a matter calling for a great deal of further
exploration. *Why* did Protestants in the early modern period place
such emphasis on the importance of sequential reading of the Bible?
How long did sequential reading of the whole Bible remain a widespread practice?[38] How might such reading practices have contributed
to what Scott Mandelbrote has described as 'the growing interest in
the Bible as an historical narrative', and how might this in turn have
interacted with the development of novel-reading in the eighteenth
century?[39]

To answer such questions we need to know more about how sequential reading practices combined with other modes of Bible reading, by
examining the reading habits of individuals and communities of readers,
and the variety of ways in which they interacted with the sacred text in
its various material forms.[40] Stallybrass's article is valuable in highlighting the significance of the paratextual and editorial apparatus found in
early modern Bibles. In his study of sixteenth-century Genevan Bibles,
Francis Higman also discusses the various kinds of aids for readers such
Bibles included, such as prefaces to each book, tables giving the meaning
of proper names, illustrations, maps and chronological tables. Higman
argues that these 'imply a particular way of reading', one which draws
attention 'to the literal meaning of the sacred text, encouraging the
reader to concentrate on the historical truth of the book'.[41] For most
readers in this period, however, the most important 'truths' of the Bible
were theological. The Geneva Bible was notable above all for its extensive
marginal annotations, explicating the text from a strongly Protestant
perspective, and further work needs to be done on how exactly readers

used these annotations.[42] Another matter which needs to be investigated is whether different ecclesiastical groupings within Protestantism may have developed markedly different modes of Bible reading, or whether, as Andrew Cambers and Michelle Wolfe have argued, the same kinds of communal Bible reading practices were characteristic of both Anglicans and nonconformists.[43] Altogether, as Kevin Sharpe has remarked, 'we have scarcely begun to ask the question of what it meant to read the Bible in early modern England'.[44]

Notes and references

1. Peter Stallybrass, 'Books and scrolls: navigating the Bible', in *Books and Readers in Early Modern England: Material Studies*, ed. Jennifer Andersen and Elizabeth Sauer (Philadelphia: University of Pennsylvania Press, 2002), pp. 42–79.
2. See Linda Pollock, *With Faith and Physic: The Life of a Tudor Gentlewoman Lady Grace Mildmay 1552–1620* (London: Collins & Brown, 1993), p. 23.
3. Stallybrass, 'Books and scrolls', pp. 50, 51, 60, 73.
4. Pollock, *With Faith and Physic*, pp. 34–5.
5. Stallybrass, 'Books and scrolls', p. 73.
6. Matthew P. Brown, for example, argues that an 'understandable disposition to see books as linear narratives' has caused book historians to be slow to recognize the implications of the codex format, 'how navigational aids were exploited, how discontinuous reading was practiced, how random access was nurtured or thwarted'. Although certainly aware that other reading practices were prescribed and followed, Brown regards 'discontinuity' as characterizing 'a standard mode of reading for early New Englanders'. See his *The Pilgrim and the Bee: Reading Rituals and Book Culture in Early New England* (Philadelphia: University of Pennsylvania Press, 2007), pp. 34, 80, and passim.
7. Stallybrass, 'Books and scrolls', p. 51.
8. *Foxe's Book of Martyrs: Select Narratives*, ed. John N. King (Oxford: Oxford University Press, 2009), p. 72. This passage is cited (from a different edition) in Patrick Collinson, 'The coherence of the text: how it hangeth together: the Bible in Reformation England', in *The Bible, the Reformation and the Church: Essays in Honour of James Atkinson*, ed. W. P. Stephens (Sheffield: Sheffield Academic Press, 1995), pp. 84–108 (p. 89).
9. Thomas Hobbes, *Behemoth, The History of the Causes of the Civil-Wars of England* (London: W. Crooke, 1682), p. 35.
10. See 'A prologue or preface made by . . . Thomas Archbishop of Canturbury', in *The Byble in Englyshe* ([London:] Richard Grafton, 1540), unpaginated.
11. For an account of a late medieval manuscript of the New Testament including a liturgical calendar and 'table of lessons' designed to enforce reading of specific sections according to their place in the ecclesiastical year, and to prevent a linear reading of the text, see Matti Peikola, 'Instructional aspects of the calendar in later medieval England, with special reference to The John Rylands University Library Ms English 80', in *Instructional Writing in English,*

ed. Matti Peikola, Janne Skaffan and Sanna-Kaisa Tanskanen (Amsterdam and Philadelphia: John Benjamins Publishing, 2009), pp. 83–104.

12. See *The First and Second Prayer-Books of King Edward the Sixth* (London: Dent, 1910), pp. 3–5.

13. Stallybrass, 'Books and scrolls', p. 50.

14. Alison A. Chapman, 'Now and then: sequencing the sacred in two Protestant calendars', *Journal of Medieval and Early Modern Studies*, 33 (2003), 91–123 (p. 106).

15 John Calvin, *Second Defense of the Faith concerning the Sacraments* (1555), cited in Chapman, 'Now and then', p. 103.

16. Cited in Chapman, 'Now and then', p. 104.

17. *A Directory for the Publique Worship of God* (London: Company of Stationers, 1645), p. 7.

18. Thomas Bisse, *The Beauty of Holiness in the Common-Prayer* (London: Henry Clements, 1716), pp. 56–7, 61.

19. See Ian Green, *Print and Protestantism in Early Modern England* (Oxford: Oxford University Press, 2000), pp. 144–51.

20. [Andreas Hyperius,] *The Course of Christianitie*, trans. John Ludham (London: Henry Bynneman, 1579), p. 204.

21. [Edward Vaughan,] *Ten Introductions* (London: A. Islip, 1594), sig. Br.

22. Ri[chard] Ro[gers] and others, *A Garden of Spirituall Flowers* (London: T. Pavier, 1609), sigs. 2Fr–3Fr. This very popular short work incorporates material from the chapter 'Of Reading' first published in Richard Rogers, *Seven Treatises* (London: Thomas Man and Robert Dexter, 1603), pp. 288–91.

23. [Lewis Bayly,] *The Practice of Pietie: Directing a Christian how to Walke that he may Please God* (1612; [London:] John Hodgets, 1624), pp. 244–7.

24. In England in the early modern period, the official calendar year began on Lady Day (the Feast of the Annunciation), 25 March.

25. Nicholas Bifeild [*sic*], *Directions for the Private Reading of the Scriptures*, 2nd edn. (London: N. Butter, 1618), Preface, unpaginated.

26. John White, *A Way to the Tree of Life, Discovered in Sundry Directions for the Profitable Reading of the Scriptures* (London: R. Royston, 1647), pp. 341–[344].

27. Walter Holmes, *An Annuall Almanacke: Shewing, how to Read the Chapters of the whole Bible, from the beginning of Genesis, to the end of the Revelation, once in the Yeare, by so many Chapters every Day* (London: n.p., 1649).

28. Elnathan Parr, *The Grounds of Divinity*, 7th edn. (London: Samuel Man, 1633), p. 48. For another recommendation to begin with 'the plainest Books first', see William Lowth, *Directions for the Profitable Reading of the Holy Scriptures* (London: H. Clements, 1708), p. 9.

29. William Burkitt, *The Poor Man's Help, and the Young Man's Guide*, 3rd edn. (London: Tho. Parkhurst, 1697), p. 74.

30. J[ohn] T[ickell], *Crums of Bread for the Dove . . . with Directions for Profitable Reading the Scriptures* (n.p., n.d. [?Oxford, 1652]), p. 69.

31. Daniel Burgess, *Proofs of God's Being, and of the Scriptures Divine Original. With Twenty Directions for the Profitable Reading of them*, 2nd edn. (London: Tho. Parkhurst, 1698), p. 21.

32. See *The Diary of Anne Clifford 1616–1619*, ed. Katherine O. Acheson (New York and London: Garland Publishing, 1995), pp. 102, 72–6.

33. See *Two East Anglian Diaries 1641–1729: Isaac Archer and William Coe*, ed. Matthew Storey (Woodbridge, Suffolk: Boydell Press, 1994), p. 60 (and cf. p. 55 for a further reference to reading the Bible 'according to Mr Bifield's book'). This passage from Archer's diary is cited (from the manuscript) by Sophie Oxenham, '"A touchstone the written word": experimental Calvinist life-writing and the anxiety of reading salvation 1650–1689' (unpublished PhD thesis, University of London, 1999), p. 134; see also her article, '"That I may tye myself under mine own handwriting": reading and writing salvation in the diaries of Oliver Heywood and Isaac Archer', *Bunyan Studies*, 10 (2001/2002), 65–87 (p. 76). I am grateful to Dr Oxenham for the loan of her thesis.

34. *Threnoikos: The House of Mourning* (1647; London: John Williams, 1672), p. 300, 248, 384. I owe this reference to the kindness of Dr Femke Molekamp.

35. *Deaths Advantage Little Regarded . . . in two Funerall Sermons . . . at the Buriall of Mistris Katherin Brettergh*, 2nd edn. (London: Felix Kyngston, 1602), p. 79.

36. Thomas Taylor, *The Pilgrim's Profession, or A Sermon Preached at the Funerall of M^{ris} Mary Gunter* (London: Jo. Bartlet, 1622), pp. 151–5.

37. Sa[muel] Clarke, *A Collection of the Lives of Ten Eminent Divines . . . and of Some Other Eminent Christians* (London: William Miller, 1662), p. 453; cited in Collinson, 'The coherence of the text', p. 91.

38. In the later eighteenth century we find Samuel Johnson recording his (many) resolutions to 'read the Bible through' over the course of a year. He forms elaborate plans to achieve this by reading six hundred verses in the Old Testament and two hundred in the New every week. In 1772 he again declares his intention to 'read the whole Bible once a year as long as I live'. See Samuel Johnson, *Diaries, Prayers, and Annals*, ed. E. L. McAdam, Jr., with Donald and May Hyde (New Haven and London: Yale University Press, 1958), pp. 133, 147 (and cf. pp. 73, 74, 84, 99, 106, 130, 135).

39. Scott Mandelbrote, 'The Bible and didactic literature in early modern England', in *Didactic Literature in England 1500–1800*, ed. Natasha Glaisyer and Sara Pennell (Aldershot: Ashgate, 2003), pp. 19–39 (p. 37).

40. For an intensive study of the variety of Bible reading practices of the non-conformist minister Owen Stockton and his wife Elianor Rant, see Jeremy M. Schildt, '"Eying and applying and meditating on the promises": reading the Bible in seventeenth-century England' (unpublished PhD thesis, University of London, 2008). I am grateful to Dr Schildt for letting me have a copy of his thesis, from which I have learned much.

41. Francis Higman, '"Without great effort, and with pleasure": sixteenth-century Genevan Bibles and reading practices', in *The Bible as Book: The Reformation*, ed. Orlaith O'Sullivan (London and New Castle: British Library and Oak Knoll Press, 2000), pp. 115–22 (p. 117). See also Femke Molekamp, 'Using a collection to discover reading practices: The British Library Geneva Bibles and a history of their early modern Readers', *Electronic British Library Journal*, article 10 (2006), 1–13.

42. See Maurice S. Betteridge, 'The bitter notes: the Geneva Bible and its annotations', *The Sixteenth Century Journal*, 14 (1983), 41–62; William W. E. Slights, '"Marginall notes that spoile the text": scriptural annotation in the English Renaissance', *Huntington Library Quarterly*, 55 (1992), 255–78; Christopher

Hill, *The English Bible and the Seventeenth-Century Revolution* (London: Penguin Books, 1994), pp. 57–66.

43. Andrew Cambers and Michelle Wolfe, 'Reading, family religion, and evangelical identity in late Stuart England', *The Historical Journal*, 47 (2004), 875–96.

44. Kevin Sharpe, 'Reading Revelations: prophecy, hermeneutics and politics in early modern England', in *Reading, Society and Politics in Early Modern England*, ed. Kevin Sharpe and Steven N. Zwicker (Cambridge: Cambridge University Press, 2003), pp. 122–63 (p. 126).

Part 2
Readers in the Enlightenment and Romantic World

3
Weeping for Werther: Suicide, Sympathy and the Reading Revolution in Early America

Richard Bell

Setting down the novel for the final time, he raised the horse pistol to his temple and fired. Beachcombers found his young, well-dressed body early the next morning; the book and the gun lying together on the ground by its side. Three years earlier, in 1804, Alexander Hamilton's blood had pooled among the dirt and rocks on this same stretch of the New Jersey shore. Like Hamilton this man was an immigrant, and like Hamilton he had been behaving strangely in the weeks before his death, telling friends that he was tired of life and ready to die; but he had his own story, as the two letters tucked in his pocket and the novel found at his feet soon made clear. His name was Bertell, he was just twenty years old, and the first letter was his suicide note, addressed to whoever might find his body. It described how he had been cast aside by the young lady he loved, how the rejection had been too much for his heart to take, and how he had made up his mind that he could only find peace in death. In the second letter, addressed to a friend in Brooklyn, he had scribbled a hasty will, leaving two-thirds of his paltry estate to the girl who had broken his heart. The third text on the scene was the book that Bertell had been reading intensively for weeks now. To readers of the dozens of news stories that spread word of his suicide, this well-thumbed and heavily underlined little volume was the most important clue as to why this young romantic had taken his own life. Bertell's copy of Goethe's *The Sorrows of Young Werther*, the most popular and vilified sentimental novel in America, lay open at the page where Werther, pistols prepared, takes his final leave by writing to the woman who has promised herself to another: 'They are loaded – the clock strikes twelve – I go. Charlotte! Farewell! Farewell!'[1]

Fiction, it seemed, could be fatal. Reading Goethe's inflammatory tale of how one adoring young man ended his anguish by pistol had led another to do the same. At least that was the conclusion many newspaper readers reached when printers from Vermont to Virginia splashed Bertell's story across their pages in the summer of 1807. In fact, Bertell's suicide came as the inevitable proof of what protective parents and anxious ministers had been warning would happen ever since the first English translation of Goethe's over-wrought romance first reached American shores in the early 1780s, the latest in a post-revolutionary deluge of new fiction aimed squarely at the rising generation. Because *Werther* and a swathe of American novels that followed in its wake each put the suicides of tremulous and tearful young characters centre stage, a generation of serious-minded adults had convinced themselves that the nation's susceptible youth would be manipulated to follow in the fatal footsteps of their fictional heroes. The discovery of Bertell's body on the Jersey shore in 1807 convinced them they had been right all along.

Johann Wolfgang von Goethe's *The Sorrows of Young Werther* takes the form of a long series of letters from a twenty-three-year-old artist to a distant friend. The letters speak directly to the reader and narrate the passionate Werther's story of love and loss during a sojourn in the fictional village of Wahlheim (based on the town of Garbenheim, in Hesse state). There he meets and falls in love with Charlotte, the fiancée and subsequent wife of Albert, a man several years her senior. Having promised her dying mother that she would marry Albert to provide security for her eight siblings, Charlotte flirts with Werther, but ultimately does not return his insistent affections; his growing obsession with Charlotte quickly starts to paralyse his mind and ravage his heart. Dressed in a blue frock-coat, yellow waistcoat and breeches, Werther pens a suicide note – 'Charlotte! Farewell!' – borrows two pistols from Albert and shoots himself.[2]

In Europe the novel was phenomenally popular. First published in Leipzig in 1774, it was translated into French (1775), English (1779), Italian (1781) and Russian (1788) and repeatedly reprinted to satisfy swelling demand across the continent. Its effect on readers was palpable. A generation of young romantics took Werther to their hearts. As historian Georges Minois writes, 'the youth of Europe learned his speeches as they learned Hamlet's'.[3]

Werther enjoyed equal success in America, and was one of the best-selling novels printed there before the War of 1812. Each of the nineteen British editions issued before 1800 circulated in American port cities, and local booksellers like Robert Bell in Philadelphia produced eight editions of their own, in three different translations, between 1784 and 1809. Only Susanna Rowson's *Charlotte Temple* (1791) was reprinted more often. During the height of the novel's popularity book-sellers placed more than five hundred notices in American newspapers to announce fresh supplies. Its readers were disproportionately adoles-cent. Many of them were boys on the cusp of manhood, like the sensi-tive young soul one British traveller came across in Georgetown in 1798 who 'delighted in the perusal of the Sorrows of Werter [and] perfumed his handkerchief with lavender'.[4] Although the story was told from the point of view of a delicate young man of feeling, booksellers also made special efforts to target young women readers. *Werther* topped a widely-circulated list of 'novels for winter evenings' recommended 'to the ladies'.[5] In her diary for Good Friday 1784, twenty-one year-old Anne Livingston of Philadelphia recorded her first encounter with the book: 'After Tea Miss Cox & myself playd. by turns on the harpsichord while Emelia work'd. Then Emelia read to us the Sorrows of Werther while we work'd. It is a very affecting little history, & made Grace & myself sob & cry like Children, but there is certainly a luxury in some kind of sorrows, as well as bitterness in others.'[6]

The unprecedented popularity of *Werther* led to a flood of imitative works. In addition to extracts of *Werther* published in American maga-zines, consumers could digest plays, poems, and even other novels that followed the story or featured its tragic hero. Editors printed dozens of Werther poems in American newspapers and literary magazines through-out the 1780s and 1790s; some poets active in this period even chose 'Werter' as their pseudonym, explicitly associating their own quickly forgotten stanzas with this literary juggernaut. Playwrights too got in on the act: in 1797 audiences in Boston, New York and Philadelphia were treated to the first American performances of a dramatic interpretation of the story. Originally performed in Dublin, the play was produced again in Charleston in 1803 and 1804 – where the cast featured Edgar Allan Poe's father – and returned once more to Boston in 1809.[7]

Such retellings testified to the American appetite for all things *Werther*, but also crystallized concern that the reading revolution famously described by Cathy Davidson – a dramatic surge in the sup-ply of and demand for fiction that so many parents and preachers had cheered as it had taken hold in the 1770s and 1780s – was producing some dangerous and unanticipated consequences.[8] Proud patriots and anxious patriarchs like Dr Benjamin Rush in Philadelphia and the Reverend Samuel Miller in New York had championed the fashion for sentimental fiction that gripped revolutionary America, convinced that the culture of sensibility promoted in works by Richardson, Sterne and Rousseau might be replicated in work by local authors and used to engineer moral reform among self-regarding young readers.[9] Between 1789 and 1796 the *Massachusetts Magazine* published more than one hundred stories, letters and poems on the theme of seduction while other home-grown literary periodicals like the *Columbian Magazine* and the *American Museum* stuffed their pages with examples of young people performing charitable acts to aid virtuous people in distress. In Susanna Rowson's *The Inquisitor; or, Invisible Rambler* (1788), the titular man of feeling is brought to tears by the deprivations suffered by the downtrodden men and women he meets on his travels. His sympathy leads him to action: he gives eighteen pounds to free a stranger from a crippling debt; he risks his reputation to save a virtuous young girl from a house of ill repute; he talks another young woman out of her plans to elope with a cad; and he leads a prodigal daughter back to her parents to be reunited and redeemed. To fund all this good work, the rambler puts his own comfort on the line, dismissing his servants, parting with one of his carriages and selling two of his horses.[10]

Before the moral and social effects of reading so many didactic plots could be measured, novels like *Werther* burst on the scene. As the number of foreign and domestic novels on sale in America proliferated throughout the 1780s and 1790s, plots and characters had begun to appear that seemed to complicate or even undermine the messages about living virtuously and acting charitably embedded in works like *Clarissa* or *The Inquisitor*. The popularity of *Werther* and its unashamedly self-absorbed and self-destructive central character now started to propel parents like Rush and preachers like Samuel Miller to the conclusion that excessively sentimental narratives might actually pervert young readers' delicate sensibilities, encouraging them to wallow in fictional tragedies while ignoring those around them in need of their sympathy. Addressing the Young Ladies Academy in Philadelphia in 1787 at the height of *Werther*-fever in the city, Rush attacked the novel for perverting sensibility:

> The abortive sympathy which is excited by the recital of imaginary distress, blunts the heart to that which is real and, hence, we sometimes see instances of young ladies, who weep away a whole forenoon over the criminal sorrows of a fictitious Charlotte or Werther, turning with disdain at three o'clock from the sight of a beggar, who sollicits its feeble accents or signs, a small portion only of the crumbs which fall from their fathers' tables.[11]

Goethe, Rush believed, had broken the cherished link between sensibility and charity, and betrayed the sacred covenant between author and reader by misusing the much-trumpeted power of sympathetic identification to stir up affection for wholly undeserving characters.

As copies continued to fly from the shelves of bookshops and libraries, more and more public figures climbed aboard Rush's anti-*Werther* bandwagon. To drive home their case against the book's unchecked sentimentality, most took to arguing that the novel's pages encouraged young readers to follow in its idol's bloody footsteps. In a frequently reprinted opinion piece published in American newspapers in 1806 one female commentator charged that Goethe could never compensate 'for the injury that vague minds receive from those publications where SUICIDE is represented as heroism; nor can the writer of the Sorrows of Werther ever make atonement for the injury he has done to society'. Goethe's offence, pundits agreed, was to tame the terrors of self-destruction, and tempt 'vague minds' to follow young Werther's example if ever their own romantic entanglements became too much to bear.[12]

Alarmingly, there was growing evidence that Goethe's sentimental rendering of romantic suicide might have already encouraged imitative acts among American readers. A report in a Boston newspaper in March 1785 described the death of a gentleman-soldier whose hopeless passion for a woman who did not return his affections had driven him to search for 'a passage from misfortune'. His suicide note, as transcribed in the paper, bore marked similarities to that of Werther's. 'The pistols are loaded', he wrote. 'ADIEU, for the last time! – Love me after I am dead, as I did you while I was alive.'[13] American columnists began to seize on reports like this as evidence of an escalating *Werther* epidemic. Writing in Philadelphia's *Weekly Magazine* in 1798 one essayist tried to persuade booksellers to remove the book from their shelves, by alleging that it had already proved 'the bane of more than one family' in the state. By way of proof she offered the 'short history' of Eleanor, a young woman wallowing in depression brought on by an unhappy marriage and an abortive affair. 'In this unhappy state of her existence the novel of Werter was never absent from her bosom; her tears moistened its leaves daily and hourly; and she dwelt, with fond and sorrowful sympathy, over these passages between which and her situation she fancied a resemblance.' When her husband wounds her erstwhile lover in a duel, Eleanor collapses by his side and 'resolved not to survive him'.[14]

News of the 1807 suicide of a twenty-year-old German immigrant on the Weehawken shore thus came as no surprise. Belief that reading the novel could lead to copycat deaths had become gospel in certain circles. In an anti-*Werther* diatribe that circulated in several newspapers in 1810, one Salem essayist claimed that its mortal effects had been felt in 'hundreds of families' over the past few years. 'Within the narrow circle of my own acquaintance', she confided, 'I have known two young men who rushed unbidden into eternity, deluded by the sophistical arguments of Werther in favor or in vindication of suicide.'[15]

In fact, *Werther's* poison seemed to be infecting much of the fiction popular with young readers. To many parents' horror, two of the very first American novels not only featured the suicides of their own avowedly-sentimental characters, but depicted these tragic climaxes as the fatal consequences of reading *Werther*. William Hill Brown's *The Power of Sympathy* (1789) placed the demonstration of the Werther effect at the heart of its convoluted plot. In a series of letters eerily similar to Werther's, Harrington informs his priggish friend Worthy of his blossoming romance with Harriot. When the two lovers learn that they are actually brother and sister, Harriot succumbs to a spiral of despair and illness that kills her. Harrington revolts at the news that their relationship was incestuous. Trembling with grief and disgust, he resolves to suicide, a decision he defends in a series of Goethian arguments laid out in his last letters. Before his moralizing friend Worthy can respond, he gets word that it is too late; Harrington has shot himself in his apartment. Arriving on the scene, Worthy sees the body for himself and reports that 'A LETTER that he had written for me, laid unsealed upon the table, and *The Sorrows of Werter* was found lying by its side.'[16]

Brown's dramatization of the connection between reading *Werther* and copycat suicide was hardly unique. By fictionalizing the Werther effect, Brown demonstrated that such fears were pervasive as early as 1789. Just four years later, the anonymous female author of *The Hapless Orphan* (1793), an epistolary novel of desire, broken hearts and multiple suicides, offered further testimony. At its climax, Fanny is shot and killed by Ashley, a young man whose affections she – like Werther's Charlotte – has persistently refused. Ashley had been reading *Werther* in the days before this murder and had taken to quoting passages to Fanny in which Werther 'argues in favor of suicide' to show her the measure of his love and sorrow. After shooting Fanny, Ashley dispatches himself, leaving a suicide note confirming the novel's influence: 'The Sorrows of Werther is now open upon my table: It animates my heart; it cheers my soul; it will sustain me through the scene which I am about to act.' Several English novels circulating in America at the same time offered similar tableau; *Werther*, it seems, had become the ultimate literary accessory.[17]

As rattled observers like Rush were acutely aware, suicide was spreading through the pages of young Americans' favourite fiction like yellow fever. Texts featuring suicidal characters reading *Werther* represent only a fraction of the narratives in which an act of self-destruction plays a central role. Indeed, as one might expect at a time when themes of seduction, ruin and comeuppance dominated literary output, no less than fifteen of the first forty-five novels written by Americans depict a character dying by his or her own hand. These fifteen early American novels portray the suicides of ten women and fourteen men, and there are dozens more attempts at, thoughts of and discussions about suicide in their pages.

This body-count takes no heed of differences in print-runs, marketing and sales, nor does it differentiate between those works that appear to valorize suicide as an extreme romantic gesture, and those which portray acts of self-destruction with studied ambivalence or as the just desserts of vice. But neither did many critics of sentimental fiction. To critics like Rush all fiction had been poisoned by the fashion among some writers for excessive sentimentality: any literary portrayal of suicide was assumed to be dangerously romantic.

There were many novels and short stories that fit Rush's emerging stereotype. In 1791 the author of a short piece in the *New York Magazine* referred to a lady's decision to shoot herself after her reputation was ruined by scandal as an 'Instance of Female Heroism'.[18] 'If [a] suicide can meet compassion from an insulted God', proclaimed another approving author in the same magazine a few years later, 'surely it must be the seduced female'.[19] Many writers of long fiction seemed to have assumed as much. In a subplot of *The Power of Sympathy*, the hapless Ophelia poisons herself after being duped and dumped by her sister's husband. As the drugs took their effect, William Hill Brown told readers, 'her sensibility became more exquisite'.[20] In Henry Brackenridge's *Modern Chivalry* (1792) readers were encouraged to share Captain Farrago's uncharacteristically emotional reaction to news of a similar suicide. The blustering hero of this subtle parody 'could not but shed tears' when he learned that a young woman disappointed in love had 'suspended herself from the bed post with her garter'. Presented as the tragic consequence of a lapse of virtue, the suicides of these fictional girls were depicted as entirely deserving of young readers' sympathies.[21]

Cognizant that a healthy proportion of their readers were adolescent boys on the verge of maturity, several turn-of-the-century authors depicted young men in similarly sentimental throes. In addition to Harrington and Ophelia, the third suicide in *The Power of Sympathy* is of Henry, a principled romantic who plunges 'into the river – to close his sorrows with his life' after discovering that his beloved Fidelia has yielded to his rival.[22] Likewise, the eponymous young hero of

John Davis's *Ferdinand and Elizabeth* (1798) joins his lover in a suicide pact when the obstacles to their earthly union become insurmountable, while in *The Gamesters* (1805) the guilt-stricken Leander Anderson throws himself into a stream after failing to act to stop a girl being seduced by another man.[23]

These novels and the many similar (sometimes illustrated) short stories suggest that suicide had become a defining element of the sentimental form, if not its apotheosis. 'Death by suicide', literary critic Herbert Ross Brown concluded in the early twentieth century, 'was the supreme luxury of the sentimentalist'.[24] As the literary language calculated to cultivate sensibility, sentimental writing was designed to stir powerful reactions among readers to scenes of acute suffering. Depicting suicide offered the supreme trial of a writer's skill, and the opportunity for readers to test their developing powers of sympathy. Confronted by characters driven to commit heinous sins for romantic reasons, readers faced an exquisite dilemma. Was condemnation or pity the proper response? As a writer for the *Massachusetts Magazine* who signed himself 'Werther' explained in 1790: 'The heart of tenderness, while it abhors the crime, cannot but feel the most real sorrow for that distress which urged him on to the fatal deed.'[25] Sentimentalized suicides provided the perfect stimuli for young readers to display their finer shades of feeling; the ubiquity of such scenes was essentially market-driven.

By the turn of the century, the presence of so many seemingly sympathetic depictions of suicide had, in the minds of many critics, transformed fiction into a blight on public health. Writing in 1803, New York Presbyterian Samuel Miller complained that self-destruction now appeared so commonly in novels that the genre amounted to 'an apology for suicide'.[26] Likewise, a piece in New York's *People's Friend* that appeared just weeks before news of Bertell's death reached that city's readers, bemoaned 'the many instances of Suicide which have lately occurred' before blaming 'those hot-beds of vice, the NOVEL SHOPS'.[27]

Such remarks usually lacked any conclusively causal evidence to prove the existence of a copycat effect. Decrying portrayals of fictional suicide was a convenient and compelling opportunity to express deep disappointment that the reading revolution had run amok. The promising cult of sensibility that Rush, Miller and others had once sponsored now seemed to have been hijacked by writers apparently unwilling to use their talents to give the nation's youth a timely moral education. Instead of instilling fellow feeling, American literature seemed, to many commentators in the 1790s and 1800s to be going in a different, darker, and more dangerous direction.

As most critics had belatedly come to realize, sympathy was a force unto itself; once elicited and unleashed it was too potent to be harnessed. While early champions of the novel had presumed that readers would be able to distinguish between characters whose positive example they were expected to emulate, and those they were supposed to pity or condemn, the pervasive power of sympathy made the task next to impossible. Novels or short stories that garbed acts of suicide in the language of sentiment only served to draw attention to this fundamental flaw in the campaign to use popular fiction to prod people toward acting correctly, and exposed the lack of control that ministers and parents had over how young people interpreted fiction. *The Power of Sympathy* was a case in point. As Elizabeth Barnes has argued, the responses of the characters that discover Harrington's body at the climax of the novel perfectly illustrate the fears of those who had come to realize that sympathy was an ungovernable force: 'Although the spectators acknowledge the young man's error, they attribute Harrington's intemperate action to his "genius", which inflamed his "violent passions" and "too nice sensibility".' Drawing the parallel between these assembled observers and the young readers of the novel, Barnes sums up their reaction to Harrington's suicide: 'In the end, they cannot condemn him, for, knowing his history, they know that he was the "dupe of nature, and the sacrifice of seduction".'[28] While authors like Brown used paratext to insist that their work was intended to warn young readers of the 'dangerous consequences of seduction', critics of sentimental fiction concluded that the opposite was true. Once hailed as the answer to the problems facing the young republic, by the turn of the century, the form's respectability had evaporated; the novel had become, in the words of a column in the *Lady's Magazine* 'a species of writing which can scarcely be spoken of without being condemned'.[29]

This onslaught of criticism about how popular fiction handled suicide is best understood as an expression of the crisis in moral authority brought about by the reading revolution; such criticism was neither fair nor balanced. Several authors were no doubt guilty of romanticizing suicide to appeal to young readers craving scenes of Goethian tenderness. However, many other American (and European) writers presented self-murder in a different light. More often than not, suicide appears in novels and short stories published in America between 1780 and 1810 either as self-inflicted retribution for villainy, or as something to be unambiguously censured. No fewer than three of the characters in the *History of Constantius and Pulchera* (1794) are saved from suicide by timely interventions, while in Susanna Rowson's *Trials of the Human*

Heart (1795) Clara 'conceive[s] the impious idea' to take her own life but is distracted from doing so when she hears 'a rustling on the other side of the hedge'.[30] Similarly, in *The Gamesters* (1805) one of Leander Anderson's first attempts to drown himself stalls when 'fancy gave him the resemblance of his father', while in *Kelroy* (1812), a novel written by Benjamin Rush's niece, Rebecca, the suicide of the Wertherian protagonist is pre-empted by a fatal illness.[31]

Refusing to resort to such fantastical plot devices to abort a suicide, one or two writers instead dramatized the power of rational discussion to deter characters from destroying themselves. The highwayman in James Butler's *Fortune's Foot-ball* (1797), for example, listens while Charles and Mercutio 'endeavoured both by moral and philosophical arguments to dissuade him from his desperate purpose – in which they happily succeeded'.[32] More conservative writers were less coy, and let characters articulate explicit anti-suicide messages. In *The Coquette* (1794), Hannah Webster Foster's alter-ego Julia Granby comforts foolish Eliza Wharton after her suitor forsakes her, telling her to resist any fatalistic daydreams. 'I hope, said I, that you have formed no resolution against your own life. God forbid, rejoined she. My breath is in his hands, let him do what seemeth good in his sight.' A few pages further on, when Major Sanford's wife leaves him after discovering his own affair with young Eliza, he briefly flirts with suicide before wrestling with his demons and resolving to live. 'I would fly to death, and seek a refuge in the grave,' the rake tells a correspondent, 'but the forebodings of a retribution to come, I cannot away with!'[33]

A few authors went further, offering their works as antidotes to the perceived power of the Werther effect. The Reverend Enos Hitchcock's *Memoirs of the Bloomsgrove Family* (1790) admiringly quotes Benjamin Rush's much-reprinted indictment of Goethe's self-absorbed characters, and describes young Rozella Bloomsgrove as the antithesis of those 'young ladies, who weep away a whole forenoon, over the criminal sorrows of a fictitious Charlotte or Werther, turning with disdain, at two o'clock, from the sight of a beggar'.[34] Hitchcock, a Federalist preacher, surely approved of a novel that appeared in the American market a decade later. Reprinted in Philadelphia in 1802 from a British original, *The Slave of Passion; or, the Fruits of Werther* attempted a thorough reworking of Goethe's story, an exercise the anonymous author hoped would 'counteract the poison in Werther's Letters'.[35]

The Slave of Passion loosely follows the outline of Goethe's narrative: a young man learns of the marriage of his intended and despairs, resolving to suicide. The protagonist, Charles, has been reading *Werther* and repeats the German's arguments to justify suicide almost verbatim in a letter to his friend, Henry. Unlike Goethe's Wilhelm, Henry writes back immediately, obliterating each and every argument that Charles has marshalled. After a moment of suspense, the plot veers drastically from the Goethian model when Charles writes back grateful and exultant to have been dragged from the metaphorical precipice by the arrival of Henry's last letter. With tragedy averted, a happy ending quickly follows as Charles learns that he has been misinformed of his beloved's marriage.

A few skilled writers even displayed the virtuoso ability to alternate between positive and negative portrayals of literary suicide. For instance, in the *Hapless Orphan* (1793) young Ashley first enacts the *Werther* effect in textbook style, before the narrator, Caroline Francis, denounces the book as a 'plausible sanction for suicide'.[36] A small minority of American authors believed they could have their cake and eat it; decrying *Werther* on one page, while offering their own romantic suicide on the next. John Davis's *Ferdinand and Elizabeth* (1798) provides another case in point. Thirty pages before the eponymous lovers agree to a suicide pact, Ferdinand comes across a servant girl and asks her if she is a fan of 'these love-inflicting volumes'. 'She replied with a coquettish air that she slept every night with the Sorrows of Werter under her pillow! I could hardly restrain my laughter, but discharging the bill, bade my novel-reading nymph farewell, whose susceptibility amused me.'[37]

In the face of rising criticism, Charles Brockden Brown began to speak up to defend novelists against accusations that their work was indulgent and corrosive. In a column in his *Literary Magazine* (1805), Brown responded to Samuel Miller's well-publicized claim that novel-reading was a leading cause of suicide. 'Suicide in truth, is very rarely to be found', Brown gamely protested. 'Wherever it occurs, so far as we remember, it is placed in such a light as to discourage rather than provoke imitation.' Choosing Rousseau's *La Nouvelle Héloïse* as an example of a well-known novel in which a suicide was averted, Brown asserted that not all prose fiction was guilty as charged:

> The faults of Rousseau's famous novel are not few, but it really does not appear to us chargeable with promoting suicide. Some readers may suppose the preponderance of argument in the epistolary controversy contained in the work to be in favour of suicide, but readers of good sense can hardly fail, we think, of forming a different conclusion; and as to the intention of the author, something may surely be inferred from his having represented his hero as influenced by his friend's reasonings to lay aside his murderous purposes.[38]

Although he might have made similar claims about *Werther*, Brown avoided any mention of it: he did not want to push his luck.

As the *Literary Magazine* found its feet, Brown slowly grew bolder. In a column for an 1807 issue, Brown charged parents and preachers with a patronizing disregard for their children's ability to discern the difference positive and negative example. Most adolescent readers, Brown argued, could readily distinguish virtue from vice and deserved more credit. For his part, he could not 'refuse to teach a child to read, because he may possibly light upon something in the form of books trifling or pernicious. It would be just as wise to sew up his mouth, because he may possibly swallow a poisoned berry, or a brass pin.'[39] By 1810, such bursts of pique had become a regular refrain in literary magazines as a growing number of writers tried to protect their reputations by disassociating themselves from the excesses of literary sentimentalism.

The turn-of-the-century struggle over suicide and sentimentality reflected a much broader reconsideration of the role of sensibility in the forging of American democracy. In its heyday during the early 1780s, 'the aesthetics of sentiment' had penetrated not just fiction, but also advice books, sculpture, painting, poetry and fashion.[40] Yet by the 1810s, the republic's problems seemed to have expanded beyond those that a keenness of perception, delicacy of feeling, capacity for sympathetic identification, and ability to be stirred to profound responses by beauty and suffering might plausibly address. The expansion of the white male franchise, the growth of factory production and out-of-home labour, rising in-migration and immigration to the nation's largest cities, ethnic fragmentation, and the insistent and insidious spread of an overtly masculine doctrine of competition and profit-seeking convinced early nineteenth-century Americans of the naivety of a middle-class culture that touted affectionate ties as tools of successful nation-building. As they groped for ways to understand and accommodate the increasingly capitalistic and individualistic culture ushered in after the War of 1812 'Americans did not become unfeeling', Andrew Burstein notes, 'but they turned away from the risks of extreme sensibility'.[41]

Literary tastes and trends were inextricably linked to these broad transformations. Between 1805 and 1825, young people's interest in sentimental novels noticeably slackened. For the first time in thirty years, *Werther* struggled to find new readers. While book-sellers had paid for more than five hundred advertisements for the book before 1809, over the next sixteen years less than 5 per cent of that number turned up in newspapers, suggesting that readers had moved on.[42] Literary magazines stopped excerpting sensational moments in the now familiar story; instead it became the subject of parody, like L. A. Wilmer's 'The Sorrows of Skwerter'.[43] Summing up the novel's dramatic reversal of fortune, one Jacksonian minister remarked that even the most feeble-minded of readers 'would now regard it as a book too silly to cry over'.[44] And it wasn't just *Werther*. Library and bookstore records show that after 1815 demand for the most overtly sentimental fiction was spiralling downwards. Fickle young readers seemed to have grown bored of it. Increasingly formulaic and predictable, plots no longer seemed fresh, fun or deliciously dangerous. Whether declining reader interest also testifies to the effects of three decades of warnings from parents and ministers, that extremely sentimental fiction was ruinous and opposed to reason, is more difficult to determine.

As the Goethian sentimentalism lost its literary currency, portrayals of suicide in American fiction became harder to find and condemn. In a sample of forty-five novels published between 1810 and 1824, only four feature characters destroying themselves. By the middle of the nineteenth century it was rare to find middle-class characters committing suicide. Authors had no desire to be accused of inciting another epidemic of copycat deaths. Instead, writers like Harriet Beecher Stowe seized on the suicides of black slaves, noble savages and desperate factory girls, turning their sentimentalized deaths to the cause of social and political reforms vastly more wide-ranging than anything imagined after the American Revolution.

Notes and references

1. Johann Wolfgang von Goethe, *The Sorrows of Werter: A German Story* (Glasgow: R. Tullis, 1804); 'Mortuary Notice', *Newburyport Herald*, 7 August 1807; 'New-York, 31 July 1807', *New-York Gazette & General Advertiser*, 31 July 1807. This chapter was abridged and adapted from an essay that first appeared in *Early American Literature*, 46.1 (2011), 93–120.
2. Goethe, *Sorrows of Werter*, p. 194.
3. Georges C. Minois, *The History of Suicide: Voluntary Death in Western Culture* (Baltimore, MD: Johns Hopkins University Press, 1999), p. 267; Fritz Gutbrodt, 'The worth of Werther: Goethe's literary marketing', *Modern Language Notes*, 110 (1995), 579–630.
4. John Davis, *Travels of Four Years and a Half in the United States of America: During 1798, 1799, 1800, 1801, and 1802* (London: T. Ostell, 1803), p. 137.
5. 'Classified Advertisement', *Independent Journal*, 31 January 1784.
6. 'Diary of Anne Hume Shippen Livingston, March, 1784', in *Nancy Shippen Her Journal Book: The International Romance of a Young Lady of Fashion of Colonial Philadelphia with Letters: To Her and About Her*, ed. Ethel Armes (Philadelphia: J. B. Lippincott, 1935), p. 312.

7. O. W. Long, 'Werther in America', *Studies in Honor of John Albrecht Walz*, ed. F. O. N[olte] and others (Lancaster, PA: Lancaster Press, 1941), pp. 106–7; O. W. Long, 'English and American imitations of Goethe's Werter', *Modern Philology*, 14 (1916), 193–216; Stuart Pratt Atkins, *The Testament of Werther in Poetry and Drama* (Cambridge, MA: Harvard University Press, 1949), p. 251.

8. Cathy N. Davidson, *Revolution and the World: The Rise of the Novel in America* (New York: Oxford University Press, 1986), pp. 113–16.

9. Benjamin Rush, *An Oration, Delivered before the American Philosophical Society . . . On the 27th of February, 1786* (Philadelphia: Charles Cist, 1786), pp. 33, 26.

10. Susanna Rowson, *The Inquisitor; or the Invisible Rambler*, vol. III (2nd edn., Philadelphia: Mathew Carey, 1794).

11. Benjamin Rush, Essays, *Literary, Moral and Philosophical* (2nd edn., Philadelphia: Thomas and William Bradford, 1806), p. 86.

12. 'Literary; Composition; Compensate; Suicide; Sorrow; Werter', *Merrimack Magazine and Ladies' Literary Cabinet*, 12 June 1806.

13. 'From the New-Hampshire Mercury. Mr. Printer', *The Independent Ledger and the American Advertiser*, 14 March 1785.

14. 'The Ubiquitarian', *Weekly Magazine*, 14 April 1798.

15. 'The Monitress', *Dartmouth Gazette*, 12 September 1810.

16. William Hill Brown, *The Power of Sympathy, or, the Triumph of Nature Founded in Truth*, 2 vols (Boston: Isaiah Thomas, 1789), II, 149.

17. *The Hapless Orphan; or, Innocent Victim of Revenge: A Novel, Founded on Incidents in Real Life* (Boston: Belknap and Hall, 1793), pp. 194, 213.

18. 'An instance of female heroism, which happened in New-York in May, 1773', *New York Magazine, or Literary Repository*, November 1791.

19. 'The seduced female – a sentimental sketch', *New-York Magazine; Or, Literary Repository*, January 1796, p. 14.

20. *The Power of Sympathy and the Coquette*, ed. Carla Mulford (New York: Penguin, 1996), p. 40.

21. Hugh Henry Brackenridge, *Modern Chivalry: Containing the Adventures of Captain John Farrago and Teague O'Reagan, His Servant* (New York: Rowman & Littlefield, 2003), p. 127.

22. Brown, *Power of Sympathy*, I, 133.

23. John Davis, *The Original Letters of Ferdinand and Elizabeth* (New York: H. Caritat, 1798), p. 135; Caroline Matilda Thayer, *The Gamesters; or, Ruins of Innocence. An Original Novel, Founded in Truth* (Boston: Thomas & Andrews, 1805), pp. 296–7.

24. Herbert Ross Brown, *The Sentimental Novel in America 1789–1860* (New York: Pageant, 1959), p. 58.

25. 'The Felo De Se. By Werther', *Massachusetts Magazine*, March 1790, p. 181.

26. Samuel Miller, *A Brief Retrospect of the Eighteenth Century* (New York: T. and J. Swords, 1803), p. 395.

27. 'Suicide', *People's Friend & Daily Advertiser*, 18 May 1807.

28. Elizabeth Barnes, *States of Sympathy: Seduction and Democracy in the American Novel* (New York: Columbia University Press, 1997), pp. 31, 40–1, 128.

29. *Lady's Magazine and Repository* (November 1792), p. 296; Davidson, *Revolution and the Word*, pp. 44, 99.

30. *The History of Constantius and Pulchera; or Constancy Rewarded* (Salem, MA: T. C. Cushing, 1795), pp. 15, 21, 60; Susanna Rowson, *Trials of the Human Heart, a Novel* (Philadelphia: Wrigley and Berriman, 1795), III, 99.
31. Thayer, *The Gamesters*, p. 280; Rebecca Rush, *Kelroy: A Novel* (Philadelphia: Bradford and Inskeep, 1812), p. 191.
32. James Butler, *Fortune's Foot-Ball; or the Adventures of Mercutio* (Harrisburg, PA: John Wyeth, 1797), I, 28.
33. *The Power of Sympathy and the Coquette*, ed. Mulford, pp. 146, 64.
34. Enos Hitchcock, *Memoirs of the Bloomsgrove Family: In a Series of Letters to a Respectable Citizen* (Boston: Thomas and Andrews, 1790), p. 296.
35. *The Slave of Passion, or, the Fruits of Werter: a Novel* (Philadelphia: J Hoff, 1802), p. 4.
36. *Hapless Orphan*, pp. 205–6.
37. Davis, *The Original Letters of Ferdinand and Elizabeth*, pp. 62–3.
38. 'Criticism', *Literary Magazine, and American Register*, April, 1805, pp. 315–16.
39. Charles Brockden Brown, 'A Student's Diary . . . No. (VI)', *Literary Magazine*, March 1806, p. 404.
40. *The Culture of Sentiment: Race, Gender and Sentimentality in Nineteenth Century America*, ed. Shirley Samuels (New York: Oxford University Press, 1992), p. 6.
41. Andrew Burstein Burstein, *Sentimental Democracy: The Evolution of America's Romantic Self-Image* (New York: Hill and Wang, 1999), pp. 323, 8–18.
42. Advertisement data drawn from Readex America's Historic Newspapers Database.
43. Lambert A. Wilmer, 'Sorrows of Skwerter', *Casket*, October 1838.
44. Andrews Norton, 'Recent publications concerning Goethe', *Select Journal of Foreign Literature*, I (1833), p. 253.

4

Reconstructing Reading Vogues in the Old South: Borrowings from the Charleston Library Society, 1811–1817

Isabelle Lehuu

In his 1960 study of the Bristol Library in the late eighteenth century, Paul Kaufman emphasized how nebulous and undeveloped the description of reading vogues remained, and called attention to the question of sources:

> The first requisite in the attempt to formulate descriptions of reading vogues is the acceptance of the need for evidence from numerous sources. Among these, quantitative library borrowing records hold great interest and no little actual importance. But they are never substitutes for reliable personal witness.[1]

In the last fifty years, students of book culture and lending institutions in Britain and in the United States have followed Kaufman's lead in researching the records of eighteenth- and nineteenth-century libraries.[2] However, book historians and literary scholars have tended increasingly to associate library records with quantitative studies, and have preferred to decipher individual accounts of reading experience and personal letters and diaries in order to produce a qualitative analysis of books and reading.[3] According to John Brewer, library catalogues, along with inventories, are 'inert sources for readership', and therefore, 'exceptionally difficult to animate'.[4]

Nonetheless, one should not conclude that only diaries and personal letters hold clues to the historical recovery of actual readers of the past. Even though library catalogues point to the library stocks, that is, the supply of books for the potential readers, in the same way as publishers' archives offer evidence of the book trade and what was available for consumption, they can be animated with the help of circulation records.

Library catalogues by themselves remain silent on the actual use of the holdings; they fail to reveal which titles gathered dust on the shelves, and which ones were sought after. For instance, older imprints could well be popular without resulting in republication.[5] Unlike catalogues, library circulation records reveal what books were actually borrowed, and who did borrow them, if not ultimately who read them. Although sometimes elusive, borrowing records deserve to be mined for evidence of reading vogues. But they also call for a new approach that takes into account the circulation of books as a dynamic process instead of losing individual borrowers in statistics of their class or their period, and book titles in categorization by literary genres. To be sure, borrowing records allow one to compare library circulation with library collections, and to measure the popularity of books. Yet the numbers alone do not tell the whole story, and reconstructing reading vogues requires a careful trailing of individual books and library users.

This article seeks to reconstruct the taste of the reading public in an urban community of the American South in the early nineteenth century. It focuses on the Charleston Library Society in the seaport city of Charleston, South Carolina, which was described as 'the social and cultural capital of the plantations'.[6] Instead of following the lead of James Raven, who analysed the library collection from the perspective of the transatlantic book trade and the London connection with the South Carolina colony, the present work explores the circulation of books and what Charlestonians actually borrowed from the Library Society.[7] The emphasis is, therefore, on the library users and the books they chose rather than the library acquisitions and holdings.

Founded in 1748 by seventeen young gentlemen who wished to read the latest publications from Great Britain, the Charleston Library Society is the third oldest library in the United States.[8] At first it was more 'a social and cultural fraternity' for low-country planters than a library, but by the time of the American Revolution, the Library Society was the town's primary intellectual institution, and as one historian pointed out, membership secured entry into the ruling class of Charleston.[9]

During his second tour of the 'Western World' from the southern states to New York, Quebec, and Cuba in 1810–1811, the Scotsman J. B. Dunlop kept a diary of his eight-month stay in Charleston, South Carolina. Like other European travellers who preceded him, he mentioned the library on the upper story of the Court House: 'Tho it cannot boast of Superior excellence [it] contains a numerous and useful collection of Books, principally in the English Language, and a number of the natural production peculiar to Carolina and her sister States.' He added: 'The

Library is private but any Stranger is at Liberty to visit it during his residence in the City by being introduced to the Librarian by one of the Subscribers, and as their (*sic*) are Seats and Desks for the use of those who visit it, it is an agreeable place to spend the forenoon.'[10] Charlestonians agreed. As Frederick Adolphus Porcher noted in the 1830s:

> One who has no direct occupation finds life often a drag in Charleston, particularly in the summer. I thought I would devote myself to reading and accordingly spend my mornings in the Charleston Library . . . At the library certain gentlemen were always to be found many of whom were like myself, unoccupied planters who made this city their summer residence.[11]

The circulation records of the Charleston Library Society from 24 July 1811 to 28 February 1817 were kept in two folio ledgers.[12] In total, 41,973 library transactions were registered, listing titles of books, names of borrowers, date and length of charges. There were 3,033 titles of books and periodicals, most of which were identified from cross-referencing short titles in printed and manuscript library catalogues.[13] The lives of the 260 library users have been documented when possible through city directories, census records, wills, inventories, family papers, as well as the minutes of the library's committees.[14] Ultimately, the prosopography of the library patrons puts the practice of reading in a context of individual stories and social networks. The history of reading vogues will take us to the book shelves and inside the books, as well as outside the library, on the streets of Charleston and in the homes of regular library users.

In an effort to explore not only the individual experience of reading, but also the social context of book consumption in a community of readers, this study follows the example of microhistorians. Characterized by either its use of narrative forms, or the primacy of irregularities and individuals over norms and social models, microhistory is best defined as a shared practice of experimental work rather than an overarching theory or a school of thought. Nevertheless, all practitioners of microhistory share an interest in multiplying the levels of observation or scales, to borrow Jacques Revel's concept of 'Jeux d'échelles'.[15] By varying the framework of reference, the historian takes into account the complexities of the context without favouring one angle over another. The change of perspective and the use of a different lens to read the evidence, allows one to connect the small and the large, the local and the global. By reconciling the individual and the social, the small scale of individual lives and the large-scale history of reading vogues, the microhistorical approach transcends the opposition between quantitative and qualitative methodologies, renewing interest in adding individual facts to popular borrowing tallies.

It is worth noting another common interest among microhistorians, one that is best represented by Edoardo Grendi's concept of the 'exceptional normal'. By using the oxymoron 'exceptional normal', Grendi underscores that a document or a testimony might be exceptional because it refers to normal events of daily life, a reality so normal that it usually remains untold.[16] Likewise, the anodyne and repetitious character of library charges constitute important historical facts, not just by their sheer numbers, but also as clues to the reading taste of the past. Apparently 'trivial and unimportant' facts of history, library transactions were rarely mentioned in personal correspondence. One occurrence was found in an undated letter by South Carolinian Martha Laurens Ramsay. She was the wife of the historian David Ramsay and the daughter of Henry Laurens, a US patriot and a wealthy merchant and planter. She wrote to one of her daughters: 'I don't know whether you have read Robertson's America. In this doubt, I have sent to the library for Anquetil [Anquetil's *Universal History*] or the first volume of Rollin [Charles Rollin's *Ancient History*], an author who, although prolix, and in some degree credulous, ought by all means to be read.'[17] In the absence of more evidence from diaries and letters, it is left to the circulation ledgers to reveal the anodyne transaction, the 'exceptional normal' fact of borrowing a book or a periodical. Even though book historians have suggested that evidence of past uses of print rest inside the book itself, through handwritten inscriptions or marginalia, borrowing records also hold valuable clues. Those records of the Charleston Library Society survived to tell the story of reading vogues, whereas many books were destroyed by excessive use or by the Civil War, when they were shipped to Columbia for safekeeping.

When David Ramsay wrote his *History of South Carolina* in 1808, the Library Society held 4,500 volumes and had 230 members; and by 1813, it had more than 8,000 volumes.[18] The membership was growing in the early republic to include low-country planters, East-Bay merchants, a few widows, and various professionals: physicians, attorneys, ministers, notaries, printers.[19] By 1816 the number of active users of the library was around 260, and by January 1818, there were 283 members.[20] Needless to say, all members were white and well-to-do, but they did not constitute a homogeneous group. The 243 patrons identified for this study included 64 planters, 86 members of the mercantile class (merchants, vendue masters, factors, bankers, and brokers), 83 professionals (37 of whom were attorneys), and 10 widows, one of whom was listed as a plantress.[21] The classification is somewhat arbitrary since most planters held another occupation and were labelled planter-attorney, planter-major, or planter-physician. The social profile of library patrons mirrored the functions of the seaport city and its rural surroundings, although one can also perceive a growing preference for a mercantile occupation with one of the many counting houses, and therefore practical affairs over 'closet and book studies'.[22]

There were native-born South Carolinians and transplanted Northerners and Europeans, owners of large estates, some with hundreds of slaves and thousands of acres, and others with 'want of judgment in the affairs of the world'.[23] There were dilettante library users and heavy users, who charged out between 300 and 500 books in less than six years, such as Mrs Ann Timothy, a widow, who checked out 444 books. Republicans, Federalists, nullifiers, unionists, partisans of colonization and others who held liberal views on slavery or favoured the instruction of slaves, all converged on the Library Society and scribbled their arguments with each another in the margins of the same books they all charged out.[24] Books thus served to strengthen a web of social and cultural relations between affluent East Bay merchants and town-dwelling planters who increasingly intermarried and shared friendships, business partnerships and residential proximity.

Some of the wealthiest patrons included John Julius Pringle with an estate of 392 slaves and more than 1,500 acres. Pringle must be counted among the heavy users of the library with a total of 310 charges during the 6-year period. However, among the top fifty members who checked out more than 220 books, only eleven were planters. By contrast, there were at least seventeen merchants, brokers and factors among the heavy users, which suggests that they turned to the Library Society for books more frequently than planters, who perhaps owned private libraries, or simply used the library on a seasonal basis during their residence in the city. And yet, a planter like Major Alexander Garden, a revolutionary soldier, who left an estate of only 14 slaves, had a private library of 480 books. He nonetheless borrowed 269 books from the Library Society. Vice-versa, one can also trace private libraries in the estate of wealthy merchants, or evidence of the ownership of other books. For instance, Robert Hazelhurst, a wealthy merchant who used the library on 255 occasions, owned some books. One of them was mentioned by Martha Laurens Ramsay in April 1811, when she asked his daughter Juliana to lend her the *Memoirs of Miss Elizabeth Smith*, which had been recommended by the Reverend Dr Kollock but was not available in the Library Society.[25] In fact, exchange of books among friends and relatives was frequent, and the Library Society represented only one other source of books.

There were also less frequent users who appear in the records and deserve our attention in spite of lower numbers of book charges. One of them is Juliet Georgina Elliott, widowed at the age of 28 with young children, who never remarried and lived as a plantress to the age of 72. She appears in a portrait made in London in 1803 when she did the traditional Grand Tour in Europe, three years before her husband's death.[26] She was a successful planter. In 1850 she left an estate of $37,000 in personal property, i.e. slaves. From the Library Society she borrowed only 66 books and periodicals, including some novels, but also books of agriculture like Curtis's *English Grass* and *American Husbandry* (1775) as well as specialized periodicals, such as *Annals of Agriculture* or *Transactions Agricultural*. Like all planters, Juliet Elliott was reading the relevant literature for the improvement of her plantation.[27]

Although Mrs Elliott was an infrequent user of the library, her interest in periodical literature was not unusual. This appears clearly when shifting the focus from the reading schedule of one library user to the larger picture of popular borrowing tallies for more than 3,000 titles during the 1810s. If ranked by popularity, periodicals came first, as the Table 4.1 shows.

These included English periodicals such as the Whig *Edinburgh Review* (483 charges), the Tory *Quarterly Review* (234 charges), and the *Gentleman's Magazine* (209 charges) – surprisingly, given its abolitionist position – but also American periodicals such as the *Port Folio* (264 charges), published in Philadelphia and featuring pieces by South Carolina authors and essayists. In total, quarterly and monthly magazines represented 3,200 library transactions or 8 per cent of all book charges. Besides offering essays and short stories, periodicals were important in guiding the library users. Book reviews may have influenced their choice of library books. For instance, travel books were sometimes charged out shortly after borrowing periodicals with reviews on those travel books.

On the popularity chart, titles of novels and history books appeared next to periodicals. As a category, novels and romances represented 38 per cent of the 41,973 library transactions (or 16,083 transactions), while they counted for only 13 per cent of the library holdings according to the titles in the early catalogues. In comparison, the category of history and biography received 6,011 book charges, i.e. 14 per cent of

Table 4.1 Borrowing records from Charleston Library Society during the 1810s ranked by popularity of titles

Short Title	Charges
Edinburgh Review	483
Sporting Magazine	268
Port Folio	264
Naval Chronicle	255
Quarterly Review	234
Gentleman's Magazine	209
Monthly Museum	203
Analectic Magazine	166
Annual Register	161
Plays	145
Rollin's Ancient History	144
Voltaire	133
Arabian Nights	125
Bell's Theatre	121
Lake of Killarney	117
Hume's History of England	116
Gibbon's Roman Empire	112
Traits of Nature	105
Clarke's Travels	102
European Magazine	97
Children of the Abbey	97
Fielding's Works	96
Self Control	96
Thaddeus of Warsaw	95
Banditt's Bride	94
Saracen	93
Scottish Chiefs	90
Lee's Memoirs	90
English Woman	88
Don Quixote	87
Ladies Museum	87
Monthly Review	86
Match Girl	85
Legends of a Nunnery	81
Romance of the Pyrenees	80
Don Sebastian	79
Monk of Udolpho	78
Monthly Mirror	77
Fashionable Life	77
Discarded Son	77
Rollin's Roman History	76
Bigland's View of the World	76
British Drama	76
Siege of Rochelle	75

(continued)

Table 4.1 Continued

Short Title	Charges
Belinda	75
Married Life	74
Hungarian Brothers	73
Sir Charles Grandison	73
Glenmore Abbey	73
Johnson's Works	72
Silliman's Travels	72
Guy Mannering	71
Castle of Inchvalley	71
Something Strange	70
Emmeline	68
English Poets	68
Anacharsis's Travels	68
Spanish Outlaw	66
Malvina	66
Gibbon's Rome	66
Milesian Chief	66
Gondez	65
Daughter of Adoption	65
Castle of Santa Fe	65
Moss Cliff Abbey	65
O'Donnell	64
Discipline	64
Rosina	64
Cecilia	64
Mysteries of Udolpho	63
Robertson's Charles 5th	63
Universal History	63
Grimm's Correspondence	62
Absentee	62
Watch Tower	62
Miser & His Family	62
Evelina	61
Santo Sebastiano	60
Monastery of St. Columb	60
Recess	60

all charges. Travel books totalled 8 per cent of charges, as did miscellanies. The other categories such as religious books, science, and law and politics were numerically insignificant. Multivolume works were tabulated separately because they overlapped categories. For instance, Voltaire's *Works*, available in a 1785 quarto edition in 70 volumes, included history books such as *The Age of Louis XIV* and tales like *Candide*. One or several volumes were charged out 133 times.

By 1816, a significant change had appeared in the circulation ledgers: novels were recorded in a separate column. This way of recording book charges offers a 'unique record of reading vogues' in the early nineteenth century. It had the advantage of including both the serious books that were the staple of subscription libraries such as Bristol Library and the lighter reading of the commercial circulating libraries in England for which evidence is lacking. While Paul Kaufman concluded that no specific record of borrowings existed for the circulating libraries, Jan Fergus has unravelled provincial readers from the rare borrowing records of commercial libraries.[28]

Combining overviews and close-ups of the record is required to accurately assess the past consumption of books. Indeed, one borrower could hide behind another one. Ann Timothy is a case in point. The widow of Benjamin Franklin Timothy and daughter-in-law of the colonial printer Elizabeth Timothy, Ann Timothy was born in Philadelphia, although biographical information about her is sketchy. Listed as a widow or a school mistress in the city directories, she outlived all her children and had important banking investments. She lent money to other city residents, both men and women. Most interesting is her 1840 will, in which she freed all her slaves and bequeathed Ohio land to a female slave.[29] Within those fragments of Ann Timothy's life, we find that she was a heavy user of the Charleston Library Society, with 444 book charges during the six-year period.

As an example, her schedule of library reading from October 1812 to July 1814 indicates charges for quite a few novels (Table 4.2). This might seem to confirm the general assumption that women read novels.[30] But if we look closer, particularly in the summer months, we see the word 'son' again and again in the column of the ledger where the librarian entered the words 'order', 'self', 'son' or a specific name.[31] The last son of widow Timothy, Peter Timothy, was 21 years old in 1815. He died of bilious fever at the age of 28.[32] Like other young barristers in Charleston, Peter Timothy seemed addicted to reading. He charged out 57 per cent of the 444 books listed under his mother's name, and took out half of the 250 novels she borrowed from the library (123 of the 251 novels).

This is a telling case, and he was not alone. Sons of planters and merchants, often teenagers, frequently picked up and returned books in the name of their father's membership, or their mother's for the sons of widows. They account for 15 per cent of all library transactions during the six-year period or close to 6,500 transactions. Moreover, a third of those books picked up by young men were novels (33 per cent), while

Table 4.2 Titles borrowed by Ann Timothy from Charleston Library Society, October 1812 to July 1814

	Ann Timothy		
Date	Title	Volume	Messenger
1812–10–01	Galatea	1 vol.	order
1812–10–09	Louisa Mathews	3 vols	order
1812–10–13	Jealousy	2 vols	order
1812–10–17	Murray House	3 vols	order
1812–10–30	Isabel	6 vols	order
1812–10–30	Infidel Father	6 vols	order
1812–11–09	Citizen & His Daughters	2 vols	order
1812–11–12	Hide & Seek	3 vols	order
1812–11–28	Scott's Tales	1 vol.	son
1812–12–02	Romance of the Castle	2 vols	son
1812–12–04	Tales of the Castle	5 vols	order
1812–12–24	Tales of the Castle	7 vols	son
1812–12–31	Don Quixote	3rd, 4th	son
1813–01–28	Saracen	3 vols	son
1813–02–08	Absentee	2 vols	son
1813–04–13	Selina	3 vols	order
1813–07–28	Discarded Son	5 vols	order
1813–08–26	Stranger	2 vols	order
1813–08–30	Vivian	2 vols	son
1813–09–14	Selima	6 vols	son
1813–09–21	St. Clair of the Isles	4 vols	order
1813–09–24	Moss Cliff Abbey	4 vols	order
1813–09–24	Missionary		order
1813–09–29	Cave of Cosenza	2 vols	order
1813–09–29	Castle on the Rock	3 vols	order
1813–11–02	Sir Roger de Clarendon	3 vols	self
1813–12–10	Abbess	4 vols	son
1813–12–24	Life of a Lover	6 vols	order
1813–12–28	Man as He Is	4 vols	son
1814–01–27	Impenetrable Secret	2 vols	son
1814–01–31	Maid of the Hamlet	2 vols	son
1814–02–10	Sicilian Romance	2 vols	son
1814–02–12	Thinks I to myself		son
1814–03–03	Nobility of the Heart	3 vols	order
1814–03–03	Monastery of St. Columb	2 vols	son
1814–03–07	Splendid Misery	3 vols	son
1814–03–08	Hatred	3 vols	son
1814–03–09	St. Leon	4 vols	son
1814–03–11	Siege of Rochelle		son
1814–03–18	Romance of the Appennines	2 vols	son
1814–03–23	Lake of Killarney	3 vols	son
1814–03–28	Married Life	2 vols	son
1814–04–15	Count Fathom	2 vols	son

(continued)

Table 4.2   Continued

Ann Timothy			
Date	Title	Volume	Messenger
1814–04–25	Desmond	3 vols	son
1814–04–27	Siege of Rochelle		son
1814–04–29	Modern Griselda		son
1814–04–30	Castle on the Rock	3 vols	son
1814–05–12	Montalbert	3 vols	son
1814–05–16	Young Candid	3 vols	son
1814–05–19	Child of 36 Fathers	2 vols	son
1814–05–24	Romance of the Castle	2 vols	son
1814–05–28	Corinna		son
1814–06–03	Delphine	6 vols	son
1814–06–11	Albinia		son
1814–06–22	Match Girl	3 vols	son
1814–06–28	Gossip's Story	2 vols	son
1814–07–14	Celestina	4 vols	son
1814–07–18	Glenmore Abbey	3 vols	order
1814–07–20	Barons of Felsheim	3 vols	son
1814–07–22	Discarded Son	2 vols	son

close to 20 per cent were history books. For instance, 38 per cent of the charges of David Hume's *History of England* were made by sons.[33] To be sure, in absolute numbers, sons checked out a small number of novels, about 2,000, by going to the library themselves. In the total of 16,083 library transactions for novels, the majority were by order from a member of the household, likely to be carried by a servant, that is, a euphemism for slave. In contrast, only about 800 book orders for novels were registered by female members.

The historical clues that individual books left in the circulation ledgers when travelling in and out of the library indicate that reading vogues in the Old South were marked by Anglophilia. Evidence from the circulation records (see Table 4.3) shows that the most popular novels in the early nineteenth century were gothic novels and historical romances, the majority of which were written by British women novelists, such as Ann Radcliffe, *The Mysteries of Udolpho* (1794), Regina Maria Roche, *Children of the Abbey* (1796), the Edinburgh sisters, Anna Maria Porter (*Lake of Killarney*, 1804; *Don Sebastian*, 1809) and Jane Porter (*Thaddeus of Warsaw*, 1803; *Scottish Chiefs*, 1810), and Mary Brunton (*Self Control*, 1811; *Discipline*, 1814). This extensive and intensive consumption of British novels by American readers – this reading vogue – took place precisely during the war of 1812, while as the result of the embargo,

Table 4.3 Records of borrowings of European (predominantly British) novels from Charleston Library Society, ranked by popularity of titles

Title	Charges	Author	Volumes	Size	Place	Edition
Lake of Killarney	117	Porter, Anna Maria	3 vols	12mo	London	1804
Traits of Nature	105	Burney, Sarah Harriet	2 vols	12mo	Philadelphia	1812
Children of the Abbey	97	Roche, Regina Maria	4 vols	12mo	Paris	1807
Self Control	96	Brunton, Mary	2 vols	12mo	Philadelphia	1811
Thaddeus of Warsaw	95	Porter, Jane	4 vols	12mo	London	1804
Banditt's Bride	94	Stanhope, Louisa Sidney	4 vols	12mo	London	1807
Saracen	93	Cottin, Sophie	2 vols	12mo	New York	1810
Scottish Chiefs	90	Porter, Jane	2 vols	12mo	New York	1810
English Woman	88	Byron, Medora Gordon	5 vols	12mo	London	1808
Don Quixote	87	Cervantes, Miguel de	4 vols	8vo	Dublin	1796
Match Girl	85	Edgeworth, Maria	3 vols	12mo	London	1808
Legends of a Nunnery	81	Montague, Edward	4 vols	12mo	London	1807
Romance of the Pyrenees	80	Cuthbertson, Catherine	4 vols	12mo	Amherst, NH	1809
Don Sebastian	79	Porter, Anna Maria	2 vols	12mo	Philadelphia	1810
Monk of Udolpho	78	Curties, T. J. Horseley	4 vols	12mo	London	1807
Discarded Son	77	Roche, Regina Maria	5 vols	12mo	London	1807
Fashionable Life	77	Edgeworth, Maria	3 vols	12mo	London	1800
Siege of Rochelle	75	Genlis, Madame de	1 vol	12mo	Philadelphia	1813
Belinda	75	Edgeworth, Maria	3 vols	12mo	London	1802
Married Life	74	Howard, Miss	2 vols	12mo	Philadelphia	1812
Sir Charles Grandison	73	Richardson, Samuel	7 vols	12mo	London	1796
Glenmore Abbey	73	Isaacs, Mrs	3 vols	12mo	London	1805
Hungarian Brothers	73	Porter, Anna Maria	2 vols	12mo	Philadelphia	1809
Castle of Inchvally	71	Cullen, Stephen	3 vols	12mo	London	1796
Guy Mannering	71	Scott, Sir Walter	2 vols	12mo	Boston	1815
Something Strange	70	Meeke, Mary [Gabrielli]	4 vols	12mo	London	1806
Emmeline	68	Smith, Charlotte	4 vols	12mo	London	1789

(continued)

Table 4.3 Continued

Title	Charges	Author	Volumes	Size	Place	Edition
Spanish Outlaw	66	Herbert, William	4 vols	12mo	London	1807
Malvina	66	Cottin, Sophie	3 vols	12mo	Paris	1811
Milesian Chief	66	Maturin, Charles Robert	2 vols	12mo	Philadelphia	1812
Gondez	65	Ireland, William Henry	4 vols	12mo	London	1805
Daughter of Adoption	65	Thelwall, John (Beaufort)	4 vols	12mo	London	1801
Moss Cliff Abbey	65	Young, Mary Julia	4 vols	12mo	London	1803
Castle of Santa Fe	65	Anon. (Female)	4 vols	12mo	London	1804
Discipline	64	Brunton, Mary	4 vols	12mo	Boston	1815
O'Donnell	64	Morgan, Lady	3 vols	12mo	London	1814
Cecilia	64	Burney, Fanny	5 vols	12mo	London	1784
Rosina	64	Pilkington, Mary	5 vols	12mo	London	1793
Mysteries of Udolpho	64	Radcliffe, Ann	2 vols	12mo	London	1799
Watch Tower	63	Curties, T. J. Horsley	5 vols	12mo	Brentford	1803
Absentee	62	Edgeworth, Maria	2 vols	12mo	New York	1812
Miser & His Family	62	Parsons, Eliza	4 vols	12mo	Brentford	1800
Evelina	61	Burney, Fanny	2 vols	12mo	unknown	

Americans, and the Charleston Library Society as well, began to turn to American editions of British bestsellers.

In this context of popular novels by British women, reconstructing reading vogues would mean following the trajectory of individual books. Mary Brunton's *Self Control* offers one example, on a small scale, of the circulation of one book, with 96 charges that are traced on the map of the seaport city of Charleston, while connecting the book to both the North and Great Britain. First published in London in 1811, *Self Control* circulated in two duodecimo volumes published in Philadelphia the same year.[34] The main character, Laura Montreville, exemplified the triumph of religion over passion but also defended women's financial independence, while the heroine earned money by painting historical pictures. The story recounts all her troubles and trials as she rejects her suitor, Colonel Hargrave, who takes her captive and transports her to America, where she miraculously escapes in a boat over a waterfall and returns to England. The story is somewhat far-fetched, as some contemporary reviewers noted, but the reading circuit of Mary Brunton's novel shows the enthusiasm of the public.[35]

The 96 library transactions of the Charleston Library Society for *Self Control* involved 68 different members of the library. Some literally took the book from their home to the home of another reader, as Thomas Bee, Jr did on 14 October 1811 when returning the two volumes from his home on 129 Church St after five days and delivering them to 55 Tradd St, the home of Major Alexander Garden, the impoverished planter, perhaps for his wife Mary Ann Gibbes. By the spring of 1812, the moralistic novel was travelling from the 69 Tradd St house of the widow Ann Timothy to the mansion of Nathaniel Heyward, at 144 East Bay, the wealthiest rice planter of South Carolina who owned 5,000 acres and more than 2,000 slaves on seventeen plantations. Or perhaps it was for the amusement of his 22-year old son, Nathaniel Heyward, Jr, who borrowed some novels and like another library user, Peter Timothy, died before turning thirty.[36]

However, one volume seemed to have stayed with Dr Ramsay around the same time, at the end of May. After entertaining the summer nights of several planters and their families, as well as two bankers (Charles B. Cochran; David Alexander) and a former Governor (Paul Hamilton), the novel reached the home of Reverend James D. Simons in the fall. In 1813 the popular book continued indiscriminately its way into the homes of factors and vendue masters with a two-day excursion into the home of Dr Dalcho, the Episcopal minister and physician, and a ten-day visit with Mrs George Read, a widow. Mary Brunton's novel is rarely mentioned in literary anthologies, but in the midst of the war of 1812, the improbable story of Laura Montreville circulated along Meeting, Broad, Tradd and East Bay. It was familiar to most book-reading Charlestonians, Federalists and Republicans alike, and perhaps to their friends and out-of-town relatives who visited during the winter or the summer.

Other English novels produced similar enthusiasm upon arrival at the Charleston Library Society, and it was later resolved that new books should not circulate before being securely bound. Nor could books charged by a member be transferred to others in a reading frenzy without being first returned to the library.[37] These popular novels began to appear in American reprints in the 1810s. For instance, Charles Maturin's *Milesian Chief* was purchased by the Charleston Library Society in the 1812 edition by Mathew Carey in Philadelphia. Beginning in January 1813, it quickly circulated from one Charlestonian to another, with a total of 66 transactions. It is particularly fitting that this work of high Gothic which portrayed Irish nationalism and animosity toward the English was so popular in Charleston during the war of 1812, when one feared a British invasion. Likewise, Walter Scott's *Guy Mannering* was purchased in an 1815 Boston edition, and was charged 71 times from August 1815 to February 1817.

Perhaps even more significant was the lasting popularity of Maria Edgeworth. In total, Edgeworth accounted for 585 borrowings for her *Match Girl* (1808), *Belinda* (1802), *Castle Rackrent* (Dublin, 1801), *Tales of Fashionable Life* (1809; New York 1809), *Vivian* (New York, 1812), *Modern Griselda* (1805), *Leonora* (1806), *Popular Tales*, *Moral Tales*, *Patronage* (1814) and *The Absentee* (New York, 1812), which circulated for the most part in London editions. The place of Edgeworth's novels in the circulation ledgers of the Library Society goes beyond the scope of this article and would deserve a study of its own, as it underscores the transatlantic popularity of British women novelists, even in the midst of the war with Great Britain, and the existence of reading vogues prior to the success of Walter Scott by the 1820s.

As for the trailing of individual books, novels were no exception and the same microhistorical approach could be applied to other books. For instance, another category of popular books among the members of the Charleston Library Society were travelogues, particularly to England and Scotland, or the so-called Northern Grand Tour. The most popular in that category was *Espriella's Letters* by the English poet Robert Southey, who offered his observations of English society through the eyes of an imaginary Spanish character, Don Espriella, and his correspondence with his confessor. One or more of the three volumes of *Espriella's Letters* in 16mo (London, 1808) were borrowed on 90 occasions during the six-year period. Another example is Benjamin Silliman's *Journal of Travels in England, Holland and Scotland, and of two Passages over the Atlantic* (2 vols, New York, 1810), which was borrowed 88 times by 67 library users.

As this chapter has shown, the daily circulation of books and periodicals in and out of the Charleston Library Society was an active process that cannot be reified by charts and numbers. The anodyne facts of library charges that were preserved in manuscript ledgers were assembled together as clues to unlock reading vogues of the early nineteenth century, and they succeeded in animating the seemingly inert catalogues. As a result, this microhistory of the Library Society offers a different image. Whereas libraries have epitomized order – the order of books – and a preference for clear, permanent classifications, the daily consumption of books by the members of the Charleston Library Society as revealed in its borrowing records give the impression that the social library was a busy place and books were in constant motion.[38] The demand for books and conversation remained constant, almost untouched by contemporary events. Marked by Anglophilia, the book culture of the public in the early republic mixed new and old fare, combining great books of history, both ancient and modern, and recent fiction, epistolary and gothic. But during the years of embargo, recent New York and Philadelphia editions of British works, particularly by British women writers, began to compete with London and Dublin imprints. The literate public of South Carolina thus partook in transatlantic reading vogues and a broader republic of letters. At the same time, it was locally, within familial and social networks that men and women of the reading public contributed to the dissemination of reading vogues, reading book reviews in periodicals, and transmitting recommendations by friends and relatives in family letters, or by word of mouth.

The evidence that books have left in and out of the library serves to unravel several stories of individuals and families that intersect in surprising ways to fashion a unique reading community. It is as if library books represented an important thread in the social fabric and helped cement the social elite of the seaport city in spite of differences of occupation, wealth or politics. In the end, southern planters, merchants, widows and their sons shared an infatuation with stories that kept them absorbed, one volume after another, for more than a thousand and one nights. Exotic oriental tales, gothic novels, narrative histories and travel journals peopled the imagination of the library users with castles and convents along with temples and ruins of ancient times. Those avid readers found solace in literary labyrinths, somewhat oblivious of their violent surroundings, as stories and histories distracted them in the midst of the war with England, financial downturn, yellow fever epidemics, hurricanes, earthquakes and fear of slave uprisings.

Notes and references

1. See Paul Kaufman, *Borrowings from the Bristol Library, 1773–1784: A Unique Record of Reading Vogues* (Charlottesville: Bibliographical Society of the University of Virginia, 1960), p. 128. For a summary of his findings, see also Paul Kaufman, 'Some reading trends in Bristol 1773–84', in *Libraries and their Users* (London: The Library Association, 1969), pp. 28–35.
2. See David Allan, *A Nation of Readers: The Lending Library in Georgian England* (London: The British Library, 2008). Examples for nineteenth-century US history include Ronald J. Zboray, 'Reading patterns in antebellum America: evidence in the charge records of the New York Society Library', *Libraries and Culture*, 26 (1991), 301–33; Robert A. Gross, 'Much instruction from little reading: books and libraries in Thoreau's Concord', *Proceedings of the American Antiquarian Society*, 97 (1987), 129–88, and 'Reconstructing early American libraries: Concord, Massachusetts, 1795–1850', *Proceedings of the American Antiquarian Society*, 97 (1987), 331–451; Emily B. Todd, 'Walter Scott and the nineteenth-century American literary marketplace: antebellum Richmond readers and the collected editions of the Waverley novels', *Papers of the Bibliographical Society of America*, 34 (1999), 495–517.
3. See, for instance, Stephen M. Colclough, 'Procuring books and consuming texts: the reading experience of a Sheffield apprentice, 1798', *Book History*, 3 (2000), 21–44.
4. John Brewer, 'Reconstructing the reader: prescriptions, texts and strategies in Anna Larpent's reading', in *The Practice and Representation of Reading in England*, ed. James Raven, Helen Small and Naomi Tadmor (Cambridge: Cambridge University Press, 1996), p. 227.
5. See Edward Jacobs, 'Eighteenth-century British circulating libraries and cultural book history', *Book History*, 6 (2003), 14–15.
6. Walter J. Fraser, Jr., *Charleston! Charleston! The History of a Southern City* (Columbia, SC: University of South Carolina Press, 1989), p. 195.
7. See James Raven, *London Booksellers and American Customers: Transatlantic Literary Community and the Charleston Library Society, 1748–1811* (Columbia, SC: University of South Carolina Press, 2002).
8. See Edgar Reinke, 'A classical debate of the Charleston, South Carolina, Library Society', *The Papers of the Bibliographical Society of America*, 61 (1967), 83–99.
9. Arthur H. Shaffer, *To Be an American: David Ramsay and the Making of the American Consciousness* (Columbia: University of South Carolina Press, 1991), pp. 34–35; Reinke, 'A classical debate', p. 87.
10. Quoted in Raymond A. Mohl, 'The grand fabric of republicanism: a Scotsman describes South Carolina, 1810–1811', *South Carolina Historical Magazine*, 71 (1970), p. 172.

11. 'The memoirs of Frederick Adolphus Porcher', ed. Samuel Gaillard Stoney, *South Carolina Historical and Genealogical Magazine*, 47 (1946), 44–8.
12. See Circulation Records, Charleston Library Society, Charleston, South Carolina.
13. See *A Catalogue of Books Belonging to the Charleston Library: January 1811* (Charleston, SC: printed by W. P. Young, 1811); *Supplemental Catalogue of Books Belonging to the Charleston Library Society Which Have Been Purchased or Presented since January 1811* (Charleston, SC: printed by J. Hoff, 1816); *A Catalogue of the Books Belonging to the Charleston Library Society* (Charleston, SC: A. E. Miller, 1826); 'A catalogue of the books &c belonging to the Charleston Library Society completed the 16th day of March 1813', Charleston Library Society, Charleston, South Carolina.
14. See 'Journall of the proceedings of the Charles Town Library Society, 1759–1790', in Charleston Library Society, Records (1758–1811), microfiche, South Carolina Historical Society, Charleston; Charleston Library Society, Minute Books (1815–1841), Charleston Library Society, Charleston. Unfortunately, the minutes for the period between 1791 and March 1815 are missing.
15. *Jeux d'échelles. La micro-analyse à l'expérience*, ed. Jacques Revel (Paris: Seuil/Gallimard, 1996). See also Giovanni Levi, 'On microhistory,' in *New Perspectives on Historical Writing*, ed. Peter Burke (University Park, PA: Pennsylvania State University Press, 1992), pp. 93–113.
16. Edoardo Grendi, 'Repenser la micro-histoire?' in *Jeux d'échelles*, p. 238.
17. The letter was appended to her posthumous memoirs published by her husband, David Ramsay, *Memoirs of the Life of Martha Laurens Ramsay* (Philadelphia: James Maxwell, 1811). Martha Laurens Ramsay died on 10 June 1811 at the age of 52. There is, therefore, no record of her actual library transaction because the manuscript ledger that is preserved began in July 1811. But on 5 September 1811 there was a book order from the Ramsay household for volumes 1 & 3 of Rollin's *Ancient History*, and in 1815, David Ramsay himself borrowed Anquetil's *Universal History*.
18. David Ramsay, *History of South Carolina*, vol. 2, p. 378. An inventory of the collection dated 17 March 1813 was appended to the 1813 manuscript catalogue. It mentioned 3,445 sets of books, or a total of 8,280 volumes. See 'A Catalogue of the Books &c.', Charleston Library Society.
19. On his admission the new member paid $50. As for the membership rate, it was $2 per quarter and only $1 per quarter after ten years. A new membership required the approval of two-thirds of the existing members. This practice precluded any radical social transformation. Widows and seasonal residents paid a lower membership rate. All women mentioned by name in the records of 1811–1817 were confirmed to be widows.
20. See Minute Books (1815–1841), Charleston Library Society.
21. All names have been included in the total: old members whose share was later owned by their widow as well as new members who requested admission within those years by either inheriting or acquiring a share. The actual readers may have been different from the subscribers as they were listed in the circulation ledgers, and it might be more accurate to speak of a 'reading household'. For instance, married women's book charges were registered in their husband's name.

22. The comment is from Charles Manigault (1846) as quoted by Michael P. Johnson, 'Planters and patriarchy: Charleston, 1800–1860', *Journal of Southern History*, 41 (1980), p. 62.

23. In his eulogy of David Ramsay, Robert Y. Hayne mentioned that 'want of judgment in the affairs of the world was the weak point of his character'. See 'Biographical memoir of David Ramsay,' from the *Analectic Magazine*, reprinted in David Ramsay, *History of the United States from the First Settlement as English Colonies, in 1607, to the Year 1808* (Philadelphia: M. Carey and Son, 1818), p. 23. The local historian and physician David Ramsay encountered many financial difficulties. Heavily indebted, by 1811 he was forced to sell his plantation of 69 acres. In 1815 he was assassinated by a lunatic he was treating.

24. The practice of writing in the margins of books was denounced in the minutes of the quarterly meeting of 20 September 1826. See Minute Books (1815–1841), Charleston Library Society, Charleston.

25. Letter to Miss Juliana Hazelhurst, 11 April 1811, in Ramsay, *Memoirs*, pp. 266–7.

26. See Maurie D. McInnis, et al., *In Pursuit of Refinement: Charlestonians Abroad, 1740–1860* (Columbia, SC: University of South Carolina, 1999), p. 178; Elliott Family, Miscellaneous Manuscripts, Charleston Library Society.

27. 'Inventory of the goods and chattels of the estate of Mrs. J. G. Elliott, 9 August 1850' and 'Inventory and appraisement of the negroes, furniture and other chattels & effects of the estate of Mrs Juliet G. Elliot made at Rosemont Plantation on the 1st February 1851,' Estate Files, Probate Court, Charleston, South Carolina; Circulation Records, Charleston Library Society.

28. See Paul Kaufman, 'The community library: a chapter in English social history', *Transactions of the American Philosophical Society*, 57 (1967), 11; Jan Fergus, *Provincial Readers in Eighteenth-Century England* (New York: Oxford University Press, 2006), pp. 28–9.

29. See 'Will of Ann Timothy', in *Wills*, Charleston County, vol. 42 (1839–45), pp. 204–7; and my article 'La place des veuves dans un monde d'hommes: genre et classe à Charleston, Caroline du Sud, au début du XIXᵉ siècle', in *Blanches et Noires: Histoire(s) des Américaines au XIXᵉ siècle*, ed. Isabelle Lehuu (Montréal: Institut de recherches et d'études féministes, 2011), pp. 85–106.

30. In opposition to this view, Jan Fergus researched cross-gendered reading in eighteenth-century England and found evidence that men were the major purchasers and borrowers of fiction. See Fergus, *Provincial Readers*, pp. 37–9, 47–52.

31. For the purpose of this research, that column was categorized as 'Messenger', although the source itself does not give any title.

32. Following the end of his studies at Princeton in 1813, Peter Timothy practiced as a lawyer in Charleston and resided with his mother at 13 Water Street.

33. For a discussion of the popularity of history books in those borrowing records, and particularly those by David Hume and William Robertson, see my unpublished paper, 'A transatlantic republic of letters: the Charleston Library Society and the diffusion of knowledge in the early nineteenth century', presented at the 2005 Edinburgh conference on 'Material Cultures

and the Creation of Knowledge'. Similarly, male students at the University of North Carolina, who were teenagers between 14 and 20 years old read volumes of British fiction and history books. See my paper, 'Carolinian students and their fathers' books: the youth culture of the early American Republic', presented at the 2008 annual meeting of the Canadian Historical Association in Vancouver.

34. The 1826 catalogue of the Charleston Library Society included an 1811 Philadelphia edition, without a publisher, and a second, unspecified copy. See *A Catalogue of the Books*, p. 143. According to Early American Imprints, the publisher of the 1811 Philadelphia edition was Farrand, Hopkins and Zantzinger. Most of the time, the two volumes were charged together.

35. See *Critical Review*, 3rd ser. 24 (Oct. 1811): 160–9, and *Monthly Review*, 2nd ser. 65 (Aug. 1811): 434–5, in *British Fiction, 1800–1829: A Database of Production, Circulation & Reception*, http://www.british-fiction.cf.ac.uk/

36. James M. Clifton, 'Heyward, Nathaniel', in *American National Biography* (1999), 10: 723. Nathaniel Heyward, Jr was born in 1790 and died in 1819.

37. At the quarterly meeting of the Charleston Library Society on 21st September 1825, a report was presented by the Committee appointed 'to inspect the library and to ascertain what books are lost, missing, or injured, &c.' The Committee listed 'the principal sources of the existing evils': for instance, 'New Books are materially injured by being circulated before they are securely bound, or before they are marked & entered in the Catalogue', and 'Books taken out in the name of one Member, are transferred to other members, without being returned to the Library as the Rules prescribe'. See Minutes Books (1815–1841), Charleston Library Society, Charleston.

38. See Roger Chartier, *The Order of Books: Readers, Authors, and Libraries in Europe between the Fourteenth and Eighteenth Centuries*, translated by Lydia G. Cochrane (Stanford: Stanford University Press, 1994).

Part 3
Readers in the
Nineteenth-Century World

5
Devouring *Uncle Tom's Cabin*: Antebellum 'Common' Readers

Barbara Hochman

Soon after its publication in 1852, *Uncle Tom's Cabin* pervaded Anglo-American culture as theatre, song, poster and game. Eric Lott, Linda Williams and others have heightened our awareness of *Uncle Tom's Cabin* as performance and visual artefact.[1] But this awareness threatens to obscure our understanding of Stowe's novel as a book that was avidly read. My chapter analyses antebellum responses to Stowe's book in order to remind us that *Uncle Tom's Cabin* had deep roots in the nineteenth-century American culture of reading, and a vital existence there for decades. I also raise questions about how we select and interpret evidence for the reading experience.

Interpreting accounts of reading is as tricky as interpreting literary texts or historical events and we need to give more thought not only to what constitutes evidence of response, but to what we mean by social context. How is response intertwined with personal as well as cultural history – are these indistinguishable? Do representations of reading in letters and diaries, autobiographies and fiction reinforce or contradict one another? How is the affect created by certain kinds of reading transformed by the act of writing or talking about it?

Antebellum commentators generally believed there was an extraordinary fit between the 'reader role' inscribed in *Uncle Tom's Cabin* and the reactions of white Northern readers. Reviews and other published discussions acknowledge the humour and the exciting plot of Stowe's narrative, but more often they highlight its moral and political impact. The encomiums of readers who claim that they wept their way through the book and emerged with renewed faith and political passion were much reprinted. 'I thought I was a thorough-going Abolitionist before', Stowe's friend Georgiana May writes in a letter after finishing the novel, 'but . . . I seem never to have had any feeling on this subject till now.' May's letter first appeared in 1879, identified as 'the letter of an intimate friend', in Stowe's introduction for a new edition of *Uncle Tom's Cabin*.[2] This introduction included letters in the same spirit by famous readers such as Lord Carlisle, Charles Kingsley, Jenny Lind, George Sand and others.

Later in the nineteenth century, commentators were firmly convinced that the emotional responses of antebellum readers had contributed directly to the abolition of slavery. In this view, readers of *Uncle Tom's Cabin* enthusiastically accepted Stowe's guidelines – experiencing sympathy for the 'lowly' and, like Senator Byrd or Ophelia, following their feelings with action.[3] The belief in a close alignment between Stowe's protocol of reading and the antebellum response has had a long life, even among scholars who explore the limitations of sentiment.[4] But many revealing as well as culturally typical responses escape from this tightly woven narrative of how *Uncle Tom's Cabin* was read.

We know that hundreds of thousands of nineteenth-century readers, North and South, black and white, old and young, consumed Stowe's tale as newsprint and book. They read it aloud, gave it to friends, talked about it, wrote about it.[5] '*Read* Uncle Tom, oh yes, literally devoured it', Maria Woodbury writes to a friend in Holden Massachusetts on 4 June 1852.[6] Such intensity often came with a price. Many of the antebellum men and women who consumed *Uncle Tom's Cabin* with gusto experienced anxiety along with pleasure. 'I have indulged myself in reading a good deal', Anna Cushing of Dorchester confides to her diary in April 1852. Cushing's words reflect some discomfort at having 'indulged' herself; but this does not prevent her from finishing Stowe's novel in three days.[7]

Men as well as women consumed the book avidly – and worried about the implications of their immersion in it. In August 1852, Carroll Norcross, a farm labourer and part-time writing master of rural Maine, describes his reading as follows:

> This morning . . . I took up a volume of Uncle Tom's Cabin. Soon I was all absorb[ed] in its interesting pages and was bound down captive by this ingenious production. . . . Eagerly I devoured the first volume regardless of the presence of those to whom at any other time I should have been happy to have tendered my whole attention. I disregarded all the rules of Ettiquit.

Norcross continues to disregard propriety by proceeding to the second volume, again 'completely bound up' and reading 'until nearly midnight'.[8] Late-night reading was itself a defiance of social norms; proper young men were regularly urged to avoid it. 'If exciting books are read at all,' William Alcott warns, 'they should be read in the forenoon, not in the evening.' As David Stewart argues, Alcott's warning reflects common fears that late-night reading would lead to masturbation, 'a practice luridly condemned in popular medical literature'.[9]

Early reviewers often describe *Uncle Tom's Cabin* as exciting and moving but it is the non-professional reader who expresses anxiety about the book's uncanny capacity to enthral, especially at night-time. An account by Henry Ward Beecher's wife exemplifies this process. One morning, she reports, after 'rising earlier than usual and eating breakfast', her husband opened *Uncle Tom's Cabin*. He 'threw himself upon the sofa, forgot his surroundings entirely and read until noon. He ate his dinner book in hand and during the afternoon frequently gave way to tears.' As his wife tells the rest of the story:

> The night came on. It was growing late and I felt impelled to urge him to retire. Without raising his eyes from the book he replied:
> 'Soon soon; you go; I'll come soon.'
> Closing the house I went to our room. . . . The clock struck twelve, one, two, three, and then, to my great relief I heard Mr Beecher coming upstairs. As he entered he threw 'Uncle Tom's Cabin' on the table, exclaiming: 'There, I've done it! But if Hattie Stowe ever writes anything more like that! I'll – well, she has nearly killed me anyhow!'
> And he never picked up the book from that day.[10]

This description evokes not only Beecher's experience of reading, but also his wife's reaction to that experience. Beecher's absorption elicits rising anxiety in his wife as she urges him to retire and watches the clock strike twelve, one, two and three. When he finally leaves the book to join her upstairs she responds with 'great relief'. Antebellum readers often express discomfort with the way *Uncle Tom's Cabin* elicited unexpected, even disquieting responses ('I have indulged myself'; 'I was bound down captive'; 'she has nearly killed me anyhow!'). In a letter to her sister, Mary Pierce Poor of Massachusetts explains that she has 'been writing home to advise Elizabeth not to attempt [*Uncle Tom's Cabin*]. I am afraid it would kill her. I never read anything so affecting in my life.'[11] Such comments suggest that some readers of Stowe's book went well beyond the instructions for reading implicit in reviews, commentaries, and *Uncle Tom's Cabin* itself.

Reading was a crucially important activity in the antebellum United States, a site of cultural enthusiasm, conflict and anxiety. Novel-reading was both an increasingly popular leisure activity and a frequent target of attack. Guidelines for purposive, useful reading proliferated in sermons, advice books and the press. Many readers rejected such recommendations of course, eagerly consuming Bulwer, Byron, Eugene Sue and other writers who were regularly savaged by American commentators, including Stowe. Prescriptions for reading are a very partial indication of real practices. Readers who were captivated by *Uncle Tom's Cabin* often rejected Stowe's own protocol of reading, inscribed in her novel and elsewhere. Such readers, so absorbed in the book that they neglected work or other duties, gave themselves over to their appetites ('oh yes, literally devoured it') and selfish needs ('I indulged myself'). These were the very effects of 'bad' reading that educators and ministers warned against.

* * *

The long-range effects of imaginative entry into a fictional world are hard to gauge, but if Stowe's tale had political impact this was accomplished by infiltrating the minds of white readers with images that held them 'captive' and by giving the idea of a slave an imaginative reality so powerful that readers, 'lost in a book', could no longer differentiate between Tom or Eliza and themselves. This dynamic goes beyond sympathy, which always requires a certain distance between subject and object.[12]

A reader's own account of reading – like any other text – often pulls in more than one direction. The letters and diary entries of antebellum readers reflect ambivalence about the extent to which Stowe's novel gained their undivided attention and elicited strong feelings. 'I *could not* leave [*Uncle Tom's Cabin*]' Georgiana May writes in her letter to Stowe, any 'more than I could have left a dying child'.[13] Like Norcross's assertion of being 'held captive' by the book, May's imagery adapts one of Stowe's own most painful tropes. Like Norcross (and others) May reproduces Stowe's words, not as explicit citation, but as a kind of deep recycling which assimilates the reader herself into the action of the book.[14]

Up to a point, the comments of readers such as Cushing, Woodbury, Norcross or May conform to widely shared expectations for reading *Uncle Tom's Cabin*. Such expectations were quickly established by advertisements, public testimonials, private exchanges and reviews of the

1850s.[15] 'Much have I heard and read about this same book', Norcross writes.[16] Some of what Norcross read and heard surely prepared him to be engrossed, and to 'feast' (albeit, as he is careful to note, 'mentally') by reading. But the recurrent image of readers gobbling up *Uncle Tom's Cabin* suggests that readers' responses often went beyond the 'mental' – exceeding what Stowe had proposed or expected.

'Charles bro't home "Uncle Tom's Cabin" the other night, & the children are devouring it', Ellen Douglas Birdseye Wheaton notes in her diary in April 1852.[17] The metaphor of reading as eating deserves attention at this point. Cultural spokesmen of the period regularly made distinctions between texts that would nourish the reader, contributing to health, and texts that would, on the contrary, foster passivity and overindulgence (as in consumption of sweets, liquor and other unhealthy food and drink).[18] While May's inability to leave the text, or Norcross's sense of being held captive by it, may suggest involuntary absorption, the image of 'devouring' also implies energy and activity. But the kind of energy implicit in 'devouring' would not have reassured the many commentators who promoted literacy in order to foster a sense of reality, order and self-control.[19] Indeed, reading as devouring suggests an almost animal-like desire and abandon. Consumed by their feelings while consuming a novel, readers such as Norcross or Beecher ignore their friends and do not join their wives in bed. This dynamic implies just the kind of merger between text and reader that preoccupied cultural guardians.

In an influential essay, Walter Benjamin emphasizes the 'isolation' of the novel-reader. This idea was a familiar source of concern for eighteenth- and nineteenth-century commentators. After Benjamin's recasting of the notion in 'The Storyteller', it became a cornerstone of fiction theory for much of the twentieth century.[20] The novel reader, Benjamin writes, 'is isolated, more so than any other reader. . . . In this solitude of his, the reader of a novel seizes upon his material more jealously than anyone else. He is ready to make it completely his own, to devour it, as it were. Indeed, he destroys: he swallows up the material as [a] fire devours logs.'[21] In Benjamin's analysis of what it means to 'devour' a novel, reading is driven by a destructive, 'jealous' appetite and passionate self-enclosure.

Reading as devouring was precisely not the kind of reading either promoted by nineteenth-century commentators or recommended by *Uncle Tom's Cabin* itself. In numerous scenes Stowe privileges the kind of reading that leads to political wisdom, moral action, thoughtfulness or faith. Within *Uncle Tom's Cabin* only the Bible enables a reader to benefit from taking textual images for reality. Fiction is presented as generally false: 'In a novel', Stowe writes, describing St Clare's state of mind after he is separated from his first love, 'people's hearts break, and they die, and that is the end of it; and in a story this is very conven- ient. But in real life we do not die when all that makes life bright dies to us.'[22] Stowe differentiates here between foolish, fantastical (inferior) novels and her own.

The kind of absorption that many antebellum readers of *Uncle Tom's Cabin* seem to have experienced is not outlined in Stowe's narrative itself – with the possible exception of the scene in which Cassie the slave woman leaves a book on a table for Simon Legree to pick up. Once he does so, Legree finds himself 'turning page after page', engrossed in 'one of those collections of stories of bloody murders, ghostly legends, and supernatural visitations, which, coarsely got up and illustrated have a strange fascination for one who once begins to read them' (p. 568). Readers such as Woodbury, Cushing, Norcross and Beecher also turn page after page, immersed, immobilized, 'strangely fascinated', heedless of others. Such readers violate Stowe's instructions; their responses are not confined to sympathy and reflection.

Stowe understood the lure of exciting fiction, for young readers in particular. She herself had been an avid reader as a child. Charles Stowe writes of his mother: 'at six years of age we find the little girl hungrily searching for mental food amid barrels of old sermons and pamphlets stored in a corner of the garret'. In this account, 'at the very bottom of a barrel of musty sermons' Harriet finds 'an ancient volume of "The Arabian Nights"' which, as Stowe's sister Isabella Beecher Hooker later recalls, Harriet committed to memory and regularly reproduced for her younger brothers at bedtime. 'Story-books were rare in those days', Hooker writes, but 'ransacking barrels in the garret' Harriet also found 'a few odd pages of Don Quixote, which she devoured with eager relish'.[23] The imagery of reading as eating in these formulations is thor- oughly conventional but though Charles Stowe (like Norcross) is careful to mark the avidly consumed 'food' as 'mental', there is no mistaking the desire and intensity in these images of a 'hungry' girl who 'ransacks' the garret and 'devours' what she finds 'with eager relish'.

Stowe's attraction to novels, as Lawrence Buell suggests, was compli- cated by 'her evangelical conditioning'.[24] 'You speak of your predilection for literature having been a snare to you', Stowe writes to her brother Edward Beecher at the age of eighteen in 1829. 'I have found it so myself. I can scarcely think, without tears and indignation, that all that is beauti- ful and lovely and poetical has been laid on other altars.'[25] In an intro- duction to Charles Beecher's fictionalized account of *The Incarnation*

(1849), Stowe justifies her brother's use of fictional devices and argues that a devout, truthful, imaginative retelling of 'the incarnation' will prevent fervent natures from turning to seductive and pernicious texts. 'For the want of some proper aliment', Stowe writes, young people seek 'strange fire from heathen altars, and cull . . . poisonous fruits and flowers from hot beds of the god of this world'. 'But', she insists, 'there is . . . bread enough and to spare in a Father's house.' Tempering her own erotic imagery (hot beds, strange fire), Stowe displaces 'poisonous fruits and flowers' with plain 'bread'.[26]

Stowe began composing *Uncle Tom's Cabin* less than two years after writing her introduction to *The Incarnation*. She had long been concerned about the potential dangers of 'heathen' texts, especially fiction, particularly fiction for the young. Her distaste for Byron, Bulwer and Sue is unsurprising: these writers were routinely criticized on moral grounds. Henry Ward Beecher condemned Bulwer 'with utter loathing' for making 'the English novel-literature more vile than he found it'.[27] Using language that effectively competes with the novels he attacks, Beecher comments:

> Novels of the French school, and of English imitators, are the common-sewers of society into which drain the concentrated filth of the worst passions of the worst creatures . . . These offspring-reptiles of the French mind, who can kill these? You might as well draw sword on a plague, or charge a malaria with the bayonet. This black-lettered literature circulates in this town, floats in our stores, nestles in the shops, is fingered and read nightly and hatches in the young mind broods of salacious thoughts.[28]

Like Stowe, Beecher was on intimate terms with the texts he denounces.[29] Through the course of the 1840s the young Stowe differentiated ever more finely among possible ends for which fictional rhetoric could be deployed. By 1851 she had come round to the idea that fiction could be legitimate fare for 'many a youthful soul' but only if clearly marked as 'a proper aliment' – not designed for 'the amusement of a passing hour', certainly not for mere pleasure and excitement.[30]

In Stowe's 'Concluding Remarks' to *Uncle Tom's Cabin* she ascribes the question 'What can any individual do' to a hypothetical reader and famously instructs her own readers to 'Feel right' (p. 624). Many claimed to have followed these instructions. 'I hope the book will do good', Cushing notes immediately after confessing that she has 'indulged [her]self in reading'; and Woodbury, who 'literally devour[s]'

Uncle Tom's Cabin, also claims 'It has done me good. But, I still need some Christian patience and meekness, those qualities that shine so brightly in the life of the poor old negro.'[31] Such explicit affirmations of Stowe's moral imperatives sometimes sound like afterthoughts which serve to rein in and make sense of the untoward feelings released while reading the book. A sizeable gap remains between high-minded formulations and other responses often noted elsewhere in a single letter or diary entry. While devouring *Uncle Tom's Cabin*, Cushing, Norcross, Beecher and others are threatened with the loss of their familiar sense of self and social positioning. By completing the novel in three days – or even in one sitting – they maximize the threat to the norms of social decorum. They regain their composure only afterwards, as they formulate the moral meaning of their reading experience (or, like Mary Pierce Poor, caution others to avoid the book).

* * *

I want to put some additional pressure on the notion of a perfect fit between Stowe's 'protocol of reading' and the antebellum response. In one much-reprinted account, Stowe describes reading completed instalments aloud to her children and they react to the story exactly as she desired. Stowe explains that when she finished reading the scene about Uncle Tom's death, her boys sobbed – the familiar prelude to moral insight and a change of heart throughout *Uncle Tom's Cabin* itself. Stowe's sons then drew the proposed moral conclusion: 'O mamma, slavery is the most cursed thing in the world!'[32] Stowe's vignette provides a prototypical narrative of the harmony between guidelines for reading and reader response. It has been taken at face value by biographers and other commentators, but testimonies of reading are shaped by multiple factors, including their intended audience.

In telling the story of her sons' response to her novel, Stowe reinforced a set of instructions for reading to which she was publicly committed: read, weep and reflect. These instructions circulated widely through antebellum culture – in letters, reviews and such artefacts as the *Uncle Tom's Cabin* handkerchief, issued by J. P. Jewett in 1852, and embossed with the famous scene in which Eva tells Uncle Tom that she will die.[33] Although we have no particular reason to doubt Stowe's testimony, her sons must have been well prepared by their life in the Stowe family to respond as their mother claims they did. According to Elizabeth Stuart Phelps, when Stowe's youngest daughter was asked to write a school composition one day, she resolutely refused; later, she wrote the words

'Slavery is the greatest curse of human Nature' on a 'slip of paper' and submitted it to her teacher instead.[34] If this report is accurate, it too suggests how well the Stowe children had absorbed their anti-slavery lesson. But the readiness of Stowe's sons and daughter to confirm their mother's expectations and convictions (in reports to their mother and teacher), does not explain the hold of *Uncle Tom's Cabin* on generations of readers beyond the confines of the Stowe family.

After the Civil War the image of antebellum readers shedding sympathetic, righteous tears over Stowe's novel became a commonplace; the idea that *Uncle Tom's Cabin* changed lives and politics was increasingly popular. Some commentators of the 1880s and 90s note that the book was no longer read 'with the intensity of other days',[35] but this idea only reinforced the governing consensus about the antebellum response.

Attention to individual testimonies of reading show us how partial and time-bound a codified consensus must be. Antebellum readers were not always riveted to the book by the responses Stowe recommended (moral contemplation, faith, sympathy). They were held 'captive' by dramatic dialogues, by a narrative voice that cajoled, exhorted and threatened; and by a swiftly paced plot that included slave suicide, a miraculous river-crossing, violence and innocent deaths. This combination of rhetorical ploys elicited excitement, fear and suspense as well as tears and sublime feelings. Unable to resist the book, antebellum readers, especially readers unaccustomed to giving themselves over to a novel, understandably express concern about their absorption.

Uncle Tom's Cabin was publicly condemned and hard to buy in the South, but Southerners often went to some lengths to acquire it, and many read it avidly there: 'I have now finally managed to obtain *Uncle Tom's Cabin*', Rosalie Roos of South Carolina writes in a letter of 4 May 1853. 'In Charleston this book cannot be bought. No bookseller has it for sale there. We have been able to borrow it from Mrs. Peronneau's sister and *Eliza read it through in a day* and has halfway become an abolitionist from it' (my emphasis).[36] When a visitor brought *Uncle Tom's Cabin* to the home of a planter in North Carolina, the master read it rapidly and with interest, sharing it with the tutor of his children (who read it to his pupils).[37] Mary Boykin Chesnut's diary and letters show that she read it, re-read it and 'could not' read it ('too sickening') in the course of 1861 and 1862. Irresistibly drawn to it as well as repelled by it, Chesnut repeatedly returns to it.[38] Southern reviewers too read the novel with intensity, as their often-cited outrage suggests.

Commentators from the South complained that by using a novel to make an abolitionist argument Stowe was hitting below the belt.[39]

This charge is informed by anxiety about the same incalculable consequences of fiction-reading that worried antebellum ministers and educators who feared that absorption in a novel might blur the boundaries between the fictive and the real, between text and reader, between self and other. Fiction-reading enables a fluid experimentation with subject positions. If readers of the 1850s came away from *Uncle Tom's Cabin* with newly formulated politics, as nineteenth-century commentators believed, they did so because Stowe's narrative drew them into a tale of racial otherness as no previous text – fiction, slave narrative or abolitionist account – had managed to do. *Uncle Tom's Cabin* challenged not only antebellum readers' assumptions about slavery but also their customary modes of fiction-reading.

Notes and references

1. See Eric Lott, *Love and Theft: Blackface Minstrelsy and the American working Class* (New York: Oxford University Press, 1995); Sarah Meer, *Uncle Tom Mania: Slavery, Minstrelsy and Transatlantic Culture in the 1850s* (Athens, GA: University of Georgia Press, 2005); Jo Ann Morgan, *Uncle Tom's Cabin as Visual Culture* (Columbia: University of Missouri Press, 2007); Linda Williams, *Playing the Race Card: Melodramas of Black and White from Uncle Tom to O. J. Simpson* (Princeton: Princeton University Press: 2001); Marcus Wood, *Blind Memory: Visual Representations of Slavery in England and America 1780–1865* (New York: Routledge: 2000).
2. Harriet Beecher Stowe, 'Introduction' to *Uncle Tom's Cabin* (Boston: Houghton Mifflin, c.1879, 1893), p. xxxviii. May's letter has often been cited. See Thomas F. Gossett, *Uncle Tom's Cabin and American Culture* (Dallas: Southern Methodist University Press, 1985), p. 167; Marianne Noble, *The Masochistic Pleasures of Sentimental Literature* (Princeton: Princeton University Press, 2000), p. 141.
3. Many recent discussions of sentiment question the link between tears and political action. See Ann Douglas, *The Feminization of American Culture* (New York: Knopf, 1978); Philip Fisher, *Hard Facts: Setting and Form in the American Novel* (New York: Oxford University Press, 1985); *The Culture of Sentiment: Race, Gender and Sentimentality in Nineteenth-Century America*, ed. Shirley Samuels (New York: Oxford University Press, 1992); Elizabeth Fekete Trubey, '"Success is Sympathy": Uncle Tom's Cabin and the Woman Reader', in *Reading Women: Literary Figures and Cultural Icons from the Victorian Age to the Present*, ed. Janet Badia and Jennifer Phegley (Toronto: University of Toronto Press, 2006), pp. 53–76.
4. Jane Tompkins writes that '*Uncle Tom's Cabin* convinced a nation to go to war and free its slaves'; *Sensational Designs: The Cultural Work of American Fiction 1790–1860* (New York: Oxford University Press, 1989), p. 41. Marianne Noble calls the book 'an undisputedly important political novel'; *The Masochistic Pleasures of Sentimental Literature*, p. 126. Recent discussions of Stowe continue to mention Abraham Lincoln's alleged statement crediting *Uncle Tom's Cabin* with starting the Civil War. See, for example, Joan Hedrick's biography

of Stowe, *Harriet Beecher Stowe: A Life* (New York: Oxford University Press, 1994), p. vii, and the Oxford World's Classics edition of *Uncle Tom's Cabin*, ed. Jean Fagan Yellin (Oxford: Oxford University Press, 1998), back cover.

5. On 10 June 1852, the *National Era* printed a reader's letter: 'there have been 25 readers of my paper since the beginning of Mrs. Stowe's story. That number goes a little higher than the one you mentioned a few weeks ago.' The *Era* replies: 'This is *too* hard usage for one newspaper. Five readers is as many as we can allow to a paper. We hope our friend will insist that every 5 at least of his circle of 25 shall take one copy of the *Era*'; 'A pretty large circle', *The National Era* (10 June 1852), p. 94. Forrest Wilson points out that *The National Era* regularly circulated from one family to another until the pages were 'quite worn out'; *Crusader in Crinoline: The Life of Harriet Beecher Stowe* (Philadelphia: J. B. Lippincott, 1941), p. 272.

6. Letter from Maria Woodbury to Miss Lucy Marshall of Holden, Mass., probably 4 June 1852, in the Marshall Family Papers, American Antiquarian Society. Woodbury lived in Fitchburg, Massachusetts but taught school in a variety of locations. The letter about reading *Uncle Tom's Cabin* was written from Westfield, New York.

7. Anna Quincy Thaxter Cushing Diary; from Vol II (April 1852–July 1853), American Antiquarian Society.

8. Cited in Ronald J. Zboray and Mary Saracino Zboray, *Everyday Ideas: Socioliterary Experience Among Antebellum New Englanders* (Knoxville: Tennessee University Press, 2006), pp. 249–50.

9. William Alcott, *Familiar Letters to Young Men on Various Subjects* (Buffalo: Derby, 1850), pp. 76–7. David Stewart, 'Sensationalism', forthcoming in *U.S. Popular Print Culture, 1860–1920*, ed. Christine Bold (New York: Oxford University Press, 2010). On the dangers of novel-reading for young men see also William Eliot, *Lectures to Young Men* (Boston: Crosby, Nichols and Co. [1853]; 1854), pp. 72–5; Henry Ward Beecher, 'The strange woman', in *Lectures to Young Men* (Salem: John P. Jewett & Co., 1846), pp. 170–214.

10. 'Harriet Beecher Stowe dead', *Philadelphia Times* (2 July 1896), p. 3. According to this article Beecher had refused to read the book as a serial; in an image that reflects some anticipatory anxiety he prepared to 'take it all at one dose'.

11. Cited in Zboray and Zboray, *Everyday Ideas*, p. 258. Mary Pierce Poor, a social reformer, was daughter of the Reverend John Pierce, for fifty years the minister of the First Church of Brookline, Mass. She was the wife of Henry Varnum Poor, a railroad journalist and economist.

12. Philip Fisher's paradigm for sympathetic response is Rousseau's image of the distant spectator watching a lion tear child from mother. Susan Ryan points out that one strain in nineteenth-century benevolent discourse 'rejected sympathetic identification', fearing that a 'too-thorough identification between helper and helped' would involve an unacceptable 'degree of social leveling'; *The Grammar of Good Intentions* (Ithaca: Cornell University Press, 2003), pp. 17, 19.

13. Stowe, 'Introduction' to *Uncle Tom's Cabin* (c.1879, 1893), p. xviii.

14. 'It is a book to sink into the heart of all readers', Maria Woodbury writes, echoing Eva's oft-repeated phrase. Such recasting of the novel's tropes suggests how deeply readers experienced the book's impact. Yet Woodbury's use of Eva's words also suggests an idea of a book as passively impressed upon

a reader rather than actively 'devoured'. The imagery used by readers raises theoretical as well as historical questions about how reading works.

15. Readers echo reviews and advertisements as well as the novel itself. In a letter to Francis Henshaw Dewey I, written 3 May 1852, Sarah Barker Tufts Wheaton reproduces a widely circulated puff which claims that the printing press and paper mills are working twenty-four hours a day, unable to meet the demand for the book (American Antiquarian Society, Dewey-Bliss Family Papers, Box 2, Folder 8). This claim is repeated in a contemporary review, 'Literature of slavery', *New Englander* X.37 [Feb. 1852] 591–2 [p. 591]). However, a direct citation is different from the kind of transmutation involved when a reader adapts Stowe's image of a 'captive' or a dying child in order to convey the experience of reading. The first kind of citing simply echoes a point in the same spirit as the original; the second kind transforms the initial image and suggests a more thorough imaginative or emotional recycling.

16. Cited in Zboray and Zboray, *Everyday Ideas*, p. 249.

17. Ellen Birdseye Wheaton, *The Diary of Ellen Birdseye Wheaton* (1923); 'North American women's letters and diaries', at: http://www.alexanderstreet2.com/nwldlive/nawld.login.htm (accessed 15 October 2006).

18. This imagery has persisted and has been put to multiple uses. On the trope of reading as eating in relation to emerging views of adolescence in late nineteenth-century America, see Steven Mailloux, 'The rhetorical use and abuse of fiction: eating books in late nineteenth-century America', *boundary* 2, 17(1990), 133–57. On the use of this trope by newly professionalized librarians in the 1870s and eighties, see Sheldrick Ross, 'Metaphors of reading', *Journal of Library History*, 22 (1987), 147–63 (p. 149). For a critique of the metaphor as used to discount popular literature in the twentieth century, see Janice Radway, 'Reading is not eating: mass produced literature and the theoretical, methodological and political consequences of a metaphor', *Book Research Quarterly*, 2 (1986), 7–29.

19. On the educational values associated with reading in the antebellum period, see Scott E. Casper, 'Antebellum reading prescribed and described', in *Perspectives on American Book History: Artifacts and Commentary*, ed. Joanne D. Chaison Casper and Jeffrey D. Groves (Amherst: University of Massachusetts Press, 2002), pp. 135–64; Sarah Robbins, *Managing Literacy, Mothering America: Women's Narratives on Reading and Writing in the Nineteenth Century* (Pittsburgh: Pittsburgh University Press, 2004); Dave M. Stewart, 'Cultural work, city crime, reading, pleasure', *American Literary History*, 94 (1997), 676–701, esp. pp. 687, 691–2.

20. Walter Benjamin, 'The storyteller', in *Illuminations*, trans. Harry Zohn (New York: Schocken Books, 1969), pp. 83–110; J. Paul Hunter, 'The loneliness of the long-distance reader', *Genre* 10 (1977), 455–84; Ian Watt, *The Rise of the Novel* (Berkeley: University of California Press, 1957), pp. 88–92; Wolfgang Iser, *The Act of Reading* (Baltimore: Johns Hopkins University Press, 1978), p. 140. More recently the social contexts of reading have gained emphasis. See Elizabeth Long, 'Textual interpretation as collective action', in *Ethnography of Reading*, ed. Jonathan Boyarin (Berkeley: University of California Press, 1993), pp. 180–211; Roger Chartier, 'Texts, printings, readings', in *The New Cultural History*, ed. Lynn Hunt (Berkeley: University of California Press, 1989), pp. 154–75; Zboray and Zboray, *Everyday Ideas*.

21. Benjamin, 'Storyteller', p. 100.

22. Harriet Beecher Stowe, *Uncle Tom's Cabin*, ed. Ann Douglas (New York: Penguin, 1987), p. 241. Future page references are to this edition and are included in parentheses in the text.

23. Charles E. Stowe, *The Life of Harriet Beecher Stowe Compiled From her Letters and Journals* (Boston: Houghton, Mifflin, 1889), p. 9; Isabella Beecher Hooker, *A Brief Sketch of the Life of Harriet Beecher Stowe By Her Sister* (Hartford: Plimpton MFC, 1896), p. 9.

24. Lawrence Buell, 'Harriet Beecher Stowe and the dream of the great American novel', in *The Cambridge Companion to Harriet Beecher Stowe*, ed. Cindy Weinstein (Cambridge and New York: Cambridge University Press, 2004), pp. 190–202, p. 190.

25. Cited in Gregg Camfield, 'The moral aesthetics of sentimentality: a missing key to *Uncle Tom's Cabin*', *Nineteenth-Century Literature*, 43 (1988), 319–45 (p. 330).

26. Harriet Beecher Stowe, 'Introductory essay', in Charles Beecher, *The Incarnation* (New York: Harper Brothers, 1849), pp. viii–ix. See also my 'Introduction' to Stowe's essay in *PMLA*, 118 (2003), pp. 1320–4.

27. Henry Ward Beecher, 'The strange woman', p. 180.

28. Ibid., pp. 210–11.

29. Beecher knew *The Mysteries of Paris* well enough to analyse its characters – Madame Lucenay's 'unblushing adultery', 'the diabolical voluptuousness of Cecily', the 'assignations of the *pure* Madame D'Harville', and the lies of Rodolphe ('The best character in the far-famed Mysteries of Paris'), ibid., p. 214. For Stowe on Byron and Bulwer see also 'Literary epidemics, 1', *New York Evangelist*, 13 (28 July 1842), p. 235; 'Literary Epidemics, 2', *New York Evangelist*, 14 (13 July 1843), p. 109.

30. Harriet Beecher Stowe, 'Introduction', *Uncle Tom's Cabin* (1896), p. xli.

31. Anna Quincy Thaxter Cushing Diary; Maria Woodbury, 4 June 1852.

32. Versions of this story appear in Stowe's 'Introduction' to the 1879 edition of the novel, reprinted by Houghton Mifflin several times during the 1890s; in Charles E. Stowe, *The Life of Harriet Beecher Stowe*, pp. 148–9; and in recent discussions of Stowe such as Sarah N. Roth, 'The mind of a child: images of African Americans in early juvenile fiction', *Journal of the Early Republic*, 25 (2005), pp. 79–109 (p. 99). E. Bruce Kirkham examines contradictions among several versions of the story in *The Building of Uncle Tom's Cabin* (Knoxville: University of Tennessee Press, 1977), pp. 72–5.

33. On the cultural work of this handkerchief, see Robin Bernstein, *Racial Innocence: Performing American Childhood from Slavery to Civil Rights* (New York: New York University Press, forthcoming).

34. Elizabeth Stuart Phelps' account of her classmate appears in a chapter on 'Mrs Stowe', in Phelps's *Chapters From a Life* (1896; New York: Arno Press, 1980), p. 135. It also appeared in *McClure's Magazine*, 7 (1896), p. 4.

35. Kate Brannon Knight, *History of the Work of the Connecticut Women at the World's Columbian Exposition Chicago 1893* (Hartford, CT: Hartford Press, 1898), pp. 24–5. On changing norms for reading *Uncle Tom's Cabin* in the 1890s, see Barbara Hochman, '*Uncle Tom's Cabin and the Reading Revolution: Race, Literacy, Childhood and Fiction, 1851–1911* (Amherst: University of Massachusetts Press, 2011), and 'Sentiment without tears: *Uncle Tom's Cabin* as

history in the 1890s', in *New Directions in American Reception Study*, ed. James Machor and Philip Goldstein (New York: Oxford University Press, 2008), pp. 255–76.

36. Letter dated 4 May 1853. *North American Women's Letters and Diaries:* http://www.alexanderstreet2.com/nwldlive/nawld.login.htm (accessed 15 October 2006).

37. Excerpts from the (Northern) tutor's diary are cited in D. D. Hall, 'A Yankee tutor in the Old South', *New England Quarterly*, 33 (1960), 82–91.

38. Mary Boykin Chesnut, *A Diary from Dixie*, ed. Isabella D. Martin and Myrta Lockett Avary (New York: D. Appleton, 1905), pp. 114, 142, 184. The cited phrases are from 2 September 1861; 13 March 1862; 12 June 1862. Chesnut's first reference to *Uncle Tom's Cabin* clearly indicates that she read the book prior to 1861.

39. Gossett notes that Southern reviewers often claimed that 'it was unscrupulous to attack an institution by means of a novel. . . . A novel was . . . [harder than an abolitionist pamphlet] to refute and Southern reviewers often complained that it was unjust to expect them to . . . comment on incidents which had not really happened . . . [I]t was unfair to use a novel as a vehicle of social criticism'; *Uncle Tom's Cabin and American Culture*, p. 195. For more on Southern readers, see Joy Jordan-Lake, *Whitewashing Uncle Tom's Cabin: Nineteenth-Century Women Novelists Respond to Stowe* (Nashville, TN: Vanderbilt University Press, 2005); Cindy Weinstein, 'Uncle Tom's Cabin and the South', in *The Cambridge Companion to Harriet Beecher Stowe*, pp. 39–57.

6
Reading in Polish and National Identity in Nineteenth-Century Silesia

Ilona Dobosiewicz and Liliana Piasecka

Reading can be approached from many perspectives and can be conceived of as a complex psycholinguistic process, a fundamental knowledge-building skill, and a cultural experience of varying levels of sophistication. It is both an ability to do something and a multifunctional activity. People read for intellectual growth, for knowledge, for pleasure, for information, voluntarily or because they have to read. Whichever the reason, reading restructures their minds and shapes their individual, social and national identities. The issue of national identity and its preservation is particularly relevant in the context of Polish history.

The unique aspect of Polish history is that the country underwent three partitions between 1772 and 1795, the effect of which was that 23 per cent of the citizens of Poland found themselves under German (Prussian) rule, 32 per cent became a part of the Austrian Empire, while 45 per cent were under the rule of Tsarist Russia. Despite the policies of the Prussian and Russian governments in particular, which were aimed at eradicating the sense of Polish national identity, the Poles living under the three partitions managed to maintain it through a number of ways, including reading Polish books. This chapter focuses on the phenomenon of reading books in Polish written by Polish authors in the region of Silesia, which remained under German (Prussian) rule. The demand for Polish books in Silesia was almost insatiable, and for many readers the act of reading in Polish became a way of maintaining their sense of belonging to Polish culture, and a substitute for a national community. We discuss the emotional attitudes of Silesians to books as manifested in their desire to possess their own home collections, and the mechanisms promoting the readership of Polish books, especially the establishment of popular lending libraries affiliated with schools, parish churches and local cultural associations.

This chapter falls into three parts. The first part sketches very briefly the relevant historical context. The second part focuses on the steps undertaken by Silesian civic activists, educators, publishers and writers to preserve the Polish language through reading. In the final section, some popular texts read by Silesians in the nineteenth century are briefly discussed.

Historical context

Originally a part of the Great Moravian Empire (Greater Moravia), Silesia became a part of Poland around the end of the tenth century, probably in the years 985–990. The beginnings of Polish statehood date back to 966 when its ruler, Mieszko I adopted Christianity, and soon after incorporated Silesia into a newly created state. The history of this region is dynamic in terms of its consecutive rulers. Silesia has always been a territory coveted by its neighbours because of its location and natural resources, and because of the Amber Road connecting the South of Europe (countries at the Mediterranean Sea) with the North (the Baltic Sea), by means of which the Silesians developed successful trade relations with other Polish lands and with foreign countries. As a border land, up until the nineteenth century Silesia was under Polish (till the fourteenth century), Bohemian, Austrian and Prussian rule. The region was inhabited primarily by Poles who, despite the foreign rule, struggled to maintain their identity manifest in their language, culture and religion. They continued to be attracted to their homeland – Poland – even when it was erased from the map of Europe.[1]

Poland lost its independence in the eighteenth century, due to three partitions (1772, 1793, 1795) which divided its territory among the three Central and East European Imperial powers of the day: Russia, Prussia and Austria. After the Napoleonic wars, and according to the provisions of the Congress of Vienna (1815), that part of the Duchy of Warsaw called the Kingdom of Warsaw or Congress Poland remained under the influence of Russia; the Grand Duchy of Poznań came under Prussian rule; and the Republic of Kraków was controlled by Russia, Prussia and Austria. Silesia remained under Prussian rule.

Poland regained its independence only after the First World War under the Treaty of Versailles of 1919. The delegates at the peace talks had a problem with Silesia because both Poles and Germans claimed the territory. Poles proposed that the part of Silesia that was inhabited mostly by the Polish people became a part of Poland. Germans refused to accept this proposal and finally the decision was made that the inhabitants of the area would decide, in a plebiscite, which state they wanted to belong to. Eventually, after three Silesian uprisings led by the Poles, Upper Silesia was divided between Poland and Germany. The region became fully Polish only after World War II. Although historically Silesia was one geographical region, it has been referred to as Lower Silesia (west of the Odra river) and Upper Silesia (east of the Odra river). German influences were strongest in Lower Silesia while it was Upper Silesia which was the bone of contention during the peace talks after World War I.

The concept of national identity determined by territory, forms of government, ethnicity, shared language and common culture is obviously multifaceted. For the purpose of this chapter, we will focus on shared language as an important constitutive factor of the national identity of the Silesians. The national identity of the inhabitants of Silesia is a complex issue. Real estate in the region originally was the property of Polish Piast dukes. As they died out, their property was gradually acquired by the aristocracy of the country which currently ruled the region. In the second half of the eighteenth century, the local Polish gentry was increasingly Germanized. Under Prussian and Austrian influence, rich German-speaking bourgeoisie came to Silesia and took over the key posts in administration and economy. Naturally, the language used in these spheres was German. Thus, the upper classes of Silesian society mostly followed the language and culture of the German-speaking Austrian and Prussian courts. Lower classes, on the other hand, especially the inhabitants of rural areas, constituted an integrated group who preserved Polish language and culture, and they were supported in this by the Catholic and Protestant churches in Silesia. It is estimated that the majority of people living in the area at the turn of the eighteenth and the nineteenth century spoke Polish.

The most dramatic period in the history of Silesia began with the commencement of Prussian rule in the mid-eighteenth century. Contacts of Silesians with the rest of Poland were gradually limited. Silesians were not allowed to study abroad, and so they could not go to Kraków to enter the famous Kraków Academy. Pilgrimages to Jasna Góra – Poland's most famous sanctuary, housing the miraculous painting of Our Lady that attracted the divided nation and supported the hope for an independent Poland – were prohibited. Silesian convents were not allowed to take candidates who did not know German.

Frederick II of Prussia decided to Germanize this area by issuing a series of regulations that pertained to education and religion. Only German teachers could be employed in Polish settlements (1751, 1754), and German was to be taught in all the primary schools (1763). Priests and ministers were expected to acquire German within one year (1764). Germanization efforts involving language and culture in the Silesian region were further intensified in the second half of the nineteenth century, when Prussian authorities took up the supervision of education.

The central importance of language as a determinant of national identity is manifest in the fact that already in the 1820s, trial language censuses were conducted in Upper Silesia. In order to increase the influence of German language and German culture among the Polish-speaking inhabitants in the region, in 1863 German became the medium of instruction in the second grade of the elementary school, and in 1872, the year after Kaiser Wilhelm I formally inaugurated the German Empire, the use of Polish was banned in education.[2] However, the steps taken by the Prussian administration were initially not very effective, mainly due to the shortage of educated people who could spread the German language and culture in the area. Moreover, the Poles living in Upper Silesia actively cultivated their language and retained traditions that were deeply rooted in their way of living, allowing them to decide who they were.

Struggle for the preservation of language and identity

Czesław Miłosz (1911–2004), the great Polish poet and the Nobel prize-winner (1980) in his collection of essays entitled *In Search of Homeland* (1992) writes of nations that are 'born out of philology'. What he has in mind are relatively small European nations which at a certain point in their history were politically and/or culturally dominated by others (Miłosz uses the phrase 'they lost in history'), but thanks to the activities of groups of people dedicated to writing in their native language and to publishing and disseminating books and periodicals in this language, managed to maintain their sense of national identity. Although Miłosz illustrates his claim with examples referring to the Lithuanians, one might argue that the sense of national identity of those inhabitants of Upper Silesia who felt that they were Polish was also 'born out of philology'.[3]

The Polish language survived because reading in Polish already had a long tradition in Silesia, one not restricted only to the upper classes, but encompassing all social groups. A common saying, 'A newspaper for the master, a hoe for the peasant', became the subject of a heated polemic in the Silesian press published in Polish, which concluded that 'the one who says so is either a liar or a fool'.[4] Nineteenth-century social commentators observed that in Silesia, in contrast to other regions of

Poland, 'the common folk began to read at the time when the art of reading was unfamiliar not only to the peasants but also to the landed gentry. Silesia is much ahead of other Polish lands.'[5] A well-known nineteenth century Silesian civic leader, Jan Karol Maćkowski, noted that the demand for Polish books in Silesia was enormous, and the number of copies sold in Silesia was much greater than in other regions. He also stressed the fact that books of such well-known Polish writers as Adam Mickiewicz (1798–1855), Teofil Lenartowicz (1822–1893) and Ignacy Krasicki (1735–1801) could be found in the homes of 'better-off peasants and workmen'.[6]

The book was a valued object in Silesia. Józef Lompa (1797–1863), a nineteenth-century schoolteacher, writer and a Silesian civic organizer described a typical Silesian country house where in the centre of the main room there was a special shelf for books. It was a common practice to sign the book with the name of its owner, or to use an ex-libris. One such bookplate contained the following inscription:

> If I lend you this book, I ask you to respect it.
> If I accidentally lose this book, I ask the one who finds it to return it to me,
> Because each thing calls for its owner.[7]

The importance of books is also manifest in the fact that in the Silesian press one could find advertisements placed by book owners who lost their possessions and offered rewards for those who would find and return them. For example, in the 1899 edition of the weekly publication entitled *Katolik* (*The Catholic*) (number 29), we find the following advertisement: 'On my way from Bogucice to Dąbrówka Mała I lost a copy of the play *The Dandy's Courtship*. I would like to ask the one who has found it to return it either to Mr. Lipinski in Dąbrówka Mała or to Mr. Sus in Bogucice. There is a reward.' The possession of books was a source of pride, and the Silesians eagerly participated in a variety of contests published in the press and almanacs whose winners were awarded book prizes. Jadwiga Kucianka, an expert on book-readership in nineteenth-century Silesia, claims that these contests were popular precisely because one could win books, and the books were considered to be 'worth striving for'. 'As far as books are concerned', writes Kucianka,

> the Silesians idolized them, and it was not enough to read them; the possession of one's own book collection was a great temptation. The Silesians would go to great lengths to build such collections, saving

and doing without essentials, in order to have money for books. They treasured their home libraries, and if they happened to have lost them, they could not bear their loss.

The already mentioned Józef Lompa, whose house was threatened by fire, feared most 'the loss of his books, his manuscripts and correspondence', as he writes in a letter of October 1862.[8]

Those who could not afford to buy their own books could join circulating libraries and reading rooms which operated in factory towns and in villages. These were affiliated first with the local schools, and later, when Polish was banned as the language of instruction, with parish churches, and with civic and farmers' associations. Józef Lompa, a pioneer of the movement to establish reading rooms in the Silesian villages, writes:

> as far as the village reading rooms are concerned, it would be beneficial for the villagers to gather in the home of a respected farmer to listen to good books being read aloud. It would be good to set up a governing committee that would recommend appropriate books [religious and historical]. It would be also good to have an itinerant bookseller who would visit villages and towns, and offer books at affordable prices, and sometimes on credit. He could visit each place at least twice a year. He would be our national librarian, always wandering, like a missionary.

In another text, Lompa describes the activities of farmers who wanted to establish a county library. Ten farmers decided that each would pay a 'monthly due of one silver *grosz*':

> Any decent and respectable inhabitant of the county could join the association called a reading society. The dues were collected by the schoolteacher, who together with the parish priest, were responsible for purchasing appropriate books. The members of the reading society were to gather each Saturday evening. The books were to remain in the school, and were to be lent to pupils.[9]

Figure 6.1 shows the title-page of one of the books which reads: 'Evening pastimes, or stories about the Holy Land, prepared particularly for common folk and school youth in order to explain "the story of the Bible". Published by Józef Lompa, the former elementary school teacher.' The second edition of the book was published in 1862.

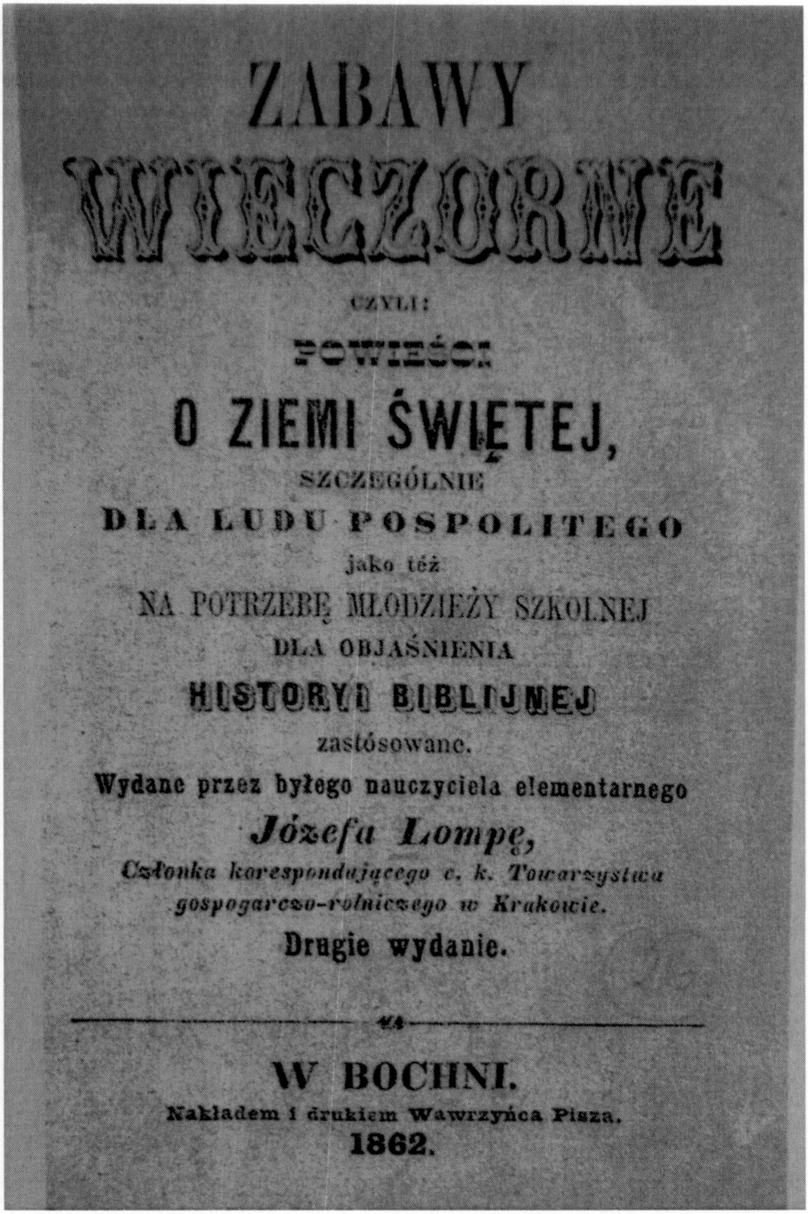

ZABAWY
WIECZORNE
CZYLI:
POWIEŚCI
O ZIEMI ŚWIĘTEJ,
SZCZEGÓLNIE
DLA LUDU POSPOLITEGO
jako też
NA POTRZEBĘ MŁODZIEŻY SZKOLNEJ
DLA OBJAŚNIENIA
HISTORYI BIBLIJNEJ
zastósowane.
Wydane przez byłego nauczyciela elementarnego
Józefa Lompę,
Członka korespondującego c. k. Towarzystwa
gospodarczo-rolniczego w Krakowie.
Drugie wydanie.

W BOCHNI.
Nakładem i drukiem Wawrzyńca Pisza.
1862.

Figure 6.1 Title-page of Józef Lompa, *Zabawy Wieczorne* [*Evening Pastimes*] (1862)

The need for establishing reading rooms and libraries in Silesian villages was stressed in the writings of another Silesian civic leader, Karol Miarka (1825–82), the editor of the Polish language weekly *Katolik* (*The Catholic*). In his manifesto entitled 'The Voice Calling in the Upper Silesian Wilderness', Miarka writes that it is of the utmost importance to popularize reading of books and periodicals, especially among the peasants. He is aware that few of them could be persuaded to buy their own books, so he points out that 'only the village libraries could bring the blessed fruit'.[10] What he means by 'the blessed fruit' is the survival of the Polish language, and the increased knowledge of Polish history and Polish culture. In addition to setting up village libraries, Miarka got involved in publishing, printing prayer books, almanacs, stories for children – all of them in Polish. When his son, Karol Miarka Jr took over, he started a series called 'The New Library of Polish Writers', which included the books of such eminent Polish authors as Adam Mickiewicz, Juliusz Słowacki, Zygmunt Krasiński and Wincenty Pol. The books were inexpensive and printed in a large number of copies, thus making the canonical works of Polish literature both affordable and available.

In the 1870s, when Polish was banned as a language of instruction in Silesian schools, Polish-language newspapers and periodicals urged parents to take responsibility for teaching their children to read in Polish. In the daily *Gazeta Górnoszląska*, one may find the following appeal: 'It is the sacred duty of the parents to teach their children . . . to read in Polish.' The importance of teaching by example was stressed: 'Your children, seeing their parents reading in Polish, will learn all these things they could not learn at school.'[11] Primers were published to help parents teach their offspring how to read in Polish. To popularize reading in Polish, the press would regularly publish advertisements with statistics concerning readership. One example of such an advertisement contains the following data:

> The folk library in Zabrze lent 1819 books in June. 1110 books were lent to male readers, and 709 books were lent to women. There are two folk libraries in Gliwice. In June, both lent 3589 books; out of which 2749 were lent by library One and 840 books were lent by library Two.[12]

At the time, the city of Gliwice had fifty thousand inhabitants, and Zabrze had twenty-nine thousand. To motivate the potential readers, the press would also advertise new acquisitions of Polish books in local libraries and print the names of benefactors who donated the books.

People like Lompa, Miarka and Franciszek Chłapowski – who became the president of the Social Circle (founded by Miarka senior) which ran a library and a reading room in the Silesian town of Królewska Huta – were very much aware that they had been involved in a struggle to maintain Polish national identity in a hostile environment. In his 1874 speech, Chłapowski said:

> Establishing the library and the reading room, organizing lectures and inviting speakers, encouraging you to read certain beneficial books, I want to inspire in all members of the Social Circle the love of your mother tongue, and your national memories. I want to motivate you to nurture in your hearts and in your words these very feelings that the inimical social conditions strive to suppress. Spreading among you the knowledge of Polish history and of Polish language, bringing to light the great treasures hidden in Polish writings, I trust that I have managed to kindle in you the love of your national past and the desire to get to know your native language, which is so beautiful, even though the strangers refuse to respect it and want to degrade and debase it.[13]

A similar sentiment was expressed by the librarian of the Social Circle, a blacksmith by profession and an amateur poet, Juliusz Ligoń (1823–1889), who encouraged others to read in the following words:

> My dear brothers, artisans, peasants and workers, we should take advantage of the spiritual nourishment provided by our benefactors. Especially now, in these turbulent times, when all forces conspire to send us to our doom, we should buy good and useful books, and we should read diligently, and we should follow good examples found in books.[14]

Perhaps the strongest testimony of the crucial role of reading in Polish in inspiring and maintaining the sense of national identity comes from a letter written by a peasant to the novelist Henryk Sienkiewicz (1846–1915), winner of the 1905 Nobel Prize for Literature. Sienkiewicz, popularly known as 'the patriot novelist of Poland', was the author of many historical novels glorifying Polish heroic past. One of the best-known of these is entitled *The Teutonic Knights* (serialized 1897–99). It contains a negative portrayal of the order of Teutonic knights who, since the thirteenth century, controlled parts of Poland, and were defeated by Poles and Lithuanians in the 1410 Battle of Grunwald.

The peasant writes to Sienkiewicz: 'I would become a German, and so would my children – and I have eleven. But the parish priest gave me your *Teutonic Knights* to read. Only then did I realize how the Germans had been fooling us. So now we know, and the children will know as well, who we are.'[15]

Popular Polish texts read in Silesia

It is important to note that in addition to books by the canonical Polish authors such as Kochanowski, Mickiewicz, Słowacki or Sienkiewicz, the so-called literature for the people, or folk literature (also known as the market-place literature) played a significant part in keeping Polish language alive in Silesia. The Silesians felt a very strong need for Polish books that were brought from other parts of Poland but also published in Silesia. Actually, many books that were banned by the Tsarist censorship in 'Congress Poland' could be published in Silesian Wrocław, under the Prussian rule, where the publishing tradition went as far back as the fifteenth century.

The folk literature was mainly of a religious and didactic nature and it was adjusted to the intellectual potential of the reader. The so-called literature for the people was sold by peddlers who travelled across the country and who frequented market places, fairs, and religious events.[16] Religious publications (see Figure 6.2) were represented by prayer books, catechisms, song books, lives of saints and occasional brochures with selected songs. For Silesians, Polish was the intimate language of prayer and of their conversation with God.

Lay literature focused around the themes connected with Renaissance romances revived for the needs of the popular reader. The books in this category described unusual and dramatic situations, using the motifs of deceit, crime and punishment. The stories were either reprinted from Warsaw editions or translated into Polish from German or Czech.[17] They included titles such as *The Story of Seven Sages: A Very Interesting and Attractive Novel for Young and for Old* (n.d.); *The Rose of Tanenburg, or the Victory of Child's Love* (1889), translated from German into Polish; *The Cradle: A Novel from the Remote Past* (n.d.); or *One Step away from Death* (1881). Such titles represent the topics available on the market. There were also texts based on the lives of contemporary people, for example miners. Figure 6.3 shows the title-page of one such book. Moreover, proverbs and songs of the Silesian people were collected.

Books for the people were also written by the local people. The example of Józef Lompa illustrates the case. As well as translating popular

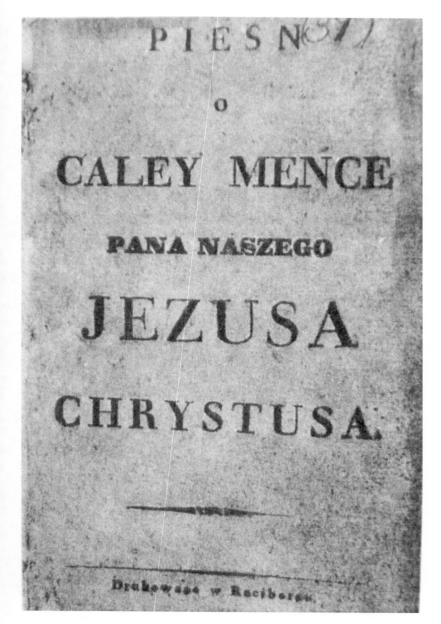

Figure 6.2   Title-page of *Pieśń o całej Męnce Pana naszego Jezusa Chrystusa* [*Songs about the Passion of Jesus Christ, Our Lord*] (*c*.1900)

Figure 6.3 Cover, Karol Miarka, *Sądy Boże: powieść z życia górników górnośląskich* [*God's Judgements: A Story about the Life of Upper Silesian Miners*] (1910)

stories into Polish – e.g., *Hirlanda czyli niewinność uciśniona* [*Hirlanda, or Innocence Oppressed*], published in the Silesian town of Lubliniec in 1846; *Historia o Gryzeldzie i margrabii Walterze* [*The Story of Gryzelda and Count Walter*], published in Mikołów by T. Nowacki in 1846 and 1847 – Lompa wrote his own original stories. An example is *Ofiara miłości niewczesnej* [*The Victim of Untimely Love*], published in Jasło by A. Rusinowski in 1858. Meeting the needs of the people among whom he lived, Lompa wrote *Pielgrzym w Lubopolu* [*The Pilgrim in Lubopole*], published in Lubliniec by J. Plessner in 1844, a work modelled after Izabela Czartoryska's *Pielgrzym w Dobromilu* [*The Pilgrim in Dobromil*], which had been published in 1818. This novel, addressed to the people of Silesia, stressed the need for learning and education and advocated the necessity of preserving the Polish language. The reader was encouraged to read in Polish as, according to the author, 'not the number of people who can read but the number of the ones who read . . . accounts for the more enlightened people'.[18] The book also had a list of ten book titles worth purchasing. Norbert Bonczyk (1837–93), known as 'the Homer of Silesia', a contemporary of Karol Miarka and Juliusz Ligoń, is another Silesian writer and civic activist who contributed to awakening the national identity of Poles residing in Silesia in the nineteenth century. A son of a soldier and a miner, he remained sensitive to the plight of the people of Silesia, and this showed in his poetry, for example in his epic poem entitled *The Old Church of Miechów*.[19]

As a response to the growing numbers of readers who had different cultural needs, needs which they wanted to satisfy by reading on a regular basis texts written in Polish and covering a wide range of issues, a variety of Polish newspapers and journals were published in Silesia. The so-called 'Spring of Nations' (the European Revolutions of 1848), which awakened and strengthened the sense of national identity in many countries on the continent, provided a stimulus for these publishing endeavours in Silesia. The following papers published in Polish attracted numerous readers in Silesia: *The Upper Silesian Journal*, *The Catholic Weekly* and *The Upper Silesian Telegraph*.

As mentioned earlier, according to the provisions of *Kulturkampf*, since 1872 Polish was banned as a subject and language of instruction. Therefore parents, particularly mothers, became responsible for teaching their children how to read in Polish. They were aided by numerous primers published especially for that purpose. Figure 6.4 shows the title-page of one such primer. The family scene depicted there reflects the fact that teaching how to read in Polish did not and could not take place at school.

Figure 6.4 Title-page of Karol Miarka, *Elemtarz polski* [*Polish primer*] (1902)

Conclusions

Despite their troubled history, and the strict measures taken by the Prussians to transform Upper Silesian Poles into obedient Prussian subjects, who would identify with German culture and use the German language, Poles, especially the ones representing the lower and middle classes, managed to preserve their Polish language and identity. Whatever the obstacles resulting from educational policies aimed at eradicating the Polish language, they wanted to learn how to read in Polish, and became avid readers of a wide variety of texts written not only by canonical Polish authors, but also by popular Silesian writers (Lompa, Bonczyk, Miarka) who were most familiar with, and sensitive to, the emotional and intellectual needs of the local people. Keenly aware of the power of the written word, Silesian civic activists encouraged and supported the development and functioning of libraries and reading rooms. This bottom-up movement resulted in maintaining the Polish language in all spheres of life. Traditionally, Polish was the language of prayer, but publications such as gardening, housekeeping or bee-keeping manuals available in the reading rooms and libraries maintained its role as a language of everyday life. Moreover it was the language of instruction about the history of Poland and the world, and the language of entertainment for the readers of both canonical Polish literature and popular books published by Silesian printing houses. Thus Polish was present in all the spheres of life. This presence may also explain why it was so important for Poles to teach their children to read in Polish. German – the language taught at schools – was the required medium of communication in the world of industry and technology. Despite this, Polish remained the language of all the spheres of life that had a particular emotional significance for those inhabitants of Silesia who felt Polish and struggled to maintain their national identity by cultivating Polish language and culture through reading.

Notes and references

1. Michał Lis, *Górny Śląsk. Zarys dziejów do połowy XX wieku* (Opole: Wydawnictwo Uniwersytetu Opolskiego, 2001), pp. 87–9.
2. Norman Davies, *Boże igrzysko. Historia Polski* [*God's Playground: A History of Poland*] (Cracow: Znak, 1989), p. 253.
3. Czesław Miłosz, *Szukanie ojczyzny* [*In Search of Homeland*] (Cracow: Znak, 1996), p. 38.
4. Krystyna Kossakowska-Jarosz, *Śląsk znany. Śląski nie znany* (Opole: Wydawnictwo Uniwersytetu Opolskiego, 1999), p. 162.

5. Alfons J. Parczewski, 'O literaturze Szląska pruskiego i Łużyc', in *Pamiętnik Zjazdu Literatów i Dziennikarzy Polskich* (Lviv, 1894), pp. 1–18.

6. Zbyszko Bednorz, *Nad rocznikami dawnych gazet Śląskich. Studium z polskiego życia literacko-kulturalnego przełomu XIX i XX wieku* (Wrocław: PWN, 1971), p. 119.

7. Otylia Słomczyńska, *Książki z kraju J. Lompy, K. Damrota, J. Ligonia* (Opole: Wydawnictwo Instytutu Śląskiego, 1990), p. 170.

8. Jadwiga Kucianka, *Śląscy pisarze ludowi* (Wrocław: Ossolineum, 1968), p. viii.

9. Jan Wróblewski, *Polskich broniły progów* (Wrocław: Ossolineum, 1981), p. 50.

10. Ibid., p. 52.

11. Kossakowska-Jarosz, *Śląsk znany*, p. 170.

12. Ibid., p. 172.

13. Wróblewski, *Polskich broniły* p. 55.

14. Ibid., p. 56.

15. Ibid., p. 63.

16. Elżbieta Gondek, *Polska książka literacka na Śląsku pod panowaniem pruskim 1795–1863* (Katowice: Wydawnictwo Uniwersytetu Śląskiego, 1995), p. 143.

17. Ibid., p. 147.

18. Ibid., p. 149.

19. Jacek Kajtoch, *Norbert Bonczyk. Epik Górnego Śląska* (Katowice: Wydawnictwo Śląsk, 1965), pp. 62–3.

7

Reading Science: Evidence from the Career of Edwin Gilpin, Mining Engineer

Lawrence J. Duggan and Bertrum H. MacDonald

'I have availed myself of all information, private and official that I have had access to', Edwin Gilpin, Nova Scotia's Inspector of Mines, claimed in his 1880 monograph, *Mines and Mineral Lands of Nova Scotia*.[1] Citations in page after page of the volume confirm, in fact, that he did read many reports on the subject, paying close attention to the documents he consulted. Reading scientific literature was an important, regular exercise for this late-Victorian scientist and mining engineer.

Even though reading in scientific contexts is a daily activity occupying tens of thousands of individuals worldwide, historians of print culture have not examined this subject to any significant degree. In her 2004 state-of-the-discipline essay, Leah Price suggested that a historiography of reading could be categorized by the 'disciplinary affiliations' of readers.[2] Yet, as Jonathan Topham points out, 'while there is . . . a growing body of literature on the history of reading practices . . . little work has been done in this area relating specifically to science'.[3] Most readers of science may have been overlooked because of the fragmentary nature of surviving reading evidence; as Price notes, reading 'destroys its own traces'.[4] Still, patchy evidence from various sources, while challenging to interpret, can be assembled to reveal the reading habits of scientists such as Edwin Gilpin. His encounters with texts may be more representative of the majority of scientific practitioners of the Victorian period in contrast to major figures like Darwin whose reading practices have been probed extensively.[5] A consideration of the evidence of Gilpin's reading can develop an understanding of the reading behaviour of typical scientists of the time. Confirmation of his reading practices arises from a number of data sources which reflect a variety of factors influencing his choice of reading materials.

This chapter shows how the accumulation of data derived from various sources and methodologies can lead to a more complete picture of a scientist's reading. This picture may only be understandable when all of the pieces are considered together. Moreover, the significance of particular pieces may only be grasped as they are corroborated by others in the puzzle. The chapter will illustrate the feasibility of undertaking a close study of the reading habits of a scientist when the surviving evidence is limited, or vaguely reveals reading characteristics. In this regard, Gilpin serves as an informative case of an exemplary reader of science.

One of Gilpin's motivations for reading arose from his scientific world view, which he outlined in his presidential address to the annual meeting of the Nova Scotian Institute of Science in November 1896. 'In every division of nature', he remarked, 'our deductions and laws remain good until rendered untenable by the unanswerable chill of fresh facts. The true student rejoices at the demolition of his fabric when he knows that the opportunity is offered of modelling it on a broader and surer foundation.'[6] To discard interpretations that new evidence no longer supports, as he suggested, required a dispassionate perspective toward scientific knowledge. Gilpin's comments emphasized that accumulation of 'fresh facts' in the conduct of scientific research and from reading scientific literature was an important and necessary activity for the members of the Nova Scotian Institute. This association and many others like it were created to share scientific information through transactions of their meetings where scientific papers were read.[7] By the end of the Victorian period the number of scientific periodicals had risen dramatically, and these printed journals and reprinted articles became the primary means for transmitting scientific information.[8]

David Livingstone noted a decade ago that 'science, in fundamental ways, is about knowledge in transit, about modes of transmission, [and] about acts of communication'. His concept of 'spaces of textual circulation' draws attention to the importance of personal and geographically separated encounters with scientific texts.[9] Complementary to this view, James Secord's *Victorian Sensation* emphasizes that 'the history of reading can best begin as local history'.[10] These related perspectives stress the importance of a subject's local surroundings along with the communication of science in casting light on reading activities.

Edwin Gilpin (1850–1908) grew up and pursued his career in Halifax, Nova Scotia, a significant port on the eastern seaboard of North America, an educational centre, and a provincial capital.[11] His scientific career can be viewed from the vantage point of his time as a university student and later as a lecturer. He was involved with local, national and international scientific and technical associations and authored over 100 published papers, reports and monographs.[12] He was also responsible for promoting mining education and improved safety of miners in dozens of underground operations in his position as a civil servant with the provincial government. Gilpin generated and used scientific information in his daily tasks. His relationships with the publications he read combined his professional obligations with his life-long interest in advancing science, particularly geology and mineralogy.

Evidence of reading arising from family influence and schooling

A scientist's family environment, schooling and childhood mentors can influence development of his/her reading habits and inculcate life-long reading practices. In Gilpin's case, he was raised in a well-to-do and well-connected family which afforded him the opportunity for a good education in Nova Scotia and for travel in his youth to the mining districts of Great Britain. His father, also named Edwin, was a prominent Anglican clergyman, active in Nova Scotia's educational circles as Headmaster of the Halifax Grammar School and later Chancellor of the University of King's College. Edwin (Senior) oversaw his son's early instruction; but specifically what he required his son to read is not known. The composition of the family library, which could reveal the home reading environment for young Edwin, has also not been determined. Details of Gilpin's home schooling and youthful reading have not survived.

Other aspects of family influence on Gilpin are evident, however. His uncle, Dr John Bernard Gilpin (1810–1892), also lived in Halifax and worked as a physician. John Bernard was well known in Nova Scotia's scientific community as a founding member of the Nova Scotian Institute of Science (NSIS), an amateur naturalist, and an accomplished visual artist. At the age of thirteen, young Edwin attended a meeting of the NSIS where his uncle presented a paper about fish species, which included some original findings and information from his readings on the subject.[13] Surviving records of early influences on Gilpin's reading are incomplete, and the evidence of reading arising from family influence is inconclusive.

Edwin's university education (BA and MA) was obtained at the University of King's College in Nova Scotia where his scientific reading was directed by the chemist, Henry How. How was raised in Britain and educated at the Royal College of Chemistry. Before coming to

Nova Scotia to teach at King's and serve as librarian, he had worked at the College for Civil Engineers, and also taught at the universities of Edinburgh and Glasgow. The King's College calendars during the years when Gilpin was a student specify the texts that How required his students to read. For instance, he listed J. Arthur Phillips's *A Manual of Metallurgy: A Practical Treatise on the Chemistry of the Metals* for his course on mineralogy and geology.[14] Through courses in geology, mineralogy and mining Gilpin and his classmates were introduced to prominent, contemporary authors. Phillips (1822–87) was a British mining engineer and metallurgist who wrote several texts of interest to Gilpin. Gilpin's familiarity with Phillips, developed during his years at university, influenced his decision to add Phillips's other publications to his private library later in his career. Gilpin read many volumes as a student, but perhaps none as notable as *Acadian Geology* by John William Dawson. Dawson was one of the most important palaeobotanists of the period in addition to being a prominent geologist. His *Acadian Geology* was first published in 1855 and in substantially revised editions in Edinburgh, London and Canada at various dates in the following years of the nineteenth century. For decades, *Acadian Geology* served as primary reading for everyone exploring and studying the geology of eastern North America. Gilpin returned to this text often and cited Dawson repeatedly.

King's College's 1870 examination report attests to Gilpin's talent and diligence: 'While the results of the examination are creditable to all the candidates, the answers supplied by Mr. Gilpin command special notice. Besides exhibiting a thorough knowledge of the subject of the examination, the concise and exact style in matters of science, so early acquired by that gentleman, is an unusual, and at the same time a very promising characteristic.'[15] Henry How's convocation address at Gilpin's graduation also praised him for his academic accomplishments, pointing out that, 'he [Gilpin] obtained the highest honour on the whole subjects he studied in the department'.[16] Gilpin's education at King's instilled a strong habit of reading current and authoritative scientific literature; however, whether this practice can be generalized to students in similar lines of study may be difficult to determine in the absence of individual records. Although evidence for Gilpin's reading as a schoolboy is lacking, considerably greater clarity exists about his reading as a college student. Course syllabi and reports in the University of King's College calendars name the books he read and confirm his mastery of those texts. His mentor at university, Henry How, directly influenced his reading by introducing him to authors and publications that Gilpin returned to time and again, as he wrote about his own scientific studies and published reports on mining topics.

Reading evidence from Gilpin's private library

To augment resources available through institutional collections, many scientists assembled private libraries of scientific publications.[17] As rich sources of evidence personal libraries can answer numerous questions about reading, and may be the source of the most convincing evidence of an individual's reading.[18] Gilpin was no different than other scientists in amassing a private library, a sizeable portion of which was acquired by the Nova Scotia Archives and Records Management (NSARM) in Halifax in the early 1990s. A small number of additional volumes are located in the Special Collections Department at Dalhousie University.[19] Consisting of over 800 titles in twenty-six bound volumes, Gilpin clearly brought this collection together to support his scientific and professional work.[20]

Several broad characteristics of Gilpin's reading behaviour can be determined from an analysis of his private library. He focused on scientific literature: geology, mineralogy, and mechanical engineering as it related to mining techniques. While the library contained international scientific publications (e.g., Canadian, American, British, Belgian and Australian), he tended to read mostly reports that overlapped with his Nova Scotia or Atlantic Canadian interests. Over 400 authors are represented in the collection, but most of the publications were from eastern North America.[21] Many of the titles in the collection are reprints of journal papers acquired through membership in learned societies. Several items were inscribed with phrases like 'With the Author's Best Compliments' highlighting direct correspondence as one of his acquisition methods. Monographs made up other titles, such as mine prospectuses and reports of the Geological Survey of Canada, which was very active in the systematic investigation of the geology and mineral wealth of Canada. The publication dates of the majority of the items show that his primary attention was on new materials. More than 700 of the titles in the collection were published between 1870 and 1904. These dates correspond with the most productive period of his career, from his university graduation until just before his death in 1908. The care Gilpin gave to this collection – professional binding, affixed bookplate and stamp, preparation of indexes – attest to its importance to him.

Even though some caution must be exercised in conclusions about reading habits based on the holdings of a private library, a large body of evidence is available for analysis; unless the entire library is currently intact (or recreated from other documentation), evidence may be incomplete. In Gilpin's case it is likely that he did own additional titles. The distinctive characteristics of the extant collection – style of binding, bookplate, etc. – served to guide searches for additional titles. However, an extensive investigation in several likely repositories failed to locate additional publications from his private library.[22] Reading evidence from private collections may remain incomplete because the entire library did not remain intact or was dispersed without obvious trace.

Reading evidence from marginalia

As Heather Jackson has ably established in *Marginalia: Readers Writing in Books*, readers' marks and notes provide some of the strongest evidence of reading.[23] But the extent to which readers annotate publications varies considerably; some add profuse jottings outlining their thoughts, others leave marks that are difficult to interpret.[24]

The page margins of publications in Gilpin's library bear ample evidence of his active reading and reflection. Slightly more than 15 per cent of the titles contain notes and other marks. He often read critically, sometimes stopping to note areas of interest or where his opinion differed from the author's. Not surprisingly, over half of the publications containing marginal notes deal with mining in Nova Scotia; marginalia validates meticulous reading. Corrections or amendments were written in the margins, and in some instances profuse marking – underlining and numerous pencil lines – imply careful attention and insertion of guides to assist his memory. Gilpin also used the pages of his books and periodicals as a place to perform brief calculations and write notes or 'see' references (pointing to other studies of interest) about the text he was reading. None of the titles he referred to in these marginal notes were found in his personal library, indicating that he had access to, and read from, other collections (possibly portions of his own library now unavailable). Blank spaces on pages were even used as scrap paper, where doodles were written in at least two instances.

In her examination of Charles Darwin's reading, Susan Sheets-Pyenson confirms that marginal notes are the footprints of reading: unambiguous evidence that Darwin read particular books and periodicals.[25] Gilpin did not annotate his books and periodicals to the extent that Darwin had; however, even some notes as simple as pencil lines indicates that he must have had some engagement with the text, even if the lines merely reminded him of his place in reading. While every title in Gilpin's collection of reprints and reports does not contain markings, their selection and organization for binding, as well as the creation of tables of contents for each volume of bound documents leaves little doubt that Gilpin must have at the very least briefly skimmed the contents. When extensive annotations do appear there is greater certainty that he read the text more closely rather than superficially perused it, even though using these notes to actually ascertain his internal thoughts would be difficult to achieve. Using evidence of marginalia to examine Gilpin's reading reveals some points of clarity, but also leaves questions arising from the ambiguity of some of the notations.

Reading evidence from membership in scientific and technical associations

Gilpin's early introduction to the benefits of scientific associations from his uncle offers another source of evidence of reading activity. By the mid-1860s when Gilpin attended his first meeting of the Nova Scotian Institute of Science, the worldwide exchange of scientific publications promoted by such organizations had become an established practice.[26] Gilpin eventually held membership in several associations both at local and international levels. In 1873, aged twenty-three, he read his first paper to the Nova Scotian Institute of Science. He published over thirty papers in the transactions of the Institute and served two years as its president. At twenty-four, he was elected a Fellow of the Geological Society of London, and subsequently he was a founding fellow of the Royal Society of Canada in 1882 and a founding member of the Mining Society of Nova Scotia. He held memberships in the North of England Institute of Mining Engineers and the American Institute of Mining Engineers, receiving copies of the journals published by the associations and numerous reprints of individual papers. Most publications in Gilpin's library that came from outside Nova Scotia arrived as benefits of his membership in the American and British societies. Membership also offered the opportunity to publish in the associations' journals, which Gilpin did. To be published in a journal such as the *Quarterly Journal of the Geological Society of London* he had to demonstrate that his research met professional standards. For example, he opened an 1886 paper on the geology of Cape Breton Island by noting the variety of literature he had read.[27] Professional memberships provide additional information about reading, although the degree to which an individual gained access to reading materials through this means varied. Documentation of an active member like Gilpin warrants consideration because additional facets of reading practices can be uncovered.

Reading evidence from correspondence

Correspondence with fellow practitioners has been commonplace among scientists since the seventeenth century. With improved postal systems in the nineteenth century, the quantity of letters circulating increased substantially.[28] Not only did scientists discuss research ideas and findings, they also disseminated publications. Gilpin documented some of his correspondence in a partial diary, and archival holdings contain copies of many letters that he sent and received. The rudimentary diary only briefly records his letter-writing activity. More substantial references to reading are found in his correspondence, which due to his position as Inspector of Mines and Deputy Commissioner of Public Works and Mines for Nova Scotia is mostly located in archival collections of government offices. For example, Richard H. Brown, General Manager of the General Mining Association in Sydney, Nova Scotia and well-informed on geological topics, discussed reports of the Geological Survey of Canada with Gilpin on 17 April 1878.[29] Gilpin corresponded with several Survey staff members; in April 1885 he sent a copy of his annual Department of Mines report and a paper about coal and manganese deposits to Hugh Fletcher (1848–1909) in Ottawa.[30]

Information and publications flowed from outside the country as well as inside. J. P. Lesley, State Geologist for Pennsylvania, wrote to Gilpin on 21 October 1877 to forward copies of his reports and to offer information in response to questions he had posed.[31] Similarly, R. Nelson Boyd wrote from London, England on 24 July 1885 to send a copy of a paper he had published on the 'petroleum fields of Europe'.[32]

While continuing to acquire reading materials through correspondence, he also exchanged unpublished information. A letter from John William Dawson of 15 February 1883 illustrates the appreciable benefit of Gilpin's correspondence network. In several pages of notes Dawson offered extensive advice regarding one of Gilpin's manuscripts, and included some of his own publications for Gilpin to read.[33] Records of reading contained in correspondence may be extensive and particularly informative if details about how reading has affected the writer are outlined. This can offer evidence about the influence of reading not available from other sources.

Reading evidence from university teaching

University researchers read current scientific publications in order to maintain awareness of new developments. While opportunities for academic appointments in the nineteenth century were limited, increasing numbers of universities by the end of the century improved options for aspiring applicants seeking teaching positions within the academy. Evidence from university contexts can disclose these reading activities.

Edwin Gilpin was a lecturer at Dalhousie University throughout the 1890s and early years of the twentieth century; the calendars of Dalhousie University document the books he assigned to students taking his course on mining. Throughout the 1890s six texts are found on the course reading list each year.[34] At the turn of the century significant changes in technical education led to a major revision of mining and metallurgical courses taught at Dalhousie and a substantially augmented list of assigned books was printed in the calendar entry.[35]

Verification of Gilpin's reading for his university teaching purposes is limited to the texts he assigned students. Surviving university records do not give any further account of reading associated with the Mining courses. As a result, this evidence lacks detailed precision when it is considered in the larger picture of Gilpin's reading. If his lecture notes were extant, or students' descriptions of his course had survived, additional features about his reading habits could be supplied.

Reading evidence from citation analysis

Over the course of the latter half of the nineteenth century, science evolved from the part-time pursuit of amateur naturalists, to a full-time profession, with higher standards for research methods and acknowledgements in communications.[36] Rising professionalism was marked by a swelling number of publications as scientists gave more attention to publishing their research. Within this growing body of literature additional confirmation of reading is found in the publications scientists cited. Questions regarding what authors were read, what types of publications were referred to, the currency of the publications that were read, and the subject and geographic spread of the literature read can be addressed by citation data. Analysis of this evidence may be the most systematic assessment of a scientist's reading habits. Since citation styles were not formalized until well in to the twentieth century, careful reading of a scientist's publications is needed in order to extract data for analysis.

Because Gilpin was a prolific author of more than 100 scientific papers and reports, we selected a sample of publications from the beginning, middle and concluding years of his career for analysis. From this sample of forty-one papers, books and reports, a total of 283 citations revealed that he read almost 100 authors (ninety-eight were cited in the forty-one publications).[37] Many of these authors (61 per cent) were represented in his private library. Those he referred to frequently were also the most common authors in his library. For example, since Gilpin studied geological and mineralogical aspects of the geographic territory similar to John William Dawson and staff of the Geological Survey of Canada, he carefully monitored and cited their work. Dawson's *Acadian Geology* (originally read when he was a student) was one of Gilpin's most used books, in terms of the number of citations.[38]

Citation data offers the clearest evidence of what a scientist found most useful to read, but we must be cautious about relying on it as a primary source of reading evidence. Authors did not cite every work they consulted, and even when they did refer to publications the references may be cryptic and incomplete, making positive identification problematic. Nonetheless, this evidence gives greater precision to our overall analysis.

Interpreting corroborative evidence

Each piece of evidence outlined above fills in a portion of the picture, sometimes with clarity, other times in outline only. An example drawn from Gilpin's reading illustrates the importance of juxtaposing different types of evidence. On 12 November 1880, an explosion in a coal mine within Gilpin's professional jurisdiction resulted in the death of forty-four miners. The accident was caused by fire-damp (a naturally occurring gas in coal mines), which if not ventilated could be ignited by the gas lamps used at the time. The impact this accident had on his reading that year becomes clear in his annual report to the provincial government in 1881.[39] Anxious to reduce mine accidents in the province, he provided detailed comments about mining products and processes documented in international publications. Gilpin's report cites twenty-five separate reports on subjects relevant to mine safety. Scientific documentation on the volatile nature of fire-damp showed that reducing open flames and sparks should be a safety priority; Gilpin recommended safety lamps and hooks, and steam powered pumps. He also cited papers on the use of barometers and gasometers to better predict the danger of explosions, and reports about safer methods of using dynamite.[40] Gilpin's reference to documents, though informal by today's standards, is hard evidence of reading, corroborated by the marginalia in copies of several reprints in his personal library from *Transactions of the North of England Institute of Mining and Mechanical Engineers.*[41] Gilpin also referred to documents from national and international correspondents from Australia, France, Belgium, the United States and Canada. He mentioned high-profile scientific serials like *Annales des Mines*, activities of associations like the North Staffordshire Mining Institute, and reports of two important commissions of inquiry on safety lamps in Belgium and France.

The most important safety step for reducing fire-damp explosions was to eliminate the use of gas lanterns – the most commonly used light source for miners during this period. Gilpin's report discusses the incandescent light bulb as a solution to the problem, and illustrates his knowledge of this recent patented technology: 'Mr. J. W. Swan, of Newcastle-on-Tyne, has recently shown that this difficult problem is on the fair way to a practical solution.'[42] Swan's lamp was patented in 1878, predating by one year Thomas Edison's patent. Though Gilpin's report was written three years later, the efficacy of the incandescent light bulb was still not proven. Even so, his report demonstrates that Gilpin had read accounts on the subject and was willing to speculate how this new lighting might reduce accidents.[43]

In this case, four types of evidence were brought together to confirm Gilpin's reading following the 1880 mine disaster. Historical accounts of the accident bear out its significance in Gilpin's work. Publications on mining in his library (contemporary with the accident) highlight his concern. However, marginalia in these publications are difficult to interpret without considering citations in his 1881 annual report. The reason why paragraphs were marked in a paper on safety lamps in mines only becomes obvious when all four sources are brought together.[44] The 1880 paper on safety lamps was timely, as Gilpin reviewed literature on this subject just months later. Likewise, the significance of his extensive pencilled marginalia becomes comprehensible when considered in relation to his report and contemporary accounts of the accident. As this example illustrates, a variety of data analysis methods may be needed to fully interpret seemingly unconnected and unrelated pieces of reading evidence.

Conclusions

Reading is an everyday occupation in the routines of active scientists. Many scientists (like Edwin Gilpin) do not keep detailed records of their reading practices; nonetheless, their research activities leave numerous traces of their reading. Publication and citation practices ensure that reading evidence is embedded in scientific literature, since authors are expected to demonstrate their findings in relation to relevant publications. If no other information than an author's own publications survives, internal citations can provide information on his/her reading.

Scientists' interactions with texts are probably more varied than citations reveal. Including each of the evidentiary traces that have informed our analysis of Gilpin's reading leads to a more comprehensive understanding of reading practice. His early participation in scientific societies and university education both shaped his desire to increase his knowledge about natural history and geology. In college courses he mastered these subjects through intensive study. His scientific reading was moulded by the community in which he lived and worked, and further influenced by his national and international networks.

These varied pieces of evidence must be brought together in order to complete a picture of his reading practices. Some of the pieces are more informative than others for the insights they provide. Just as Gilpin sought out 'fresh facts' in his quest to advance scientific knowledge, understanding his reading requires an assortment of data. As new data is assembled in the complex puzzle of reading, earlier interpretations may require revision.

A prolific author, active in scientific circles locally and internationally, Gilpin is both a typical late-nineteenth-century scientist and an exemplary reader. By probing his 'spaces of textual circulation'[45] we have begun to map the history of reading in a largely unexplored area and have made a case for how reading practices can be assembled from disparate but interrelated evidence. As this study of Gilpin demonstrates, the reading practices of scientists need not be relegated to the backwaters of reading research, especially since 'by the early twentieth century the sciences had become absolutely central to the workings of modern society'.[46] Richer understanding of reading throughout society will occur when reading scholarship engages scientific fields.

Notes and references

1. Edwin Gilpin, 'The mines & mineral lands of Nova Scotia', manuscript, Dalhousie University Special Collections; Edwin Gilpin, *The Mines and Mineral Lands of Nova Scotia* (Halifax: Robert T. Murray, 1880).
2. Leah Price, 'Reading: the state of the discipline', *Book History*, 7 (2004), 303–20 (p. 306).
3. Jonathan R. Topham, 'Scientific publishing and the reading of science in nineteenth-century Britain: a historiographical survey and guide to sources', *Studies in History and Philosophy of Science*, 31 (2000), 559–612 (p. 572).
4. Price, 'Reading', p. 312.

5. See, for example, Susan Sheets-Pyenson, 'Darwin's data: his reading of natural history journals, 1837–1842', *Journal of the History of Biology*, 14 (1981), 231–48; Peter J. Vorzimmer, 'The Darwin reading notebooks (1838–1860)', *Journal of the History of Biology*, 10 (1977), 107–53, Sydney Smith, 'The origin of *The Origin* as discerned from Charles Darwin's notebooks and annotations in books read between 1837 and 1842', *Advances in Science*, 16 (1960), 393–4; and R. Alan Richardson, 'Biogeography and the genesis of Darwin's ideas on transmutation', *Journal of the History of Biology*, 14 (1981), 1–41.

6. Edwin Gilpin, '[Presidential address]', *Proceedings of the Nova Scotian Institute of Science*, 9 (1897), lxxix–lxxxv (p. lxxx).

7. Sarah Gibson, 'Scientific societies and exchange: a facet of the history of scientific communication', *Journal of Library History*, 17 (1982), 144–63 (p. 152).

8. Scientific periodicals grew from about 100 at 1800 to 10,000 by 1900. See William H. Brock, 'Science' in *Victorian Periodicals and Victorian Society*, ed. J. Don Vann and Rosemary T. Van Arsdel (Toronto: University of Toronto Press, 1994), pp. 81–96. Technical journals in this period are less well known.

9. David N. Livingstone, 'Science, text and space: thoughts on the geography of reading', *Transactions of the Institute of British Geographers*, 30 (2005), 391–401 (p. 392).

10. James A. Secord, *Victorian Sensation: The Extraordinary Publication, Reception, and Secret Authorship of Vestiges of the Natural History of Creation* (Chicago: University of Chicago Press, 2000), p. 157.

11. Gilpin's biography has been sketched in Donald MacLeod, 'Gilpin, Edwin', *Dictionary of Canadian Biography Online*: http://www.biographi.ca/EN/ShowBio.asp?BioId=40859. Additional detail is found in Donald MacLeod, 'Miners, mining men and mining reform: changing the technology of Nova Scotian gold mines and collieries, 1858–1910' (unpublished PhD thesis, University of Toronto, 1981), and Donald MacLeod, 'Practicality ascendant: the origins and establishment of technical education in Nova Scotia', *Acadiensis*, 15 (1986), 53–92. For further information, see Lawrence J. Duggan and Bertrum H. MacDonald, 'Reading scientific and technical literature: the case of nineteenth-century Nova Scotian mining engineer Edwin Gilpin', *Journal of the Royal Nova Scotia Historical Society*, 11 (2008), 146–67.

12. On his over 100 papers see R. Alan Richardson and Bertrum H. MacDonald, *Science and Technology in Canadian History: A Bibliography of Primary Sources to 1914* (Thornhill, ON: HSTC Publications, 1987).

13. J. Bernard Gilpin, 'On the common herring (Clupea elongate)', *Proceedings of the Nova Scotian Institute of Science*, 1: 1 (1867), 4–11. Gilpin states at p. 9, 'In this paper I have endeavoured to prove by facts seen myself, by others gleaned from old and experienced fisherman, and from the best American writers – Dekay and Storer – and from the very able report of the late Moses Perley, Esq., . . . that our common herring makes no long migrations as those of the British Isles are said to.'

14. *The Calendar of King's College, Windsor, Nova Scotia . . . 1871–72* (Halifax: James Bowes & Sons, 1871), p. 24.

15. Henry Youle Hind to President of King's College, in *The Calendar of King's College, Windsor, Nova Scotia . . . 1870* (Halifax: James Bowes & Sons, 1870), p. 45.

16. Henry How, 'Address on scientific education delivered at the Encoenia of King's College, Windsor, NS . . . Thursday, June 30th, 1870' (Windsor, NS: Printed at the Office of the 'Windsor Mail', 1870?), p. 8.

17. See Bertrum H. MacDonald, 'Canadian naturalists and their private libraries: case studies from the Victorian period', paper presented to the Society for the History of Natural History, Dublin, 25 March, 2006, and idem, '"Public knowledge": the dissemination of scientific literature in Victorian Canada as illustrated from the geological and agricultural sciences' (unpublished PhD thesis, University of Western Ontario, 1990). Additional accounts of private science libraries include: Raymond Duchesne, 'La Bibliothèque scientifique de l'Abbé Léon Provancher', *Revue d'histoire de l'Amérique française*, 34 (1981), 535–56; Dennis R. Dean, 'John Playfair and his books', *Annals of Science*, 40 (1983), 179–87; M. R. Williams, 'The scientific library of Charles Babbage', *Annals of the History of Computing*, 3 (1981), 235–40; and Thomas R. Trautmann and Karl Sanford Kabelac, *The Library of Lewis Henry Moran* (Philadelphia: American Philosophical Society, 1994).

18. Some libraries tend not to survive their owners. See Bertrum H. MacDonald, 'Searching for gold: the reconstruction of a private library – the case of Dr. Robert Bell', *Canadian Bulletin for the History of Medicine*, 12 (1995), 385–410.

19. David J. McDougall, of Lachine, Quebec, donated twenty-three volumes of reprints and monographs, which he had acquired from Concordia University, Montreal, to the Nova Scotia Archives and Records Management (NSARM) in 1992.

20. Each title was catalogued in a database containing fields that document bibliographic details as well as the geographic focus of each publication and presence of marginalia.

21. Of the 403 authors, some were represented by multiple publications in the collection.

22. Searches were conducted in Nova Scotia and Quebec. Halifax institutions included Dalhousie University Libraries (the Sexton Design and Technology Library and the Faribault-Fletcher Collection in the Faculty of Engineering), University of King's College Library, Library of the Nova Scotia Department of Natural Resources, Nova Scotia Legislative Library, Library and Archives at the Nova Scotia Museum, and searches in Sydney were conducted at the Beaton Institute at Cape Breton University and the McConnell Library of Cape Breton Regional Libraries. In Montreal, a search was undertaken in the Concordia University Library and Archives.

23. H. J. Jackson, *Marginalia: Readers Writing in Books* (New Haven: Yale University Press, 2001), and idem, '"Marginal frivolities": readers' notes as evidence for the history of reading', in *Owners, Annotators and the Signs of Reading*, ed. Robin Myers, Michael Harris and Giles Mandelbrote (New Castle, DE: Oak Knoll, 2005), pp. 137–51.

24. Readers' markings can be 'mysterious' as Robert E. Stoddard points out in *Marks in Books, Illustrated and Explained* (Cambridge, MA: Houghton Library, 1985), p. 34.

25. Sheets-Pyenson, 'Darwin's data', p. 232.

26. Such societies were 'messianic' in their efforts to disseminate information and exchange periodicals around the globe. See Gibson, 'Scientific societies', p. 152.

27. See Edwin Gilpin, 'The geology of Cape Breton Island, Nova Scotia', *Quarterly Journal of the Geological Society of London*, 42 (1886), 515–26.

28. Krista Cooke, 'One hundred years of postal processing in Canada', in *More than Words: Readings in Transport, Communication and the History of Postal Communication*, ed. John Willis (Gatineau, Quebec: Canadian Museum of Civilization Corporation, 2007), Mercury series, 5, p. 54.

29. R. H. Brown to Gilpin, 17 April 1878. NSARM – Incoming Correspondence, 1860–1906. Series of the Department of Public Works and Mines fonds [hereafter SDPWM], RG21, Series A. Volume 3. Brown studied at Harvard University (1860–61), and succeeded his father (Richard Brown) as general manager at Sydney Mines (1864–1901).

30. Hugh Fletcher to Gilpin, 4 April 1885. NSARM – Incoming Correspondence, 1860–1906. SDPWM fonds, RG21, Series A. Volume 3.

31. J. P. Lesley to Gilpin, 21 October 1877. NSARM – Incoming Correspondence, 1860–1906. SDPWM fonds, RG21, Series A. Volume 3.

32. R. Nelson Boyd to Gilpin, 24 July 1885. NSARM – Incoming Correspondence, 1860–1906. SDPWM fonds, RG21, Series A. Volume 3.

33. J.W. Dawson to Gilpin 15 February 1883. NSARM – Incoming Correspondence, 1860–1906. SDPWM fonds, RG21, Series A. Volume 3.

34. The texts included: George André, *A Practical Treatise on Coal Mining* (London & New York: E. & F.N. Spong, 1876); Henry M. Chance, *Report on the Mining Methods and Appliances Used in the Anthracite Coal Fields* (Harrisburg, PA, 1883); James D. Dana, *Manual of Mineralogy* (London: Trübner & Co., 1873); Archibald Geikie, *Outlines of Field-Geology* (New York: Macmillan & Co., 1881); John H. Merivale, *Notes and Formulae for Mining Students* (London: Crosby Lockwood & Co., 1887); and W.W. Smyth, *A Treatise on Coal and Coal Mining* (London: Virtue Brothers and Co., 1867). These texts were first listed in *Calendar of Dalhousie College and University, Halifax, Nova Scotia, 1891–92* (Halifax: Printed for the University by the Nova Scotia Printing Company, 1891). The brief titles in the calendar were searched in several databases and the closest edition selected.

35. *Calendar of Dalhousie College and University, Halifax, Nova Scotia, 1900–01* (Halifax: Printed for the University by the Nova Scotia Printing Company, 1900). Textbooks listed for the new course on Mining and Metallurgy increased from six to fourteen.

36. Suzanne Zeller, '"Merchants of light": the culture of science in Daniel Wilson's Ontario, 1853–1892', in Marinell Ash, et al. *Thinking with Both Hands: Sir Daniel Wilson in the Old World and the New*, ed. Elizabeth Hulse (Toronto: University of Toronto Press, 1999), p. 127.

37. Most authors were identified; in a few cases definitive confirmation was not possible. For example, in 1877 in a paper on iron ores of Nova Scotia Gilpin wrote that a group of fossils were identified by 'Billings' and 'Professor Hall'. He likely meant Elkanah Billings (1820–76), palaeontologist with the Geological Survey of Canada, and James Hall (1811–98), a noted American geologist. See, Edwin Gilpin, 'The iron ores of Nova Scotia', *North of England Institute of Mining and Mechanical Engineers. Transactions*, 26 (1877), 71–89 (p. 75).

38. Whether Gilpin owned a copy of any of the four editions of *Acadian Geology* has not been confirmed, but he cited this work frequently, suggesting he had

a copy of one or more of the editions. *Acadian Geology* was referenced well into the twentieth century, attested by T. H. Clark's statement in 1966 that it 'is still an authoritative source of information essential to any worker in geology'. See, T. H. Clark, 'Sir John William Dawson, 1820–1899', in *Pioneers of Canadian Science*, ed. G. F. G. Stanley (Toronto: University of Toronto Press, 1966), p. 108.

39. Edwin Gilpin, 'Report on the mines of Nova Scotia', *Journal and Proceedings of the House of Assembly of the Province of Nova Scotia. Session 1881* (Halifax: Robert T. Murray, Queen's Printer, 1881).

40. Four out of sixteen authors clearly identified in the twenty-five citations are represented in Gilpin's private library: W. J. Bird, A. R. Sawyer, and J. W. Swan, who published papers in the *Transactions of the North of England Institute of Mining and Mechanical Engineers*, and G. C. Hoffman, a Geological Survey of Canada staff member.

41. Papers that he marked extensively are: W. J. Bird, 'Condensation in steam pipes', *Transactions of the North of England Institute of Mining and Mechanical Engineers*, 29 (1880), 7–14; 'Safety lamps for mines: report of the commission instituted in Belgium by ministerial decree dated the 20th of January, 1868', *North of England Institute of Mining and Mechanical Engineers. Transactions*, 29 (1880), 113–40'; A. R. Sawyer, 'Notes on the Muesseler Lamp', *Transactions of the North of England Institute of Mining and Mechanical Engineers*, 29 (1880), 141–4; and James Ashworth, 'Improved safety lamps of the Davy and Mueseler types', *Transactions of the North of England Institute of Mining and Mechanical Engineers*, 29 (1880), 145–56.

42. Edwin Gilpin, 'Report on the mines of Nova Scotia', *Journal and Proceedings of the House of Assembly of the Province of Nova Scotia. Session 1881* (Halifax: Robert T. Murray, Queen's Printer, 1881), p. 26.

43. For the history of electric lamps see J. B. Harris, 'Electric lamps, past and present', *Engineering Science and Education Journal*, 2 (1963), 161–70.

44. 'Safety lamps for mines: report of the commission instituted in Belgium'.

45. Livingstone, 'Science, text and space', p. 392.

46. James A. Secord, 'Science, technology and mathematics', in *The Cambridge History of the Book in Britain. Volume VI, 1830–1914*, ed. by David McKitterick (Cambridge: Cambridge University Press, 2009), p. 474.

8
Reading in an Age of Censorship: The Case of Catholic Germany, 1800–1914

Jeffrey T. Zalar

One of the most resilient interpretive paradigms in the historiography of modern Germany is the metanarrative of the 'Catholic confessional milieu'.[1] It argues that in response to the challenges presented by modernity, Catholics found unity and mutual succour in an insular subculture, whose boundaries were policed by a rigidly authoritarian clergy. The story begins with the seizure of church property by state officials in the secularization of 1802/03 and then catalogues the series of indignities in the Restoration era (1814–48) that encouraged among Catholics a siege mentality. Such indignities included the ostentatious celebrations of the Protestant Reformation in October 1817, the uneven application of press laws that privileged anti-Catholic rhetoric in public, the gross social inequalities among inhabitants of mixed confessional regions – above all in Prussia – due to anti-Catholic bias, denunciation of clerical resistance to mixed marriages, and outright Liberal howling at Catholic educational 'inferiority' in an era of enlightenment, symbolized above all by the mass pilgrimages to the so-called Holy Shroud of Trier in 1844. Intelligent, urbane Germans, Liberal opinion declared, did not go on pilgrimage.[2] Hoping to capitalize upon this siege mentality, and in order to tidy up the disciplines separating the Catholic *Volk* from secular evils like dancing, the hierarchy built a *Sondergesellschaft*, a Catholic 'milieu', which was structured to enhance the cohesiveness and restore the confidence of the German church in an age of emergency. The institutions of this milieu, such as themed associations and reading clubs, were authentically modern, as were the milieu's modes of communication, such as diocesan publications and Sunday news sheets. The message of the milieu, however, transmitted by an intrusive, nay-saying, increasingly homogeneous and militant clergy, was patently anti-modern. Thus, in the words of the historian

Urs Altermatt, the Catholic milieu 'promoted anti-modernism with modern means'.[3]

The metanarrative of the Catholic milieu is rendered as a success story. As 'milieu managers', to use Olaf Blaschke's influential term, the clergy flexed a remarkable intellectual and cultural control – unprecedented in the history of Catholicism – despite all the temptations of modernity, over the lower-class laity.[4] This is the core of the milieu thesis, the metanarrative at its most tenacious. It is taken for granted that lower-class laypeople in Germany existed under and acquiesced in a penetrating clerical domination. The entire interpretive edifice of the milieu idea seems to rest upon it. With the exception, perhaps, of the Iberian, Irish and Eastern European peasantries, no population in the historiography of modern Europe appears more docile and flat, more undifferentiated and malleable, than the German Catholic *Volk*, and few ideological leaders without access to state power appear more confident and successful than German priests. These clerical 'managers' policed the milieu by compelling anti-modernism with modern means, and this pervasive control helps to account for the milieu's integrating force so surprisingly, and so far, into the twentieth century.[5]

This confident assertion of clerical control intrigues. Can it be true that Catholic readers for example, despite their exposure to the most dynamic print market in Europe, and in a developing *Kulturnation* that assigned the most pregnant social and cultural meanings to the possession, consumption and display of books, restricted themselves, in the long era from 1800 to 1914, to 'naïve' religious literature?[6] Can it be possible that these many millions, a full third of the population under the German Empire (1871–1918), therefore remained frozen in intensive reading practices, which featured the repeated consumption of simple, trusted, very often religious texts, without adopting, like every other literate group in Europe, those extensive practices of mature readers, which featured ephemeral consumption of diverse material by inclination and personal taste? And can we accept the idea of powerful clerical oversight of these practices?

Recent research on state censorship in modern German lands demonstrates that censors were 'victims' of their own frustrated endeavour.[7] In theory, they wielded considerable cultural power, but in reality they suffered keenly from the unrealistic expectations of their administrative superiors and basic disagreement among authorities in general about what constituted acceptable rules of publication. They were also a weak and timid group, in large part because they so dreadfully feared exposure in public as backward, narrow-minded or inconsistent. How was it, then, that parish priests, many of whom were poorly educated and read, were able to do what no other censors in Germany were capable of doing, and with far fewer resources and less coercive methods available to them? How successful were these priests, finally, in so dictating the reading interests of their parishioners, that, as Dieter Langewiesche and others have concluded, Catholic laypersons avoided public lending institutions in consideration of their faith commitments, when by 1900 reading books from public libraries was one of the most distinctive practices of German everyday life?[8]

In the light of such puzzling questions, assertions about the reading discipline of the Catholic milieu place severe strain on a historian's sense of the probable. Scepticism only swells when one realizes that these assertions of clerical control over the cultural activities of the *Volk* are precisely that: assertions, which have never been established on the basis of research evidence. The paradigmatic requirements of the milieu thesis themselves seem to insist upon (and account for) a punitive clerical–lay relationship. In a recent study of 'lived religion', historian Robert Orsi observes that scholars have 'long represented religious leaders and followers like this, setting them within religious contexts in which everyone does what he or she is supposed to do, in which authority is obeyed and ritual rubrics carefully followed. Yet no one has ever seen anything like this in the real world.'[9] What did the real world of literacy among the Catholic *Volk* look like in modern Germany? What does the research evidence allow?

The research evidence for Prussia's western and predominantly Catholic provinces comes from eighteen months of work in the diocesan archives of Trier, Cologne, Münster and Paderborn, and from almost a hundred parish archives located throughout the region. It includes letters from Catholics to their bishops about access to forbidden literature, priests' descriptions of cultural behaviour in their parishes, data on Catholic patronage of German lending institutions, accounts of home book collections, and secret clerical observations of domestic intellectual consumption filed with diocesan authorities. These many, various and mutually reinforcing sources demonstrate that indeed there was a great deal of reading activity among the lower-class laity throughout the 'long nineteenth century,' but that 'disciplined' is hardly the word to describe it. This chapter discusses this evidence. It also reflects on an interpretive paradigm thrown into crisis by the history of popular reading.

Clerical reports and pastoral letters

Let us begin with the singular commitment of the laity to religious literature. That lower-class Catholics consumed a great volume and variety of religious literature seems beyond doubt.[10] And yet historians readily concede that lower-class Catholic communities before 1848 were also shot through with proscribed publications which lay readers took up with alacrity. These publications included Protestant apologetics, hack medicine manuals, racy short stories, and irreverent social commentary. The avid consumption of this literature is understood as a principal reason for the creation of a more restrictive and disciplined milieu in the first place. 'You go on a walk and find some sheets on the path', one priest near Cologne complained in 1850.

> You travel on a steamer, on a locomotive, in a mail cart. There a traveller has left behind this small item by accident, and better judgment is abandoned. There is a great crush of people in the street and an unfamiliar person presses something amiably in your hand. You receive alms and, as food for the soul, a pamphlet to go with it. You work in a factory [and so on] . . . The honourable clergy . . . probably know of many similar examples to relate. Such mischief must be brought under control.[11]

Examples of this concern may be summoned from the other Rhenish diocese of Trier and the Westphalian sees of Münster and Paderborn.[12] Historians working with these examples are necessarily careful of being fooled by the exaggerations of hyper-conservative priests. We have to take the testimonies of these priests on the absence of lay discipline seriously, as Jonathan Sperber argues in his classic study of popular Catholicism in the Rhineland. 'Should we dismiss these observations as just the perennial ruminations of the clergy, a group professionally inclined to view public morality with alarm, or as the product of a paternalistic bureaucracy, intent on finding excuses to interfere in the private lives of its "administrees"? These are weighty objections', Sperber writes, 'but not altogether convincing ones.' Priests, he continues, 'did not always complain of deteriorating public morality', and their testimonies reveal 'a certain internal logic', because they corresponded to the evidence on secularization and 'the laicization of formerly clerically supervised practices'.[13] David Blackbourn, a leading authority on German confessional history, also endorses the reliability of these reports.[14] One would expect, then, that by 1870, when the bishops' discrete reading regime of pious books was firmly set in place as a critical feature of the Catholic milieu, testimonies of ill-disciplined reading behaviour among the laity would diminish or even disappear from the record. The fact of the matter, however, is that these negative clerical testimonies increase vastly in number and intensify sharply in vehemence, leaving little room but for the conclusion that in the Catholic milieu after national unification, reading discipline was *even more relaxed*.

There are manifold sources that describe the free-wheeling reading behaviour of the laity in defiance of the church's book rules, but let us focus on bishops' pastoral letters and sermons, which drew upon clerical reports of actual cultural practices in parish communities. Throughout the Imperial era, these pastoral letters and sermons inveighed repeatedly against the consumption of forbidden literature, which continued unabated and became more flagrant in all four dioceses of the western provinces. The bishops' language could have left little doubt in its hearers about the perils of disobedience. 'I warn you most emphatically', admonished the Cardinal Archbishop of Cologne in 1872, 'against this so terrible and widespread evil of our times', which threatens souls with eternal damnation. The bishop of Münster concurred: 'Catholics who read forbidden literature', which the bishop defined broadly to include overtly anti-Christian texts, the secular press, and even popular fiction with immoral content, 'show through [their choices] which spirit they [serve]. They may call themselves Catholics, but they do not belong to us. They sympathize with the [Devil], and support him against their own Mother, the Church, to whom they owe their spiritual life and from whom they must hope for their very salvation.' Thirty years later, the bishops were making the same desperate arguments, to no discernible avail.[15] 'Are you so dumb, so certifiably dumb', a surrogate for the Archbishop of Cologne asked an assembly of Catholic men in 1901, 'that you go to confession every year and do not confess [your sinful reading habits]'?[16]

Confirmed by a vast array of corroborating reports from priests in local communities everywhere in the region (in both urban and rural areas), and addressing the cultural practices of men, women and children (both regular churchgoers and the lapsed), this evidence lends little support to the idea that the establishment of the Catholic milieu had a positive effect on lay reading practices. In fact, if it had any effect at all it was negative. A number of accounts demonstrate that attempts at censorship only whetted appetites among the laity for these forbidden fruits.[17] But here is the more surprising interpretive fact: whereas a relatively small number of reports of lay misbehaviour in the Restoration era are taken as indications of an *absence* of clerical control, many dozens of longer, more detailed and intense reports of lay misbehaviour in the Imperial era, such as these pastoral letters and sermons, are taken as evidence of precisely the opposite: a calculated and successful attempt on the part of the clergy to 'dictate' cultural tastes from above and to rule the laity with a 'theology of fear' and a 'pastorship of torment'.[18] This is a curious use of evidence, because its methods of evaluating similar reports filed just a generation apart differ so completely. It also suggests that in this particular relationship of power, one need only establish the intentions of the dominant in order comprehensively to understand and predict the intellectual attitudes, intentions and behaviour of the subordinate, regardless of social position, age, gender or even extent of involvement in the institutional life of the church. By this account, Catholic priests were powerful indeed.

Literary policing

Or were they? The interpretation of pastoral visits in the home for the purpose of literary policing reveals the same curious use of evidence. Priests did practice 'literary espionage' during pastoral visits, in order to ensure the removal from the domestic sphere of offensive material, such as Liberal newspapers and journals, immoral fiction, or Social Democratic tracts. Olaf Blaschke offers these visits as evidence of the 'strict censorship' priests exercised over the behaviour of the laity 'and even [over] their bookcases'. The supervision of reading, he writes, was an important 'control mechanism' used by priests to enforce confessional cohesion and 'loyalty to the church'.[19] But this evidence, again, merely establishes clerical intention; it tells us nothing at all about the response the laity made to clerical interference, their relationship to the confessional milieu, or their loyalty to the church. In fact, the evidence of lay response demonstrates quite the opposite. Sometimes readers listened to the warnings of their priests – I do not wish to overstate my case – but only if these warnings were repeated and if they were not strident.[20] Most families, however, deeply resented clerical meddling in their reading choices. Most often they ignored priests' admonitions outright, since follow-up visits revealed that they had not abandoned offending materials.[21] Nor did they shrink from abusing priests verbally as hypocrites, when they knew that their priest himself read forbidden newspapers or novels, or as 'monastic escapists', when they suspected their priests wanted to prevent them from accessing information deemed vital for making one's way successfully in the world.[22] The majority of priests, for their part, hated challenging the laity, not only because doing so elicited such animosity, but because the expectation of flawless judgement imposed on them by their bishops was unrealistic, and also because the book rules of the church were so contested and unclear.[23] Clerical censors, it seems, experienced the same 'victimization' of censorship and for the same reasons as non-Catholic censors everywhere else in Germany. One priest referred to the literary police work he reluctantly conducted in the homes of his parishioners as 'the odium' of his office.[24] It is hard to believe assertions of clerical discipline when priests themselves admitted that literary policing in the German Empire was, according to one pastor in the Diocese of Trier, all but totally 'without success'.[25]

The evidence described here, and the way I suggest it has been mishandled, has left us with a flawed understanding of lay involvement in German everyday life. A fascinating encounter between a priest and a Catholic woman evokes my meaning.[26] In February 1905, Father Georg Reitz, pastor of St Martin's church in Damscheid, which lies between Koblenz and Mainz on the Rhine River, strolled through his quiet rural community. Approaching from the other direction he espied one of the prominent women of his parish, a regular communicant on whom he relied to bring off the parish's annual fair. As they moved closer together, Reitz noticed a large, heavy envelope hidden within the folds of her winter coat. He suspected the worst. Like other priests in Imperial Germany, Reitz read the clerical journals. He was well aware that by the turn of the twentieth century, even loyal Catholics in country villages lived not only in a religious sub-culture, but also in overlapping cultures of leisure and consumption that powerfully shaped their tastes and values. These cultures – vibrant, pervasive, beckoning – overwhelmed their resolve. A colleague had recorded in 1901, 'Also in rural areas the desire to read or often even the frenzy to read [*Lesewut*] is always becoming greater and stronger and reading material is truly not lacking.' His parishioners preferred, he continued, '[religiously indifferent] newspapers or inexpensive, dangerous brochures that some foreign peddler brought in, so-called trashy, harmful, dangerous love stories, frightful stories about robbers, or harmful popular-medical treatises – in short, worthless or manifestly detrimental books'.[27] Another country priest observed despairingly: 'I see it as an important need to obtain good reading material for the *Volk*; the people read all trashy merchandise at a cheap price; it is even brought by them into the home.'[28]

When they met in the street, Father Reitz asked the woman to reveal the envelope's contents. She said nothing, stood shocked and rigid, and held tightly to her secret. His suspicion confirmed by the evident guilt so characteristic of the Catholic book culture, he grabbed the envelope from her arm and tore it open. And what did he find inside? The first instalments of two 'sensational serial novels'. One novel bore the title *A Martyr for Love*, which told the tale of a woman's unsuccessful romance with a man who was not her husband. The other was that model of Catholic family values, *Sonja Kovalevsky: the Husband Killer*. The Sonja Kovalevsky of the story was none other than the famous Russian mathematician of the same name, the sudden death of whose husband had been the stuff of salacious gossip throughout Germany since the early 1880s. Both of these novels fell under the opprobrium of the Index of Forbidden Books, which the German bishops interpreted broadly in the 1890s to include all 'lascivious and obscene' material of whatever type that could undermine faith or good morals.[29] And well the woman ought to have known it, since the book rules of the church had been proclaimed by every conceivable Catholic medium since the 1850s, even in the tranquil countryside of the Diocese of Trier.[30] Father Reitz, at least, was certain of these books' power to corrupt. 'Both novels', he recorded angrily of the encounter later on, were 'of the basest kind, with character portrayals and corresponding pictures that lure the imagination of [the people] onto forbidden paths'.[31] Thus did Father Reitz learn that despite all of the protections of the Catholic clerical milieu, despite all the preaching, exhortations and threats, this devout woman of his parish was no match for the seductions of Germany's secular book market, which he was all but powerless to control.

And still there is more to tell. What about, for example, Catholic patronage of public libraries? Historians tell us that no self-regarding Catholic would be seen in a secular public library; he or she patronized confessional collections instead.[32] However, the Association of Saint Charles Borromeo, which had led the Catholic library movement since the creation of the milieu in the 1850s, had decayed badly by 1890. In order to survive it had to abandon the bishops' regime of pious books and completely revamp its collections in light of lay demands for secular histories, classic literature, popular science and escapist fiction. So many Catholics in Cologne were using public libraries that in 1903 the Cologne Pastoral Conference recommended closing underutilized *Borromäus* libraries altogether.[33] Similar concerns for the 'existence and livelihood' of Catholic libraries were raised in Münster, Paderborn and Trier, where heavy lay patronage of the 'so-called "*paritätischen*", interconfessional [and] in very many cases utterly anti-Catholic public libraries' ran unchecked.[34] The futility of attempting to safeguard the laity from public book collections also registered in the matter of subscriptions to secular newspapers. So many Catholics preferred secular to confessional newspapers in the diocese of Trier that in 1905 priests here discussed the advisability of quoting from the secular press during their Sunday sermons, in order more avidly to hold their congregations' attention.[35]

Conclusions

This research encourages the following conclusions. The history of lay reading within the boundaries of the Catholic confessional milieu is not the history of the good government of souls. In fact, these boundaries were all but non-existent, as Catholic communities everywhere were saturated by texts from the broader German secular and/or Protestant culture, which lay readers took up with impunity. Almost from the moment they became literate, reading illicit books was a chronic apostasy that made literary policing one of the most pressing – and vexing – pastoral dilemmas of the 'long nineteenth century'. The milieu thesis, then, which argues that disciplined maintenance of the church's *Weltanschauung* held the laity in clerically supervised patterns of behaviour, simply does not explain the actual reading experience of most believers.[36] The effect of the milieu thesis, in other words, has been to encourage scholars to exaggerate the power of priests to impose standards of cultural taste and rules of literary consumption, an exaggeration all the more unwarranted because it is largely unsupported by the evidence available to us. Lost in the spatial metaphor of the milieu is a view of the full tableau of Catholic culture, whose colour and complexity would make us recognize the particularity of individual Catholics as cultural consumers emancipating themselves from the gravitational field of the church. Without succumbing to teleological theories of modernization, we might then understand the Catholic *Volk* as authentic agents in a complex process of inculturation, occurring over decades of time, by which they developed apposite habits of the heart and mind that reflected their own increasingly confident self-governance.[37] For if we but listen to their voices, we will find that they rejected clerical discipline in the area of reading, because they just did not feel a conflict of conscience over the consumption of illicit texts.[38] They responded to this intellectual control in the nineteenth century in the same way their descendants responded to birth control in the twentieth and after: with a shrug of the shoulders and rebellion.[39]

Notes and references

1. See, for example, Dominik Burkard, 'Ökumenische Tradition? Zum Verhältnis der Konfessionen in Württemberg im 19. und 20. Jahrhundert', *Blätter für württembergische Kirchengeschichte*, 101 (2001), 114–52.
2. A superior study of such attitudes is Michael B. Gross, *The War against Catholicism: Liberalism and the Anti-Catholic Imagination in Nineteenth-Century Germany* (Ann Arbor, MI: University of Michigan Press, 2004).

3. Urs Altermatt, 'Katholizismus: Antimodernismus mit modernen Mitteln?', in *Moderne als Problem des Katholizismus*, ed. by Urs Altermatt et al. (Regensburg: Friedrich Pustet, 1995), pp. 33–50.

4. Olaf Blaschke, 'Die Kolonialisierung der Laienwelt. Priester als Milieumanager und die Kanäle klerikaler Kuratel', in *Religion im Kaiserreich: Milieus – Mentalitäten – Krisen*, ed. by Olaf Blaschke and Frank-Michael Kuhlemann (Gütersloh: Kaiser, Gütersloher Verlagshaus, 1996), pp. 93–135. Urs Altermatt, for example, refers to the era from 1850 to 1950 as an 'Ausnahmperiode' – an exceptional period.

5. Most historians date the milieu's demise in the post-war era. For recent discussions of the topic, see Mark Edward Ruff, *The Wayward Flock: Catholic Youth in Postwar West Germany, 1945–1965* (Chapel Hill, NC and London: University of North Carolina Press, 2005), and Wilhelm Damberg, 'Entwicklungslinien des europäischen Katholizismus im 20. Jahrhundert', *Journal of Modern European History*, 3 (2005), 164–82.

6. Reinhard Wittmann, *Geschichte des deutschen Buchhandels: Ein Überblick* (Munich: C. H. Beck, 1991), pp. 172 and 266.

7. Grzegorz Kucharczyk, 'Zensoren und Zensoramt. Studien über Aspekte der Zensurpraxis um 1848', in *Kommunikation und Medien in Preußen vom 16. bis zum 19. Jahrhundert*, ed. by Bernd Sösemann (Stuttgart: Franz Steiner Verlag, 2002), pp. 421–35.

8. Dieter Langewiesche, '"Volksbildung" und "Leserlenkung" in Deutschland von der wilhelminischen Ära bis zur nationalsozialistischen Diktatur', *Internationales Archiv für Sozialgeschichte der deutschen Literatur*, 14 (1989), 108–25. On German reading practices at the *fin-de-siècle*, see Peter Fritzsche, *Reading Berlin 1900* (Cambridge, MA: Harvard University Press, 1996), and Gideon Reuveni, *Reading Germany: Literature and Consumer Culture in Germany before 1933*, trans. Ruth Morris (New York: Berghahn, 2006). The indispensable resource for modern German book culture is *Geschichte des Deutschen Buchhandels im 19. und 20. Jahrhundert*, Vol. 1: *Das Kaiserreich 1870–1918*, Teil 1, ed. Georg Jäger (Frankfurt am Main: Buchhändler-Vereinigung, 2001).

9. Robert Orsi, 'Everyday miracles: the study of lived religion', in *Lived Religion in America: Toward a History of Practice*, ed. David D. Hall (Princeton, NJ: Princeton University Press, 1997), p. 12.

10. Rudolf Pesch, *Die kirchlich-politische Presse der Katholiken in der Rheinprovinz vor 1848* (Mainz: Matthias-Grünewald-Verlag, 1966), and Susanna Schmidt, *'Handlanger der Vergänglichkeit': Zur Literatur des katholischen Milieus 1800–1950* (Paderborn: Ferdinand Schöningh, 1993).

11. 'Was ist das Evangelium?', *Monatsblatt des Vereins vom heiligen Karl Borromäus*, 38 (April 1850), 150–1 (p. 151).

12. See, for example, 'Warnung antikatholische Schriften', *Kirchlicher Amtsanzeiger für das Bisthum Trier*, 1, 4 (1853), pp. 13–14, and 'Verbreitung abergläubischer Gebetsformulare', *Amtliches Kirchenblatt für die Diöcese Paderborn*, 4, 21 (1855), pp. 101–2.

13. Jonathan Sperber, *Popular Catholicism in Nineteenth-Century Germany* (Princeton, NJ: Princeton University Press, 1984), pp. 17–18.

14. David Blackbourn, 'Progress and piety: Liberalism, Catholicism and the state in Imperial Germany', *History Workshop Journal*, 26 (1988), 57–78 (p. 59).

15. Sources for this section are 'Stimmen des deutschen Episcopates über die Presse unserer Zeit', *Münsterisches Pastoral-Blatt*, 10, 2 and 3 (1872), pp. 23–4

and 35–6; 'Kann ein Katholik mit Gewissensruhe eine schlechte Zeitung lesen?' *Sankt Paulinus-Blatt für das deutsche Volk*, 1, 23 (1875), 255–6 (p. 255); Michael Felix Korum (Trier), 'Über die schlechte Lektüre', in *Hirtenbriefe des deutschen Episkopats anläßlich der Fastenzeit 1910*, ed. by Albert Pape (Paderborn: Junfermannschen Buchhandlung, 1910), pp. 22–37; and Felix von Hartmann (Münster), 'Über die schlechten Bücher und Schriften', in *Hirtenbriefe des deutschen Episkopats anläßlich der Fastenzeit 1912*, ed. by Albert Pape (Paderborn: Junfermannschen Buchhandlung, 1912), pp. 19–27.

16. This diatribe was republished in Trier in Nikolas Racke, 'Zur Abwehr der neuesten kirchenfeindlichen Angriffe', *Extra-Beilage zum 'Paulinus-Blatt'* (28 April 1901), 1–5 (p. 5).

17. Read, for example, a Münster priest's concern that repeated denunciations of liberal newspapers had enhanced their notoriety and, as a consequence, increased their circulation among his parishioners in 'Was kann der Seelsorger zur Verbreitung guter Lektüre in seiner Gemeinde thun?' *Münsterisches Pastoral-Blatt*, 33, 11 (1895), 165–6 (p. 166).

18. Blaschke, 'Die Kolonialisierung der Laienwelt', pp. 102–3 and Altermatt, 'Katholizismus: Antimodernismus mit modernen Mitteln?', p. 45.

19. Olaf Blaschke, 'Das 19. Jahrhundert: Ein zweites konfessionelles Zeitalter?' *Geschichte und Gesellschaft*, 26 (2000), 38–75 (p. 63). See also Helmut Walser Smith, *German Nationalism and Religious Conflict: Culture, Ideology, Politics, 1870–1918* (Princeton, NJ: Princeton University Press, 1995), pp. 84–5.

20. For example, 'Die katholische Presse und die Seelsorger', *Pastor Bonus*, 19 (1906/07), pp. 520–1.

21. 'Was lesen meine Leute?' *Der katholische Seelsorger*, 8 (1896), pp. 292–3 and 'Der katholische Seelsorger und die Presse', *Münsterisches Pastoral-Blatt*, 37, 1 (1899), 3–6 (p. 5).

22. For example, 'Der katholische Seelsorger und die Presse', p. 5; 'Wie soll man die langen Winterabende verbringen?' *Zweite Extra-Beilage zum Paulinus-Blatt*, 38 (23 September 1906), p. 1; 'Eine Mahnung zur Vorsicht im Lesen', *Zweite Extra-Beilage zum Paulinus-Blatt*, 33, 37 (15 September 1907), p. 291; and 'Ueber Hausseelsorge', *Pastor Bonus* 22 (1909/10), 107–11 (p. 109).

23. 'Der katholische Seelsorger und die Bücher', *Pastoralblatt*, 4, 9 (1870), 104–8 (pp. 106–7).

24. 'Der Klerus und die Lektüre in der katholischen Familie', *Pastoralblatt*, 30 (1896), pp. 293–8 and 'Soziales: Eine praktische Resolution', *Die öffentliche Meinung*, 7, 1 (1896/7), pp. 2–3.

25. 'Wie soll man die langen Winterabende verbringen?', p. 1. Consider also the despairing surrender of a pastor in the Diocese of Trier, who observed that even if attempts to enforce reading discipline failed, at least priests could reside in the comfort that they tried to do their duty, in 'Der Seelsorger in der Gemeinde', *Extrabeilage zum Paulinus-Blatt*, 33, 7 (17 January 1907), p. 50.

26. Georg Reitz, 'Kolportage und Romane', *Pastor Bonus* 18 (1905/06), p. 186. The month of February is an estimate based upon the date and other features of the article.

27. 'Der Verein vom hl. Karl Borromäus in den Landgemeinden. Erfahrungen und Winke eines Landgeistlichen', *Borromäus-Blätter (frF)*, 7 (November 1901), 185–93 (p. 187).

28. P. Walterbach, 'Katholische Kolportage', *Borromäus-Blätter (frF)*, 7 (November 1901), 174–84 (p. 181). See also 'Gesetz und Selbsthülfe im Kampfe gegen die unsittliche Litteratur', *Münsterisches Pastoral-Blatt*, 43, 7 (1905), 97–100 (p. 97).

29. 'Die kirchliche Repressivcensur', *Pastoralblatt*, 25 (1891), 331–6 (p. 332): 'Hieraus schließen wir, daß die Tendenz des Index sich nicht darauf beschränkt, Bücher im eigentlichen Sinne zu verbieten, sondern überhaupt alle geschriebenen oder gedruckten Sachen, welche dem Glaube und der guten Sitte gefährlich sind, von den Gläubigen fern zu halten. Hieraus ergibt sich denn auch weiterhin, daß nicht bloß glaubens- und sittenfeindliche Bücher im eigentlichen Sinne, sondern auch Manuscripte und kleinere Schriften, wie Zeitungen usw. dem Indexverbote unterliegen.' See also 'Constitutio Apostolica Leonis PP. XIII. de prohibitione et censura librorum', *Kirchlicher Anzeiger für die Erzdiözese Köln*, 37, 7 (1897), pp. 43–8.

30. Jeffrey T. Zalar, 'Knowledge and nationalism in Imperial Germany: a cultural history of the Association of Saint Charles Borromeo, 1890–1914' (unpublished doctoral thesis, Georgetown University, 2002), pp. 62–3.

31. Reitz, 'Kolportage and Romane', p. 186.

32. Langewiesche, pp. 108–25 and Urs Altermatt, *Katholizismus und Moderne. Zur Sozial- und Mentalitätsgeschichte der Schweizer Katholiken im 19. und 20. Jahrhundert* (Zurich: Benziger Verlag, 1989), p. 160.

33. 'Hebung der Borromäusvereine', *Pastoralblatt*, 40 (1906), pp. 171–3.

34. 'Versammlung der Leiter der Borromäusvereine betreffend', *Kirchliches Amtsblatt der Diöcese Münster*, 44, 4 (1910), pp. 27–8; 'Diözesankonferenz des Borromäus-Vereins', *Extrabeilage zum Paulinus-Blatt*, 47 (20 November 1910), 1–2 (p. 1); and J. Bergmann, 'Volksbibliotheken in kleinen Gemeinden', *Pastor Bonus*, 10 (1898), pp. 195–6.

35. 'Die Zeitung auf der Kanzel?', *Pastor Bonus*, 18 (1905/06), pp. 65–74.

36. Burkhard, 'Ökumenische Tradition?', p. 129.

37. Jonathan Sperber ably discusses the pitfalls of modernization theory in the study of German religion in 'Kirchengeschichte or the social and cultural history of religion?', *Neue Politische Literatur*, 43 (1998), pp. 13–35.

38. Priests were one in this assessment. For example, see 'Die mit dem kirchlichen Bücherverbote verbundene Exkommunikation', *Münsterisches Pastoral-Blatt*, 10, 4 (1878), pp. 1–4; 'Vom Lesen schlechter Bücher und Zeitschriften', *Sankt Paulinus-Blatt für das deutsche Volk*, 8, 23 (1882), p. 322; 'Clerus und Presse', *Münsterisches Pastoral-Blatt*, 34, 9 (1896), pp. 129–32; 'Der katholische Seelsorger und die Presse', p. 4; and 'Unser Motto', *Paulinus-Blatt. Sonntagsblatt für die christliche Familie*, 33, 50 (15 December 1907), pp. 394–5.

39. Hermann Herz, the head of the *Borromäusverein*, reported that the laity 'shrugged their shoulders' at the Index of Forbidden Books. See Herz, review of Albert Sleumer, *Index Romanus. Verzeichnis der sämtlicher auf dem römischen Index stehenden deutschen Bücher; desgleichen aller fremdsprachlichen Bücher seit dem Jahre 1870*, 2nd edn. (Osnabrück: Pillmeyer, 1906) in *Die Bücherwelt*, 4, 4 (January 1907), p. 80.

Part 4
Readers in the Twentieth-Century World

9

Understanding Children as Readers: Librarians' Anecdotes and Surveys in the United States from 1890 to 1930

Kate McDowell

Public librarians documented children's reading choices and activities in surveys and articles published from 1890 to 1930, a period in the United States that coincided with popular interest in childhood, the rise of children's publishing and the emergence of mass media. Librarians worked alongside other Progressive Era professionals, including teachers, journalists and educational researchers, to gather data on children's reading patterns in order to better guide their reading. Librarians emphasized building personal relationships with their young patrons, and this value appears explicitly in statements of professional ethics and implicitly through frequent quotation of children's own words about the public library. Perhaps in no other realm of Progressive Era work with children were the voices of children reprinted with such frequency and accorded such status in professional publications.

This chapter examines historical traces of children as readers, analysing quantitative and qualitative evidence of children's reading. Although historical readers are notoriously difficult to study because evidence of their interactions with texts is ephemeral, there are abundant traces of children's reading preferences, choices and descriptive statements in these documents. That librarians collected both kinds of data – surveys and anecdotes – provides an unusually rich basis for historical analysis of children's reading experiences. Of course, these children's voices were recorded in librarians' words and for professional purposes. Librarians typically quoted children to bolster their claims of professional efficacy; these records are inevitably partial, mediated by adults, and complicated by power relations between children and adults.[1] Nevertheless, analysing these documents of children's reading experiences promises to shed greater light on this often overlooked population – children as readers.

Historical analysis has seldom attempted to understand children's reading practices in libraries or other institutions. The development of children's literature has been the subject of full-length scholarly treatment, including histories of the children's publishing industry, prominent author biographies, and studies of the critical (adult) reception of children's literature.[2] Missing from these studies of the culture of print around childhood have been analyses of the actual voices of child readers as participants. In journals such as *Library Journal*, *Public Libraries* (later *Libraries*), and the *American Library Association Bulletin* (*ALA Bulletin*), as well as in popular publications such as *Outlook* and *The Bookman*, librarians wrote about child readers' experiences and quoted the words of their young patrons. In seeking to understand what librarianship may offer to a history of children as readers, two kinds of evidence from the above sources are relevant: surveys of child patrons investigating their reading and library use, and anecdotal writings about child patrons in librarians' articles about their work. Both forms of evidence are complicated by power relations between children and (professional) adults. Even answers to seemingly straightforward queries about favourite books or authors must be read with an awareness of the influence librarians had over children.

In many of the surveys that appeared in library literature from 1890 to 1930, librarians reported children's replies to questions about reading or libraries. A total of thirty-six surveys were described in library literature of this period; of these, twenty-one were conducted by librarians and fifteen by non-librarians (teachers, superintendents and academics). Almost half the surveys were conducted by professionals from other fields but published in library literature. In assessing children's reading, librarians were not isolated from developments in other fields, but instead developed their ways of collecting evidence in relation to other professions.[3]

While other groups working with children made more frequent use of surveys, librarians' writings are replete with stories about individual children: their words, reading choices and relationships to librarians and the public library. These anecdotal records of children's voices distinctively show aspects of relationships between individual librarians and children. The records were kept by adult librarians, who evinced a wide range of attitudes toward the children they served, including pride in children's learning through reading, amusement at children's foibles, frustration with (and condescension toward) immigrants' perceived ignorance, and admiration for immigrant groups who placed a high value on reading and learning. This analysis focuses on anecdotes in which librarians quoted children's own words verbatim, through which it is possible to glean some sense of children's (and their family's) attitudes toward reading, libraries and librarians.

Most of the history of youth services is missing from library history, as Christine Jenkins notes.[4] Historical research indicates that children's rooms, particularly in urban areas, were burgeoning with young patrons during this period.[5] Recent scholarship on the cultural history of children's librarianship sheds some light on youth services history, though it focuses primarily on professional attitudes toward children rather than on children themselves.[6] In cities, large swaths of the reading public were recent immigrants, and their children sought out libraries for entertainment and educational opportunities. Librarians met these children with an array of programmes and services; some were tailored to the children's demands, but all reflected the reading-based values of the recent profession of librarianship. Those values included strong opinions about what kinds of books children should read, and how those choices would foster their education and self-improvement. How librarians kept records has, in part, to do with their continuing process of establishing their authority as professional and situating children's librarianship as a valid specialty within librarianship. Understanding children's reading through these records requires examining when librarians conducted surveys, why they collected anecdotes, and how librarians' published articles view children's reading through the lens of librarians' professional values and authority.

Surveys of children

Librarians used questionnaires to gather a wide range of information from children, including their favourite books, authors and genres, their opinions of library services, the decor of the children's room, story hours and exhibits and the collection itself. The varied forms and contents of each questionnaire reflect the value that librarians placed on addressing their local communities. Librarians usually surveyed children in their libraries, by distributing and collecting questionnaires during a child's visit. Frequent users were the most accessible target for these in-house questionnaires. However, there were instances in which librarians enlisted teachers or community groups such as Boy or Girl Scouts to distribute surveys to children who were not already frequent library users.[7]

When librarians used surveys, they joined professional groups dedicated to either reform or to the development of the social sciences. Such groups were beginning to use survey methodology to gather empirical evidence of poverty, illiteracy and other social ills that they hoped to ameliorate.[8]

Surveys in the late nineteenth century were not the quantitative tools we see today. Social changes such as industrialization and urbanization inspired the 'flowering of a variety of forms of social investigation'.[9] Among these were basic questionnaire-based surveys that asked children questions related to their reading preferences and habits, and behind these questionnaires was the assumption that reading could improve children's characters. Most often, librarians' writings described surveys as qualitative information, situating quantitative facts within a narrative framework that highlighted individual readers' experiences (and included some quotations from children). This emphasis on situating survey results in narrative, qualitative frameworks followed in a tradition of surveys in youth services work started by director of Hartford Public Library pioneering youth services provider, Caroline Hewins, in 1882.[10]

Librarians' surveys typically asked children for information about their favourite books, authors, genres and general reading habits; reports were typically in narrative form. Children were asked from one to eight questions about their reading preferences and library use; their answers were recorded quantitatively but embedded in a qualitative narrative that included children's own words. Questions included queries about favourite books, favourite authors, frequency of library use, whether children held library cards, and many more questions related to children's reading. Some surveys were administered through public libraries, while others were distributed in nearby schools. In-house surveys often deliberately targeted the 100 or 150 children who were the most frequent patrons and asked them to name their favourite books, favourite aspects of the library, or to suggest new library services. Surveys that librarians asked teachers to administer in schools were more likely to ask questions about use, including whether children had library cards and knew how to use the library.

Mary Wright Plummer of the Pratt Institute Free Library in Brooklyn conducted a typical survey, consisting of six questions posed to 150 regular child patrons. She collected about 100 replies, and reported 'specimen answers' in her article. Queries included how long children had been library users, whether they received reading suggestions at home, whether they preferred help in choosing books, how many books they read, and the 'best book the child had ever read'. Plummer summarized responses to the question of whether children preferred to have help or not:

49 [children] said that they came to the library to get help in writing their compositions or in other schoolwork, while 51 said they did

not, one proudly asserting, 'I am capable of writing all my composi-tions myself' and another, seeming to think help a sort of disgrace, 'I do not come to the library for help about anything at all.'

This quotation demonstrates how these surveys reported quantitative data in narrative that included children's voices. Asked about their best book, Plummer noted that children's responses came in 'bewildering variety' which assured her there had been 'no copying or using of other children's opinions'. Plummer mentioned a few titles as popular favour-ites, including *Little Women*, *The Swiss Family Robinson*, *Uncle Tom's Cabin*, and *Grimm's Fairy Tales*.[11]

   Some librarians reported the results of surveys while also promoting the need for their own professional intervention. Librarian Electra Doren of the Dayton, Ohio public library surveyed children in a classroom regard-ing their use of the library. She asked eight questions about their reading and library use, including 'Have you a card to draw books from the public library?' and 'Do you take books from any library other than the public library?'. Doren described their responses vividly, if not objectively:

To the question, 'Do your parents ever tell you good books to read, and help you to select them?' the answer, 'Not very often', 'Nobody helps me', 'I choose my own books', from pitiful little 10-year-olds, had a most mournful aspect. In one case a small urchin of the eighth grade who had read 58 books since Christmas, 'an average', accord-ing to his calculations, 'of three to five books a week', naively replies to the question, 'Do you choose your own books?', 'Yes, by the help of ——, one of the librarians'.[12]

These children's voices are framed in terms of their need for guidance. The 'urchin' who 'naively replies' to the librarian is betrayed by his own reading habits; Doren, writing for an audience of librarians familiar with emerging standards of children's librarianship, relies on readers' knowledge of the assumption that no children's librarian would encour-age a child to read as many as 'three to five books a week' lest they detract from schoolwork. This example highlights the danger of bias in such narratives. Given that she used children's written survey replies as the basis for her article, it is hard to imagine how Doren attributed a 'mournful aspect' to their written words. Although she gathers evidence from readers, the narrative frame is that of a professional who already knows that children need help with their reading and interprets the results to emphasize that message.

Librarians also collected qualitative data about how children understood their reading preferences and motivations. One survey asked
children not only to name favourite books, but to offer explanations
for their preferences. Librarian Mary Root surveyed children in a school
to discover more about their library use, asking for both 'a few books'
they liked and 'a few books you do not like' (Horatio Alger was both
the most liked and most disliked author). Alger's books were frequently
banned from libraries and disapproved by librarians; this polarized
response shows both compliance with and resistance to librarians' values. Root reported some of the children's reasons for disliking books:
'*Tale of Two Cities* – too deep; Alger – too much alike; *English Orphans* –
too sad; Henty – too monotonous; *From Cattle Ranch to College* – too
much description; *Life's Shop Window* – too much work to figure out;
The Halo – too mushy.'[13] This demonstrates that some librarians were
striving to understand not only what children read, but why they made
those choices and how their preferences were motivated.

Children's behaviour in the library was an ongoing concern, and the
power of the survey was occasionally used to make children compliant
with library rules. One survey elicited children's own opinions about
how to enforce the rules of the reading room. The librarian displayed a
mutilated book and asked children to respond in writing to the question of what they thought should happen to the perpetrator of this
crime. A portion of the children's replies read:

'In such a case as that the person ought to be suspended from the
library and also be compelled to pay a heavy fine, or else sent to jail.
(Signed) One of the boys that protects the children's room.'

'I think the boy or girl who would injure a book in such a way ought
to be promptly discharged from the library.'

'No, they don't deserve any prevliages [*sic*, privileges]. I never did
such things as that to any book and I hope no more will injure
any.'

'I think that a boy or girl who inger [*sic*, injure] a book like this outo
[*sic*, ought to] pay as much as the book cost and not to come to the
library.'[14]

These replies are representative of a complex power relationship
between librarians and children, and deserve further analysis. First,

children express a protective stance toward their library and a punitive attitude toward the transgressor, demonstrating the social commitment that the librarian sought to elicit. Second, the librarian reprints the children's words exactly as written. This strategy reinforces the authenticity of the replies as children's own opinions. The fact that other children are outraged serves expressly to bulwark the librarians' authority and the library's rules. Third, the librarian devoted the bulk of her writing to the verbatim replies from children. Rather than summarize their attitudes toward the perpetrator, she gives their words as written. Why devote this kind of space to these words? Given that the column in which these quotations appeared was written to suggest similar techniques for modifying children's behaviour to other libraries, the librarian may have been offering this as an example to colleagues who feared that children's unruly behaviour could decimate library collections. By quoting children directly, she was showing her fellow librarians that they had nothing to fear; at least in her library, young patrons embraced their civic duty to protect library collections.

This explicit emphasis on the group is relatively unusual in librarians' writings, which tend to focus on individual over collective behaviour. This is evident in one survey from Redlands, California, for which the librarian reported that 'Scott's novels', 'Ben Hur', and 'Miss Alcott' were the top choices, but also included the full list of favourites from one child 'because of its being so good a list'.[15] This strategy situates collective results as comprised of individual readers. It also suggests that the efficacy of librarians' work was most visible at the individual level. A survey of favourite books from San Antonio gave results of 1,317 children's votes, listing all books with more than twenty votes and the authors in order of popularity. However, the survey authors also noted that '432 different titles were named' by the children.[16] Like the list from an individual reader above, describing the wide range of favourite books situates the survey-based emphasis on the collective preferences of child readers drawn from individual responses.

At least one librarian was overtly critical of the way that surveys tended to obscure individuality. Caroline Hewins solicited 'twelve hundred papers' that contained answers to questions about their reading, noting that the methodology was problematic in that papers required by teachers as school assignments were marked by a much lesser 'degree of spontaneity' than those requested of children in the public library. Hewins was dismayed at finding that very few of the children's responses had any 'individual flavour'.[17] Her disappointment in finding 'individual flavour' emphasizes the orientation of children's librarianship toward offering guidance to individual children. This sentiment implies a resistance to standardization, and explains why librarians did so few surveys of their own relative to their colleagues in education. Although Hewins relied heavily on numerical evidence in other surveys she conducted, the article that she wrote based on this survey eschewed any counting and instead used extended quotes from children to illustrate the kinds of replies received.

Anecdotes about children

Children's librarians frequently used anecdotal evidence to justify and demonstrate the efficacy of their work. Narratives, stories, quotations from children and anecdotal evidence must be analysed more rigorously as part of the historical record of librarianship. Rather than seeing these writings as less legitimate than surveys, historians should re-evaluate librarians' anecdotal evidence in context as their preferred kind of evidence, even when questionnaire methods were available. The anecdotes that librarians collected and published about children in their libraries have the advantage of great contextual granularity, allowing for historical analysis of specific times, places and interactions.

Librarians' anecdotes captured surprisingly detailed records of individual children's reading paths. Mary Root described the response of one child to a query about favourite reading by quoting a boy who said:

> I have read and liked Three Muskateers [*sic*], Out with Garabaldi, Ben Hur, Swiss Family Robinson, King Arthur and His Knights and the Round Table, Robin Hood, most all of Shakespeare's tragedies, Operas Every Child Should Know, Life of Napoleon Bonaparte, Two Young Patriots, Lives of Washington and Lincoln, Heroes of Chivalry, and Story of the Cid.

Root praised this list as evidence of the boy's 'increased ability to read a finer type of book'.[18] Such anecdotes are best read as librarians' attempts to demonstrate that readers improved and expanded their knowledge through library use, serving as proof of the widely held belief that well-chosen reading provided a ladder of learning. Catherine Ross analysed the use of this metaphor in librarians' nineteenth-century writings as a means of justifying their pushing reading toward better 'taste' in their selections.[19]

In many of these anecdotes, race, class and gender feature prominently as descriptors of children that accompanied their words as librarians recorded them. As Matthew Jacobson writes in his book *Whiteness of a Different Color: European Immigrants and the Alchemy of Race*, these ways of describing children were common at the time and were part of a larger process of the historical development of categories of race, including 'whiteness'.[20] Early children's librarian Minerva Sanders of the manufacturing town of Pawtuckett, Rhode Island described one young working-class reader's experience in her library:

> An Italian boy of thirteen years, who attends school but twelve weeks in the year, and is employed in one of our manufactories, has read, for the entertainment of his mother and invalid sister during the winter and spring, 'Livingstone's Travels in Africa', Lamb's 'Tales from Shakespeare', and the 'Life of Savonarola' from 'The Makers of Florence'; in speaking of which his dark eyes light up, and he expresses the most sincere gratitude for the privilege of reading books of such character.[21]

In this case, the gender, ethnicity and class of the reader in the librarians' description indicate not only that users came from diverse social situations, but that the public library was specifically useful to recent immigrants in manufacturing communities, a topic that Sanders addressed at length in another article.[22] That this Italian boy was enjoying reading about Italian history also suggests that librarians were aware of ethnicity as a factor in children's reading choices. In another case, a librarian noted that 'books of Italian national interest' attracted young Italian-American readers, such as 'the small Italian boy who came asking for a story of the "biggest stone cutter that ever lived". It proved to be Michelangelo, and the youngster went home happy with his book.'[23]

Gender also factored into librarians' commentary about the progressive 'improvements' of individual readers through library use. One librarian described a girl's 'progress' in reading science books:

> Another little girl from the public school asked one day for books on the sponge. Simmons' 'Commercial products of the sea' was handed to her. The same child then became interested in the beaver, and took home Woods' 'Homes without hands'. Then she took out 'Life and her children', by Arabella Buckley, and 'The fairy-land of science', by the same author, and since then she has been studying Champlin's 'Child's catechism of common things', two little books by the Kirby sisters, 'World brought home', and 'The sea and its wonders', and another book, 'The broad, broad ocean'.[24]

This anecdote indicates this girl's significant engagement with reading scientific topics in children's literature. Another librarian commented on a girl's request for 'an aquarium' in the library, because 'children would enjoy seeing pollywogs change to frogs every time they came to the library', by noting that 'This is the comment of a little girl, I am glad to say.'[25] Though the era of the New Woman was in full swing, this would seem to be an unusually forward-looking comment regarding gender and science. However, the librarian's gladness also indicates two other values in librarianship at the time: the promotion of nonfiction and broader reading, designed to extend children's tastes beyond fiction.[26]

Although there were frequent anecdotes about such individual readers, librarians also facilitated connections between readers with common interests. In the same article, the librarian noted that several boys who were around ten years old came into the library looking for books on microscopes, botany, sea shells and insects. She was circumspect about her role in making introductions, but notes that the 'four boys now made a scientific society of their own, meeting regularly at one another's houses'.[27]

In some cases, identity appears to have been a factor in how librarians approached children. Many librarians worked closely with individuals and reading groups to provide them with reading they would enjoy. One librarian described her work 'on the lower West side, where the Irish-Americans live in large numbers, where street fights and fires contribute a constant source of excitement' with 'a library club of girls who have been meeting twice a month for two years'. The librarian was concerned about selecting books that would capture the children's interest, so she asked them directly, 'What kind of books do you really like to read?' After a few moments of silence, one girl mentioned *Huckleberry Finn* and another added 'that she had enjoyed the chapter on whitewashing the fence in Tom Sawyer'. She decided that adventure books would appeal to these girls, and so 'a reading club of adventure was formed, and though we began with the Prisoner of Zenda we have wandered with Odysseus, and sighed over the sacrifice of Alcestis, and thrilled over the winning of Atalanta this winter'.[28] The librarian was explicit in her knowledge not of the racial or ethnic identities of these girls, but of their social environment. Eliciting reading interests was a means of bridging a cultural divide between Irish immigrant children and the public library.

Some librarians wrote about the barriers to children's use of the library. One librarian quoted two girls who had trouble understanding the expectations of the library. The first girl stopped using the library because of overdue fines: 'I forgot about my book once until I owed twenty cents, and I couldn't get no money, so I sent the book back with another girl and quit.' The second girl had an even more daunting experience of the library, and the librarian quoted her as saying: 'I didn't get a book; I was hardly ever in a place as big as that before; it was all so quiet and everything that I didn't like to go past the door, and besides I thought I mightn't do the right thing.'[29] Another librarian described children who did not have the freedom to use the library, quoting a former library user as saying:

> I ain't got no more time to read books . . . My ma is gone to Cleveland, my pa is out all the time and comes home drunk, I got to mind the store, look after the kids, cook and wash, it don't leave me much time for reading. I am terrible sleepy at night.[30]

That barriers to participation in the library (whether real monetary or perceived cultural ones), were prohibitive for some library users comes as no surprise. However, the fact that librarians quoted children whose experiences were not positive, shows they were aware of the difficulties of using the library.

A serious conflict arose in one library because of a misunderstanding regarding the common practice of immigrants taking on American-sounding names. Children whose families were changing their names were, deliberately or inadvertently, violating a basic library presumption of honest identification for the purpose of holding library cards. As one librarian wrote:

> To them a name is a small matter; Hyman Slutzky, prevented by a two-cent fine from using his card, starts a new life in the library as Hyman Simon. Rebecca Lubarsky for the same reason becomes Rose Barr, thus killing two birds with one stone, as she avoids paying her fine, and advances a step toward respectability by assuming a more American name![31]

Changing names may or may not have been intended to deceive, but the librarian certainly considered it to be a deliberate deception. Although the librarian acknowledges the dynamics of name changing by calling it a 'step toward respectability', she ultimately decries it by calling names a 'small matter' and implies a lack of morality in the act. She does not acknowledge that entire families could have been changing their names at the same time.

Children's voices were sometimes subsumed in librarians' words about them, as they emphasized their own professional authority, utility and success. Despite the plethora of direct quotations, it can be difficult to know to what extent the surveys and anecdotes indicating library successes recount the lived experiences of children. Moments when children resisted rules can therefore be especially valuable for understanding their actual experiences of reading. One form of children's resistance that repeatedly appears is that of cleanliness. The expectation that children should have clean hands when using the library was exemplified in the motto of the Cleveland Public Library club for children, the Library League: 'Clean hearts, clean hands, clean books.'[32]

Children did not always comply. One librarian described a group of boys who had been sent home to wash their hands. They returned 'in an incredibly short time with purified palms and suppressed giggles, and on persistent inquiry confessed, "We just licked 'em".'[33] Another librarian was trying to educate a boy as to the 'necessity for clean hands' in the public library, and so she asked him whether he would 'rather take a clean book or a dirty one?' The boy replied, 'A dirty one everytime', and explained: 'I always pick for real dirty ones, then the little spots I get on 'em don't show.' Such examples of children finding ways around library rules demonstrate their inventiveness and provide clear examples of agency. Both strategies (licking hands clean and choosing dirty books) were ways of accommodating library expectations while resisting rules.

Another conflict over cleanliness became a conflict with the child's parent, when a boy 'brought back a book with its cover soiled and greasy' and 'refused to pay the fine', until his mother came in to the library. She argued that the librarians 'had been very unjust and unkind to her boy' because, 'he is very careful; he puts his book in the ice box where the baby can't get it, and nothing but our food and Willie's books ever goes in that ice box'.[34] Like the boy with soiled hands, this boy was attempting to comply with library rules but interpreting them in his own way. This anecdote is also framed as humorous in the librarian's writings, another example of the cultural gap between middle-class library settings and immigrant households. Such moments of non-compliance are scarce in librarians' writings, but they are all the more important for understanding how and when children asserted their agency.

Conclusion

Christine Pawley has recently called for more historical investigation of readers' experiences in libraries, to reveal how and why people read and to better understand the impact of public libraries as institutions.[35] Children deserve special consideration both as a population served by public libraries and as a uniquely proscribed, controlled and diverse category of readers. Histories of reading have tended to value statistical evidence over more local, contextualized narratives of readers' agency. Roger Chartier has argued for 'localizing social difference in practices more than in statistical distributions'.[36] This chapter addresses both of these calls by analysing not only statistical information collected in surveys, but also children's own words collected by librarians that reveal their reading practices.

Recent scholarship in the history of childhood has touched on children's reading. Some histories incorporate children's writing practices, especially diary writing, to trace their paths from childhood to adulthood. Harvey Graff has traced the paths of individual child readers from dependency to adulthood.[37] Karen Sanchez-Eppler's cultural history of children in the nineteenth century draws on children's diaries as a source for understanding the cultural importance of the activity of writing.[38] Howard Chudacoff has consulted children's diaries in constructing his history of children's play.[39] Children's reading is related to both writing and play, but few studies have specifically addressed these connections in relation to their reading practices. One exception is Deirdre Stam's analysis of the unusually comprehensive diaries of a single child that reflected her book collecting, reading and writing activities.[40]

Scholarship has just begun to look at what children (a distinctive age group defined and constrained by particular social norms), might contribute to the history of reading. Jonathan Rose in *The Intellectual Life of the British Working Classes* drew attention to the fact that studies that addressed race, gender and class typically gave short shrift to class. Though Rose included schoolchildren in his analysis, children are often excluded even when other aspects of identity are addressed. Indeed, considering what children may offer to the history of reading adds another dimension to these considerations of identity. Children are diverse in race, gender and class, although, particularly at this time period, they were subject to emerging age-based laws and institutions, from child labour prohibitions to mandatory schooling.

Robert Darnton's communications circuit positioned booksellers as the agency between publishers and readers.[41] For many children – especially poor children in the USA in the early twentieth century – the library served this intermediary function. Children as readers were not passive recipients of library services and values, but actively engaged with the institution in a variety of ways that demonstrate their agency;

they were active borrowers, proud cardholders, and sometimes resisted the libraries' rules and regulations. The records that librarians kept provide rich data for analysing the ways in which young readers' were able to make their voices heard in libraries as cultural spaces. This evidence contributes to a history of children as readers by situating children as agents in their use of the public library. Reading was a part of many children's lives, even though they came from radically different walks of life. Libraries were important sites for child readers as an intermediary institution that both connected and came between children and their reading materials.

Notes and references

1. Kate McDowell, 'Toward a history of children as readers', *Book History*, 12 (2009), 240–65.
2. Anne Lundin, 'Victorian horizons: the reception of children's books in England and America, 1880–1900', *Library Quarterly*, 64 (1994), 30–59; Leonard S. Marcus, *Minders of Make-Believe: Idealists, Entrepreneurs, and the Shaping of American Children's Literature* (New York: Houghton Mifflin Harcourt, 2008), p. 402; Leonard S. Marcus, *Golden Legacy: How Golden Books Won Children's Hearts, Changed Publishing Forever, and Became an American Icon Along the Way* (New York: Golden Books, an imprint of Random House Children's Books, 2007), p. 245; Leonard S. Marcus, *Margaret Wise Brown: Awakened by the Moon* (New York: W. Morrow, 1999); Leonard S. Marcus and Children's Book Council, *75 Years of Children's Book Week Posters: Celebrating Great Illustrators of American Children's Books* (New York: A. A. Knopf, 1994), p. 74; Jacqueline Eddy, *Bookwomen: Creating an Empire in Children's Book Publishing, 1919–1939* (Madison, WI: University of Wisconsin Press, 2006), p. 211.
3. Though beyond the scope of the present study, it would be interesting to examine the frequency with which librarians' surveys were reported in other professional literatures.
4. Christine A. Jenkins, 'The history of youth services librarianship: a review of the research literature', *Libraries & Culture*, 35 (2000), 103–40.
5. Fannette H. Thomas, 'The genesis of children's services in the American public library: 1875–1906,' (unpublished doctoral dissertation, University of Wisconsin, 1982), pp. 1–357; Kate McDowell, 'The cultural origins of youth services librarianship, 1876–1900' (unpublished doctoral dissertation, University of Illinois, 2007), pp. 1–280.
6. Melanie A. Kimball, 'From refuge to risk: public libraries and children in World War I', *Library Trends*, 55 (2007), 454–63; Chris Lyons, '"Children who read good books usually behave better, and have good manners": the founding of the Notre Dame de Grace Library for Boys and Girls, Montreal, 1943', *Library Trends*, 55 (2007), 597–608; Jennifer Burek Pierce, '"Why girls go wrong": advising female teen readers in the early twentieth century', *Library Quarterly*, 77 (2007), 311–26.

7. Caroline Maria Hewins, 'Report on list of children's books with children's annotations', *Library Journal*, 27 (1902), 79–82; Rex Gary, 'Survey of leisure time reading of school children', *Iowa Library Quarterly*, 10 (1928), 199–201.
8. Jean M. Converse, *Survey Research in the United States: Roots and Emergence, 1890–1960* (Berkeley: University of California Press, 1987), pp. 11–25.
9. Martin Bulmer, Kathryn Kish Sklar and Kevin Bales, *The Social Survey in Historical Perspective, 1880–1940* (Cambridge and New York: Cambridge University Press, 1991), p. 11.
10. Kate McDowell, 'Surveying the field: the research model of women in librarianship, 1882–1898', *Library Quarterly*, 79 (2009), 279–300.
11. Mary Wright Plummer, 'The work for children in free libraries', *Library Journal*, 22 (1897), 683.
12. Electra Doren, 'School libraries', *Library Journal*, 22 (1897), 191.
13. Mary E. S. Root, 'Children's library work', *Library Journal*, 45 (1920), 828.
14. Mary E. Dousman, 'Object lessons', *Library Journal*, 24 (1899), 516.
15. Antoinette M. Humphreys, 'Some statistics on children's reading', *Public Libraries*, 4 (1899), 321.
16. Leah Carter Johnson, 'Favorite children's books in San Antonio', *Library Journal*, 49 (1924), 426.
17. Hewins, 'Report on list of children's books with children's annotations', p. 79.
18. Root, 'Children's Library Work', p. 829.
19. Catherine Sheldrick Ross, 'Metaphors of reading', *Journal of Library History, Philosophy, and Comparative Librarianship*, 22 (1987), 147–63.
20. Matthew Frye Jacobson, *Whiteness of a Different Color: European Immigrants and the Alchemy of Race* (Cambridge, MA: Harvard University Press, 1998), p. 338.
21. Minerva A. Sanders, 'Report on reading for the young', *Library Journal*, 16 (1890), 59.
22. Minerva A. Sanders, 'The possibilities of public libraries in manufacturing communities', *Library Journal*, 12 (1887), 395–400.
23. Anon, 'Notes on children's reading', *Library Journal*, 29 (1904), 476.
24. Anon, 'Fiction at the Boston Public Library', *Library Journal*, 6 (1881), 205.
25. Plummer, 'The work for children in free libraries', 684.
26. Kate McDowell, 'Which truth, what fiction?: librarians' book recommendations for children, 1876–1890', in *Education and Print Culture in Modern America*, ed. Adam Nelson and John Rudolph (Madison, WI: University of Wisconsin-Madison Press, 2010), pp. 15–35.
27. Anon, 'Fiction at the Boston Public Library', p. 205.
28. Anna C. Tyler, 'Library reading clubs for young people', *Library Journal*, 37 (1912), 549.
29. Margaret Drew Archibald, 'Teen age girls as booklovers', *Library Journal*, 52 (1927), 857.
30. Aniela Poray, 'The foreign child and the book', *Library Journal*, 40 (1915), 234.
31. Ibid., p. 155.
32. Linda Eastman, 'The library and the children: an account of the children's work in the Cleveland Public Library', *Library Journal*, 23 (1898), 143.
33. Plummer, 'The work for children in free libraries', p. 683.

34. Mary Pretlow, 'The opening day – and after – in a children's library', *Library Journal*, 33 (1908), 179.
35. Christine Pawley, 'Retrieving readers: library experiences', *Library Quarterly*, 76 (2006), 379–87.
36. Roger Chartier, *The Order of Books: Readers, Authors, and Libraries in Europe Between the Fourteenth and Eighteenth Centuries* (Stanford, CA: Stanford University Press, 1994), p. 23.
37. Harvey Graff, *Conflicting Paths: Growing Up in America* (Cambridge, MA: Harvard University Press, 1997), pp. xiii, 426.
38. Karen Sanchez-Eppler, *Dependent States: The Child's Part in Nineteenth-Century American Culture* (Chicago: University of Chicago Press, 2005), p. 260.
39. Howard P. Chudacoff, *Children at Play: An American History* (New York: New York University Press, 2007), p. 269.
40. Deirdre C. Stam, 'Growing up with books: Fanny Seward's book collecting, reading, and writing in mid-nineteenth century New York State', *Libraries and Culture*, 41 (2006), 189–218
41. Robert Darnton, *The Forbidden Best-Sellers of Pre-Revolutionary France* (New York: W. W. Norton, 1995), p. 440.

10
Letters to a Daughter: An Archive of Middle-Class Reading in New Zealand, *c.*1872–1932

Susann Liebich

I

In 1891, Fred Barkas, then thirty-seven years of age and living in Christchurch, New Zealand, wrote to his brother in England about his usual reading habits.

> Another result of this delay in mail delivery is that both Amy & I have got ahead of our supply of Home papers, this is a very unusual state of things . . . We get Spectators, weekly Chronicles, Truth, &c. &c. and should we fail in our steady reading it's wonderful how our 'Papers-to-be-read' baskets get crowded – now they are empty. We don't go out much of an evening and usually read our papers for an hour or so between finishing our nightly game of cards and going to bed. Not having any papers I have this week again taken up 'Lorna Doone' and I think I'm enjoying it even more than I did upon my first and second readings. Amy has taken to 'Treasure Island' again – but we miss our papers as we like to keep up a nodding acquaintance with the events in the Great World.[1]

More than thirty years later the same man wrote to his daughter, then also living in England.

> I have finished Stephen Graham's 'Priest of the Ideal' and I must say that I enjoyed reading it greatly; there is a subtle poetic charm about Graham's writing which appeals to me and when in his book he talks of Glastonbury, Holy Island, Durham – places one loves – with an undercurrent of 'England, My England', what lover of his country can resist him.[2]

Much had happened during these thirty years. The intellectual and cultural landscape of New Zealand had changed, and yet, for Barkas the same sense of keeping a connection to places outside New Zealand, particularly to Britain, remained. While the reference to the 'Great World' in the letter to his brother might have been a bit 'tongue-in-cheek', in both letters Barkas positioned himself geographically and literally in relation to his correspondent. While he was situated in New Zealand, his addressees were living in England, and Barkas connected and identified as much with his local place as with his British identity. In both instances, and – as the chapter will show – over the course of his life, it was Barkas's reading, the sharing of texts and the mobility of print which enabled those connections to a number of cultural spaces.

Who was Fred Barkas and why is the archive of his reading experiences so significant? Born in 1854 in Newcastle-upon-Tyne, England, into a middle-class family, his father owned a bookstore, and later a gallery and newspaper reading room.³ In 1881, aged twenty-seven, Barkas migrated to New Zealand to take up a teaching position in Science at Lincoln College near Christchurch. Two years later he left the college to work as a clerk with the New Zealand Loan and Mercantile Agency. In 1887 he married Amy Parker, who had emigrated from England in the early 1880s, and in 1889 their only child Mary was born. In the early 1900s Barkas was transferred to the firm's Wellington office, and the family moved to the capital city for a few years. In 1909 he was promoted to General Manager of the Timaru branch, a position he filled until his retirement in 1919. He remained in Timaru for the rest of his life (Figure 10.1), until his death in 1932.

Fred Barkas was middle class; he and his family lived a financially secure life. He was well educated and moved within middle-class circles in Christchurch, Wellington and Timaru, enjoyed musical or theatrical entertainments, 'evenings at home' and visits to sport clubs where he played tennis and golf. In 1903 he described himself and his family as 'ordinary middle-class folk'.⁴ Earlier, he had confessed to his brother Charlie that 'for myself – year by year I am more & more convinced that my proper role is respectable and ordinarily useful Mediocrity'.⁵ Barkas titled his reminiscences 'Some Memories of a Mediocrity',⁶ expressing a sense of failed aspirations felt by an elderly man looking back at his life.

Despite his professed inconspicuousness, Barkas created and bequeathed a substantial record of his reading and of his correspondence. Barkas engaged in extensive correspondence with relatives and friends, keeping copies of a large proportion of this correspondence. The Fred Barkas archive comprises sixty-seven bound volumes of letters,

Figure 10.1 Photograph of Fred Barkas, c.1915 (South Canterbury Museum, 2002/300.072)

diaries and notebooks and is housed at the Alexander Turnbull Library, within the National Library of New Zealand, Wellington.

This chapter uses the Barkas archive to pose some questions about the reading culture and experiences of a middle-class male reader in the context of the wider intellectual and cultural climate between 1909 and 1932. While Barkas was based in provincial New Zealand, examining this archive enables us to explore the history of reading and print culture in the wider Anglophone world. Recently, studies in the history of reading have used diaries, letters and autobiographies to offer a more vivid picture of the reading experience and explore traces of 'the reader's emotional engagement with the text . . . or the underlying set of practices that helped determine reading'.[7] With this in mind, the Barkas archive offers a case study of a historical reader, situated in New Zealand and within the wider Anglophone world, helping us to interpret both his intellectual life and his place within a community of readers. What did he read and how? What role did reading play in his life, and how was his reading experience shaped by social and cultural activities, or by political or private circumstances? By illustrating the richness and the possibilities of this archive, this chapter assesses whether a case study of one individual historical reader can be representative for a specific group of people in a particular place and time.

II

The Barkas papers include letters, reminiscences and travel diaries from 1872 to 1932. Amongst his letters there are collected ephemera, theatre programmes, photographs, pamphlets and a notebook titled 'Books read'. The majority of the collection consists of correspondence with his daughter, Mary Rushton Barkas (1889–1961). After 1913, when Mary left New Zealand permanently for England, Barkas wrote her a 'daily page', describing in exact detail his cultural and social life, in which reading literature was an integral part.[8] For the years after 1913 in particular, when Barkas started using a typewriter for his correspondence, and conscientiously kept all his 'daily pages' to Mary, the records give an almost complete picture of his activities and social life. In retirement, Barkas transcribed most of the letters or kept carbon copies of the originals, which he then 'had bound "into handy volumes"' which he fancied would 'afford amusing, and perhaps instructive, reading for my daughter or my nephews and nieces in the years to come'.[9]

Barkas's effort to preserve his letters (and the underlying imperatives of recording his reading) needs to be considered when assessing the representativeness of the archive. The act of letter writing and of keeping copies – not just the content and extent of his correspondence – is in itself a very conscious act of his middle-class existence. The title of the collection ('Some Memories of a Mediocrity') and the extent and detail of the material included suggests that this autobiographical collection had some future audience in mind, even if this comprised just his friends and relatives. His overseas travel diaries, amusingly called his 'Obs & Imps', were passed on to friends for their enjoyment.[10] Barkas even considered having his memoirs published, possibly posthumously.[11] While he never actively sought a publisher for his letters and memoirs during his life, his desire for his collected writing to be published emerges from the archive. This indicates higher literary aspirations than those expressed in his letters. They alert us to the characteristics and conventions of the particular genres (letters and diaries), and remind us of the care needed when used and interpreted as a historical source.

Large parts of the archive (especially the intimate letters Barkas wrote to his daughter Mary), must be read against the background of his failed marriage. Amy Parker had been an independent young woman travelling though Europe and Australia before settling in Christchurch in 1886, where she taught music and acting. At the time of their wedding, Amy was thirty-seven and Fred three years her junior. The two were attracted to each other's intellects, enjoyed conversations about music and literature, and he admired her independence and strength. By 1905, the relationship had cooled. When Barkas prepared many of his letters and notes to be bound many years later, he also included retrospective comments. The entry in his recollections for 3 September 1909 reads: 'The 22nd Anniversary of our Wedding day – and we had very distinctively begun to drift apart.'[12] This is certainly an understatement. 1909 was the year in which Amy left New Zealand permanently for England, never to return.

One main point of disagreement between Fred and Amy was the cultural and social landscape of New Zealand. It is evident from the correspondence that Amy became increasingly unhappy in New Zealand; she described it as a 'one horse country' fit only for 'cabbages and sheep'.[13] Shortly before her permanent departure from New Zealand, while Fred was on a business trip, she wrote to her husband:

> I have had quite enough of the kind of society N.Z. offers to me, yesterday afternoon spent with Mrs Geo. Ross and Mrs Clarke Johnson being a sort of climax. I took a map to show them where Mary and I had been, and where I proposed to go, and I came to the conclusion that neither of them knew what the Riviera was, and as to the Tyrol, Botzen etc. etc. I might as well have talked to Maoris. You remember when I first came here, my meeting a room full of Hobson St. ladies who none of them knew what Chamber Music was.[14]

Fred, on the other hand, had an established social network; he was happy with his job and was not inclined to return to England. Amy returned alone in 1909, living off an allowance from Fred, but not seeking a divorce; in the same year, Fred and his daughter Mary moved to Timaru.

This chapter focuses on the last twenty-three years of Fred's life in Timaru (1909–32); the archive is particularly rich and records an active social and cultural life during this period. A port town on the east coast of the South Island, Timaru is the centre of a large, prosperous pastoral region (South Canterbury) and is located half-way between the larger cities of Dunedin and Christchurch. By the 1910s the population was just over 11,000 citizens, rising to 18,000 by 1930.

III

Barkas was essentially a typical reader of middle-brow literature; he read some English classics (Shakespeare and poetry by Matthew Arnold), as well as well-known contemporary writers such as Hugh Walpole (1884–1941) and Laurence Housman (1865–1959). Novels formed the largest proportion of his reading matter. Among them were Constance Fenimore Woolson's *Jupiter Lights* (1889), Mrs Humphry Ward's *David Grieve* (1891), Gertrude Atherton's *Rulers of Kings* (1904) and Rudyard Kipling's *Puck of Pook's Hill* (1906).[15] Robert Louis Stevenson was one of his favourite writers and he read most of Stevenson's novels, some of them repeatedly.[16] There is no modernist or avant-garde literature on his list, and none of the influential Russian writers, such as Tolstoy and Dostoyevsky. There are also very few New Zealand titles. Katherine Mansfield fails to appear in his letters, but in 1928 he was reading *Three Plays of New Zealand* (1922) by Alan Mulgan, and also Mulgan's *Home: A New Zealander's Adventure* (1927), which Barkas found 'very good indeed'.[17] In addition to New Zealand newspapers, English and North American papers and periodicals were part of his regular reading. *The Review of Reviews*, *The Nation*, and *The Round Table* were all journals he enjoyed reading, though the *Spectator* was his lifelong favourite.[18] Barkas appears to have been a mainstream, fairly conservative but open-minded consumer of literature.

He was a remarkably steady reader. Over the entire period of his correspondence he read an average of three books per month, in addition to newspapers and periodicals. However, there are years in which he kept no letters and there are long periods when he did not write about his reading activities; there are no records of his reading between 1893 and 1906, and for 1913 there is only evidence for three books. In reality he probably read more than three dozen titles per year. He liked reading novels, and often if he liked one particular author, he read several titles within a short period of time.[19] He seemed to have been rather indiscriminate in his choice of novels, often merely commenting that he liked a book, or that it bored him. He also enjoyed reading non-fiction, particularly history, biography and political essays. He read Edward Gibbon's *The Decline and Fall of the Roman Empire* (1776–89) in an eight-volume edition several times between 1908 and 1913.[20] His political interests in Socialism and Fabianism were reflected in his reading of H. G. Wells's *New Worlds for Old* (1908), which in Barkas's opinion was the 'best, clearest, most reasonable statement of Socialism I have come across'. He read Edward Bellamy's *Equality* (1897), Henry Hyde Champion's *The Root of the Matter* (1895) and George Bernard Shaw's *Intelligent Woman's Guide to Socialism and Capitalism* (1927), among others.[21]

Because the archive covers a long period, it is possible to draw a few conclusions about Barkas's reading over his lifetime. Unsurprisingly, he read a lot more after he retired and lived alone. Time was a crucial factor. While he was still working he complained about not being able to read as much as he would like: 'of course, the evenings are not long enough and there are not enough Sundays in the week – that's the trouble'.[22] The absence of family commitments also contributed to his retreat into books, with reading becoming a diversion and a kind of silent conversation. The amount of reading varied in relation to his circumstances, but the pattern also changed. With advancing years he preferred to re-read old favourites, non-fiction titles and plays. In 1922 he told Mary that novels increasingly bored him.[23] Of the 131 titles he read in 1928, just over half were fiction (forty-five were plays); the others were non-fiction titles, mainly political and historical works.

IV

After Barkas moved to Timaru in 1909, a large part of his reading matter came from the Timaru Public Library, one of the first free libraries in the country.[24] The chief librarian, Miss Evelyn Culverwell,[25] was mentioned regularly in his correspondence with Mary. Barkas evidently valued highly Culverwell's advice and trusted her recommendations. When she applied for a position at the Public Library in Dunedin in 1918, he wrote a flattering reference:

> Since Miss Culverwell took charge I have found the management so good, the attention so prompt & courteous, the arrangement of the

books so systematic and the supply of first class literature so well chosen & 'up to date' that all my one time dislike for using a Public Library for supplying my reading wants has gone.[26]

Likewise, Culverwell regarded Barkas as representative of ordinary readers in Timaru, even though he was perhaps better informed than most library users. He often recommended titles for acquisition, although the library committee did not always approve of his suggestions.[27] On numerous occasions, Culverwell handed him newly acquired books to see whether they would be suitable for general circulation.[28] Although the public library was a space which created and fostered a particular reading culture, this space was flexible in its boundaries and allowed input from readers, as well as being formed by the agencies controlling it.

Institutional control is evident from the 'Cupboard of Doubtfuls': volumes only distributed if asked for. One of the authors kept in the 'cupboard' was the ethical socialist Edward Carpenter. After Barkas had read his *My Days and Dreams* (1916), he expressed his surprise to Culverwell that he had never come across Carpenter's books in the library. He noted her response:

> She opened a cupboard near her desk and brought out two small red-bound volumes explaining that they had been among the considerable collection of books which old Wood had presented to the Library when his eyes failed and he had to give up reading. They were 'England's Ideal & other essays' and 'Civilization; its cause & cure'; I asked why they were not on the shelves – she'd never had time to read them and some one of the committee had heard that Ed. Carpenter was a writer on sex problems, a defender of Oscar Wilde, – so these books had been stowed in the cupboard of 'Doubtfuls' and forgotten.

As often before, Barkas was asked to give his opinion:

> They were handed to me and I'm to read & report: as yet I've only read the essay on 'England's Ideal' and that entitled 'Desirable Mansions' – both of which I thoroughly enjoyed because they contain so much that I, myself am inclined to preach on Simplification of Living – if the 'Cause & Cure of Civilization['] are no more dangerous or subversive of 'Sound Morality' than these, it's quite time both books were put into rapid circulation.[29]

This judgement is not surprising for a reader with an active interest in politics. While Barkas was never an active member of any political organization, he described his own political stance as centre-left and followed closely the activities of political movements (particularly Socialism and Fabianism) in New Zealand and elsewhere in the British Empire.

Another source for borrowing reading matter was his friends in Timaru. From the 'daily pages' to Mary it is possible to establish a local readers' network that recommended, loaned and discussed books and other reading material amongst themselves. One place they met was the Timaru Public Library:

> When I was at the Library yesterday morning returning Walpole's 'Green Mirror', Jack Cotterill came in & naturally annexed it, so we got talking of [Hugh] Walpole's books and I mentioned that I had not yet read 'The Duchess of Wrexe'. 'I'll mark it to be kept for you' said Miss Culverwell, and then added, 'but I'm afraid you'll find it rather dirty by this time – it seems to be always out'. Then Jack Cotterill chipped in to say he had a copy, that [he] thought it was at his office, & he'd be pleased to lend it to me. Sure enough when I got back to my office after lunch it was there nicely wrapped up awaiting me; so you see I've got plenty to read this week.[30]

Unsurprisingly, the middle-brow author Hugh Walpole's books are 'always out' and much desired, confirming the assumption that public libraries in the Anglophone world in the first decades of the twentieth century predominantly stocked middle-brow literature to be consumed by middle-class readers such as Barkas and his clique.[31] This connection to other readers was significant for Barkas's general reading experience. Frequently, he told Mary that he had spent the evening reading aloud with friends the latest essays or articles in *The Review of Reviews* or the *Spectator*.[32]

V

This shared reading experience is also an element in some of the groups to which Barkas belonged. In 1918 a number of Timaru men established the 'Round Table Discussion Group' as part of a British worldwide movement, with similar groups all around the Empire.[33] Inspired by and keeping a strong orientation on *The Round Table* magazine,[34] the men involved in this group focused on political and economic topics of the day, especially the future of the British Empire and the possibility of a

League of Nations or Commonwealth.[35] They met approximately every three weeks and spent the evening engaging in debate based on the chosen issue and reading. Interestingly, the group soon developed its own dynamics. Certain topics that were suggested in the accompanying magazine were ignored or condemned, others picked up. When by the early 1920s the Round Table movement had diminished in significance, the men involved in the Timaru group had come to appreciate a cultivated and 'systematic' discussion amongst each other to such an extent that it was decided to carry on under the new – and rather playful – name of 'Club for the Cultivation of Enjoyable Conversation'.[36]

Despite his obvious interest in imperial politics and his British loyalties, during the First World War Barkas was accused of being a German national or of having pro-German attitudes. He vehemently defended himself against such rumours, explaining his British origins and his general condemnation of war; he clearly thought these accusations were ridiculous.[37] It is likely that these rumours arose because of his unusual (and non-English sounding) surname and his open appreciation of German culture (especially music). In 1917, his manager at the Loan and Mercantile Agency insisted that 'it would be more than wise that (in the meantime) [he] would refrain from singing German songs'.[38] This episode is a prime example of the anti-German hysteria that befell New Zealanders of all intellectual backgrounds during the First World War, uneasy about the prospect of being attacked by 'enemies in their midst'.[39]

In the 1920s and early 1930s Barkas was also a member of a group called 'The Readers', made up largely of the same friends from the Round Table Group, and the more informal 'network' of readers Barkas belonged to, but not restricted to men. 'The Readers' met regularly (usually once a month), and re-enacted plays chosen at an earlier meeting. The organization of the group was strict, with a committee deciding on plays, the respective casts of actors and other organizational matters:

Thursday, 23 June 1932

Tweedy, Secty. to 'The Readers' looked in and left me a volume of 3 Plays by A. A. Milne so that I could read the middle one – 'The Dover Road' – and thus be ready for the casting committee who are to meet in this Parlour at 7 pm. tomorrow. Rereading 'The Dover Road' (which I'd read before, but some time ago & had mostly forgotten) afforded me good entertainment this afternoon; I just skimmed the other two – 'The Great Broxopp' and 'The Truth about Blaydes' by way of refreshing my memory.

Friday, 24 June 1932, Evening, 8.15 pm.

The Readers committee has just gone; we fixed up the cast for 'The Dover Road' which is to be read at Mr. Thomas' on Monday week; we also practically settled about 'The Readers' play to be got ready for the Drama League competitions.[40]

Amateur drama groups were a common feature of New Zealand life, especially after the establishment of a local branch of the British Drama League.[41] 'The Readers' was one of many such community groups in Timaru, all of which competed at annual competitions, but primarily provided entertainment and a cultured pastime in a semi-private setting for their members.

Barkas's wider cultural life is reflected in his reading; his interest in music, theatre and politics is interwoven with his reading experience. In the late 1920s a high proportion of his reading matter consisted of plays, clearly relating to his involvement in 'The Readers'. The Book diary he kept from 1927 until his death is full of annotations remarking that a particular play would be suitable for 'The Readers' and often with specific ideas of who could take which part.

VI

Through this archive it is possible to observe Barkas's development as a reader over time, and to sense alterations in his reading practices and patterns in relation to other events in his life. During the First World War his concern with geopolitical questions is evidently reflected in his choice of titles. After the outbreak of the war he resorted much more often than before to non-fiction material, often of political or historical content in relation to Continental Europe (especially Germany or Russia). In September 1918 he gave Mary a very detailed account of his reading of *Germany at Bay* by Major Haldane (1918):

The other book Miss Culverwell has given me to read 'Germany at Bay' is not at all easy reading, the man Major Macfall has about as 'rocky' a style as even I should care to tackle, he seems to be hammering at some idea and trying to make it as difficult and roundabout as he is able – I'm sticking to it but must say it's very hard to keep awake over it. What he appears to insist upon is that the Man-in-the-Street must study the Psychology of the Nations, more especially that of Prussia & the New Germany, so as to understand

International Strategy, the inevitableness of the present war, and the absolute necessity for the Allies to win and wipe out Autocratic Prussianism.[42]

Three days later his judgement had softened somewhat; he told Mary that the book 'is turning out fascinatingly interesting; I have just read his account of the Great retreat & the Battle of the Marne – one of the best and most illuminating I have yet found.'[43] Like many readers during this period, he developed a great interest in war stories, whether biographical or eye-witness accounts or novels. When the war lasted longer than anticipated, and its far-reaching consequences were beginning to be felt, his fondness for battle stories vanished. In 1922, after reading Robert Keable's *Simon Called Peter* (1921), he concluded:

I'm rather fed up with accounts of the war, its muddles, stupidities & wickedness, so I rather fear I should fail to get through the rather dismal story – the end of which seems to point to Rome as the only way of salvation & peace.[44]

VII

Reading was an integral part of Barkas's whole life, not just in his cultural and literary life. His reading was influenced by events, personal circumstances and by his wider cultural interests. Often he shared his reading experiences with friends and family, literally reading aloud or discussing books, and passing reading material on. This testifies to the complexities and multi-layered nature of reading experiences, the overlap of individual and collective reading experiences and the diversity of reading practices. For Barkas, reading was a way of social interaction within the middle classes of Timaru, enabling him to maintain his middle-class identity.

While it is only the archive of one individual, Barkas's connections to other readers and his frequent interactions with the Public Library confirm that he was not a unique or isolated reader. This case study of an individual historical reader can help interpret the wider intellectual and cultural life of particular reading communities in a specific context: Timaru, New Zealand, between 1909 and 1932. Barkas clearly existed within the extensive circulation of (and discussion about) printed matter in his community. At the same time, Barkas's reading connected him to a global print culture. His reading practice was similar to that in other places (particularly Britain), and he read newspapers and periodicals published in Britain and North America throughout his life. In a personal sense, Barkas was connected to British print culture through the frequent letters to his daughter Mary in England. While physically located in New Zealand, Barkas's reading enabled him to participate in a wider circulation of texts and ideas.

An in-depth case study of an historical reader like Fred Barkas highlights the significance of the connections between different, single reading experiences and activities; and between all the cultural activities and involvements of one individual. It reminds us that if we are to understand how reading and reading material leaves traces on the reader's mind and shapes social positions, we must locate reading within cultural and intellectual practices, not in an isolated and separated manner.

Notes and references

1. Fred Barkas to Charlie Barkas, 13 March 1891, 'Some Memories of a Mediocrity' [hereafter SMM], MS-Papers-2491-06, Alexander Turnbull Library [hereafter ATL].
2. Fred Barkas to Mary Barkas, 13 September 1918, 'Letters to a Daughter' [hereafter LD], MS-Papers-2491-28, ATL.
3. Newspaper clippings, in SMM, MS-Papers-2491-06, ATL.
4. Kay Sanderson has demonstrated the uniqueness of the archive, approaching it from the angle of women's history. See Kay Sanderson, 'A cabbage, a bohemian, and a genius, or ordinary middle-class folk?', *Turnbull Library Record*, 19 (1986), 61–75. On Mary Barkas, see also Kay Sanderson, 'Mary Barkas', in *The Book of New Zealand Women, Ko Kui Ma Te Kaupapa*, ed. by Charlotte Macdonald, Merimeri Penfold and Bridget Williams (Wellington: Bridget Williams Books, 1991), pp. 45–7.
5. Frederick Barkas to Charlie Barkas, 15 April 1892, SMM, MS-Papers-2491-06, ATL.
6. This is the title of the collection of letters from Fred Barkas to relatives and friends, now at the ATL.
7. Stephen Colclough, *Consuming Texts, Readers and Reading Communities, 1695–1870* (Basingstoke: Palgrave Macmillan, 2007), p. viii.
8. Included in the collection are eighteen volumes of Mary's letters to her father.
9. SMM, MS-Papers-2491-01, ATL.
10. Abbreviation of 'Observations & Impressions'.
11. Fred Barkas to Mary Barkas, 24 August 1922, LD, MS-Papers-2491-30, ATL.
12. Presumably, Barkas made this comment when preparing his work for binding in 1930. It appears on a sheet entitled 'From the old exercise book', and bound amongst the copies of his letters. SMM, MS-Papers-2491-07, ATL.
13. Cited in Sanderson, 'Mary Barkas', p. 63.
14. Amy Barkas to Fred Barkas, 3 November 1909, 'Some letters from my wife', MS-Papers-2491-38, ATL.

15. Years in brackets refer to the date of first publication.
16. '"Memorandum of books read", 26 June 1907, "Kidnapped", for the Nth. time, read it with greatest enjoyment', in SMM, MS-Papers-2491-07, ATL.
17. Fred Barkas to Mary Barkas, 08 January 1928, in Mary Barkas Papers, 89-339, folder 2, ATL.
18. For the *Spectator* being the most suitable publication for his centre-left political stance, see Fred Barkes to Mary Barkas, 05 June 1922, LD, MS-Papers-2491-30, ATL.
19. E.g., in November 1892 he read three titles by Constance Fenimore Woolson within a few days; in November 1907 he read A. C. Benson's *Beside Still Waters*, followed by *From a College Window* by the same author; and in late 1927 and early 1928 he read four plays by the British playwright Harley Granville Barker within less than a month. See SMM, MS-Papers-2491-06 and -07 and Mary Barkas Papers, 89-339, folder 5, ATL.
20. See several entries in SMM, MS-Papers-2491-07 and -08, ATL.
21. References in order of mentioning: the first three titles are included in a list of books read, entries for December 1908 and 15 September 1909, SMM, MS-Papers-2491-07. The rationalist Barkas concluded about Bellamy's utopia: 'A delightful society, if only it were possible'. For G. B. Shaw, see Fred Barkas to Mary Barkas, 23 July 1928, Mary Barkas Papers, 89-339, folder 5, ATL.
22. Fred Barkas to Mary, 30 July 1917, LD, MS-Papers-2491-27, ATL.
23. See letters of 18 January 1922 and 7 July 1922, LD, MS-Papers-2491-30, ATL.
24. Established with the Timaru Public Library Act in 1906 and opened in new premises as a free library in June 1909. See M. J. O'Connor, 'The development of the Timaru Public Library as an educational institution' (unpublished MA thesis, University of Otago, 1955), pp. 13–14.
25. Miss Evelyn Culverwell was appointed the first female chief librarian in New Zealand in April 1913; see O'Connor, 'The development', p. 18.
26. Reference for Miss Culverwell, dated 15 July 1918, in LD, MS-Papers-2491-28, ATL.
27. Fred Barkas to Mary Barkas, 24 February 1919, LD, MS-Papers-2491-28, ATL.
28. For example: '[Miss Culverwell] had handed me a book on Friday morning with a request as to how I considered it should be classified; the title is "LIMANORA" and the sub-title "The Island of Progress", the author signs himself Godfrey Sweven . . . [It] is rather long, I might almost say prolix, and certainly very fantastic; it has a sort of kinship with "The Coming Race" with a touch of "Erewhon" and a general flavour of Utopias.' Fred Barkas to Mary Barkas, 25 August 1918, MS-Papers-2491-28, ATL.
29. Fred Barkas to Mary, 12 July 1922, LD, MS-Papers-2491-30, ATL. The category of 'doubtful' books stocked but only loaned on request was also used by the main British circulating libraries such as Mudie's. See Mary Hammond, *Reading, Publishing and the Formation of Literary Taste in England, 1880–1914* (Aldershot: Ashgate, 2006), p. 28.
30. Fred Barkas to Mary, 24 July 1818, LD, MS-Papers-2491-28, ATL.
31. Also part of this network was the rector of the local Boys High School, William Thomas, the editor of the *Timaru Herald*, William Frederick Alexander and the book collector Percy Watts Rule.
32. There are numerous references to this shared reading experience, e.g. in July 1918 he read an Empire Service League pamphlet to his friends Lilian and

Blanche Hall, which 'they thoroughly enjoyed'. Fred Barkas to Mary, 8 July 1918, LD, MS-Papers-2491-28, ATL.

33. Formed in 1908 and restricted to men; see John Kendle, 'The Round Table movement: Lionel Curtis and the formation of the New Zealand groups in 1910', *New Zealand Journal of History*, 1 (1967), 33–50.

34. The quarterly *The Round Table* was published by Macmillan, London from 1910. The editorial note in the 1910s stated: 'The affairs of *The Round Table* in each portion of the Empire [are] in the hands of local residents who [are] responsible for all articles on the politics of their own country'. The Timaru Group contributed an article on New Zealand for the March issue of 1919, elaborating on 'The Imperial War Cabinet and conference, political tendencies, industrial disputes and the liquor traffic', *The Round Table*, 34 (March 1919), 412–28.

35. For example, at a meeting on 31 August 1918 the men met at Mr W. Thomas's, Rectory, Boys' High School to discuss 'Problems of the Commonwealth', but without much agreement. The group continued with this subject and a few weeks later Barkas wrote: 'Campbell has presented me with a copy of Lionel Curtis's "The Problem of the Commonwealth"; I am to read a chapter or two at our future "Round Table Group" meetings so as to form a basis for our study of the "Problem" . . . By way of rehearsal I read the Introduction & Chap 1 to the Halls after supper last night – it is very clearly written & quite interesting.' Fred Barkas to Mary Barkas, 31 August 1918 and 30 September 1918, LD, MS-Papers-2491-28, ATL.

36. Fred Barkas to Mary Barkas, 8 and 12 July 1922, LD, MS-Papers-2491-30, ATL.

37. Letter to Clarke Johnson, 10 October 1917, SMM, MS-Papers-2491-08, ATL. See also Fred Barkas to Mary Barkas, 10 October 1917, LD, MS-Papers-2491-27, ATL.

38. Letter dated 16 October 1917, included in LD, MS-Papers-2491-27, ATL.

39. The most prominent example of anti-German public sentiment and its far-reaching consequences was the case of George von Zedlitz, Professor of Modern Languages at Wellington's Victoria University College until his dismissal in October 1915. See Andrew Francis, 'Anti-alienism in New Zealand during the Great War: the von Zedlitz affair, 1915', *Immigrants and Minorities*, 24 (2007): 251–76; and Andrew Francis, '"To be truly British we must be anti-German": patriotism, citizenship and anti-alienism in New Zealand during the Great War' (unpublished PhD thesis, Victoria University of Wellington, 2009).

40. Fred Barkas to Mary Barkas, in Mary Barkas Papers, 89-339, folder 2, ATL.

41. On amateur drama groups in New Zealand see Howard McNaughton, 'Drama', in *The Oxford History of New Zealand Literature in English*, ed. Terry Sturm (Auckland: Oxford University Press, 1998), pp. 331–9.

42. Fred Barkas to Mary Barkas, 5 September 1918, LD, MS-Papers-2491-28, ATL.

43. Fred Barkas to Mary Barkas, 8 September 1918, LD, MS-Papers-2491-28, ATL.

44. Fred Barkas to Mary Barkas, 19 April 1922, LD, MS-Papers-2491-30, ATL.

11
Books Behind Bars: Mahatma Gandhi's Community of Captive Readers

Ian Desai

> Why does one read books? To instruct oneself, amuse
> oneself, train one's mind . . . certainly all this and
> much more. Ultimately it is to understand life with
> its thousand faces and to learn how to live life. Our
> individual experiences are so narrow and limited, if
> we were to rely on them alone we would also remain
> narrow and limited. But books give us the experiences
> and thoughts of innumerable others, often the wisest
> of their generation, and lift us out of our narrow ruts.
> (Jawaharlal Nehru, 'Prison Diary', 1935)[1]

Mohandas K. Gandhi, popularly known as the Mahatma, first discovered the power of reading in the confines of colonial penitentiaries. Although Gandhi had been exposed to the routines of rigorous reading as a law student in London, he maintained a sceptical attitude toward the benefits of bibliographic pursuits well into his adulthood. Gandhi rhetorically eschewed book learning for much of his life, and yet he also developed a sophisticated print-based knowledge enterprise, including thousands of books that served as the intellectual basis of his engagement with imperial rule and efforts toward the development of an independent India. Ironically, the origins of this knowledge enterprise evolved from Gandhi's experiences in colonial prisons during the first part of the twentieth century. From his first imprisonment in 1908 until his final jail sentence, between 1942 and 1944, Gandhi developed and refined a reading programme that played a major role in his public life. He extended this programme to include his most trusted colleagues and advisors so that jail sentences became opportunities for collective engagement with books and collaborative mobilization of the information and ideas within them. These reading practices were exported from one penitentiary to another, meaning that the colonial system itself helped circulate the very conditions, materials and people that ultimately were able to overcome its power.

This chapter examines the advent of Gandhi's reading practices and his cultivation of a community of readers in the context of prison life in colonial South Africa and India. Beginning with Gandhi's own experiences and then turning to the book-based intellectual network that he and his closest associates maintained in prison, what follows provides an overview of a group of individuals who 'read obsessively, in a dedicated and concentrated way, seeking self-improvement, enlightenment [and] emancipation'.[2] Ultimately, Gandhi and his associates were able to subvert the British attempt to use prison as a place of control by transforming it into an intellectual resource that benefited their resistance to imperialism. For Gandhi's community, books behind bars became the material basis for inverting the power relations between inmate and jailer, subject and ruler – and the subversive power of reading became a key aspect of the authoring of the end of empire.

Good behaviour: Gandhi's reading practices in jail

Between January 1908 and August 1933, Gandhi was arrested fourteen times and cumulatively spent more than four years behind bars in South Africa and India. During this quarter of a century, he transformed from a relatively unknown provincial barrister into a political and social reformer with an international reputation. Gandhi's repeated jail terms facilitated this transformation, allowing him to rest, read and reflect in an otherwise tumultuous period in his life. Gandhi's experiences as an inmate were important building blocks in the making of his 'Mahatmaship'. During his career as a prisoner, he was able to practice rigorous self-discipline and capitalize on the opportunities for personal development that prison provided.[3] Most histories of his life and career gloss over his time behind bars, thereby creating lacunae in the otherwise detailed historiography. Prison-going was a critical part of the Gandhi phenomenon: it simultaneously drew widespread positive publicity for Gandhi; forced the Raj to manage negative publicity in India and Britain; inspired masses to court arrest in the cause for *swaraj* (home rule), thereby instilling courage and a spirit of sacrifice in them; afforded many of the political prisoners the opportunity to engage in significant intellectual undertakings; and served to bond Gandhi's political allies and personal associates into an tightly-knit intellectual community around the Mahatma.

Beginning with his first imprisonment in 1908, Gandhi took advantage of the ample time jail provided for reading, and he immersed himself in a cosmopolitan selection of books. Gandhi read works including Francis Bacon's annotated essays, Thomas Carlyle's *Life of Robert Burns,* and T. H. Huxley's *On Education.* He also read extensively about the life and work of Socrates and produced a series in Gujarati entitled 'Story of a Soldier of Truth' paraphrasing Plato's account of the life of Socrates.[4] Several years later, while serving time in a Pretoria jail, Gandhi returned to Carlyle, this time investing his energies into that author's history of the French Revolution. He also read Giuseppe Mazzini's *The Duties of Man and Other Essays* (which he recommended to his son Manilal), Robert Louis Stevenson's *The Strange Case of Dr Jekyll and Mr Hyde,* and works of Emerson. As the breadth of his reading expanded, Gandhi encouraged his family and colleagues at the Phoenix Settlement and Tolstoy Farm also to invest their time in intensive reading. Writing to Henry Polak from Pretoria Jail, Gandhi recommended that the 'inmates' of Phoenix and Tolstoy Farm read practical manuals relevant to communal living (such as a how-to manual on laundering) and Tolstoy's *Life* and *My Confessions* among other books.[5] Writing to Tolstoy himself, Gandhi related that he and his colleague Herman Kallenbach were so inspired by the writer's work that they had agreed to name their second experimental community in South Africa 'Tolstoy Farm' in his honour.[6]

Gandhi's time in prison enhanced his enthusiasm for reading and provided him the opportunity to develop his intellectual capacity in significant ways. Prison changed his approach to book-learning by forcing him to turn to books where previously he had relied on experience (especially of people) as his primary resource of information and knowledge. As he learned how to mine books for knowledge he could employ in his work, Gandhi reflected on the importance of prison in the development of this aspect of his life:

> Amongst the many benefits that I received in these three months, one was the opportunity I got to read. At the start, I must admit, I fell into moods of despondency and thoughtfulness while reading, and was even tired of these hardships, and my mind played antics like a monkey. Such a state of mind leads many towards lunacy, but in my case, my books saved me. They made up in a large measure for the loss of the society of my Indian brethren. I always got about three hours to read . . . So I was able to go through about thirty books, and cover others, which comprised English, Hindi, Gujarati, Sanskrit and

Tamil works . . . This kept my mind in a state of cheerfulness, night and day. If disappointment or despair attacked me at times, I would think over what I had read and my heart would instantly become gladdened and thank God . . . I would only say, in this world good books make up for the absence of good companions, so that all Indians, if they want to live happily in jail, should accustom themselves to reading good books.[7]

In South Africa reading became Gandhi's principal method for coping successfully with incarceration, thereby creating a template for his future terms in prison.

Gandhi's next major imprisonment occurred a decade later, after he had moved back to India. In March 1922, he was arrested and sentenced to six years imprisonment at Yeravda Central Prison in Poona. This institution became his residence for the following twenty-two months.[8] During that time, he was once again able to focus on books.

At 6-30 a.m. I commence my studies. No light is allowed. As soon therefore [as] one can read, I commence work. It stops at 7 p.m. after which it is impossible to read or write without artificial light . . . My studies include reading the Koran, Ramayana by Tulsidas, books on Christianity given by Mr. Standing, study of Urdu. These literary studies receive six hours. Four hours are given to hand-spinning and carding.[9]

Gandhi then described how he 'used books or my extra clothing as a pillow' and how he was provided a separate cell in which to do his work during the day. With ample time and office space devoted to his intellectual pursuits, Gandhi was extremely productive while in prison. He read more than one hundred books during this incarceration on a broad array of subjects, including Edward Gibbon's *The Decline and Fall of the Roman Empire*, Goethe's *Faust*, Ernst Haeckel's *Evolution of Man: A Popular Scientific Study*, William James's *Varieties of Religious Experiences*, *The Laws of Manu*, and *Natural History of Birds*. In the last four months of this confinement he wrote more than half of his memoir of his experiences in South Africa. Reading at least a book a week, in addition to keeping up his correspondence, writing and performing his daily spinning, was an enjoyable routine for Gandhi. These intellectual practices that he developed during his early imprisonments became an important model for his own future incarcerations and those of his colleagues.

Everybody's Boswell:[10] Mahadev Desai and Gandhi's brain trust behind bars

Mahadev Desai began working as Gandhi's secretary in 1917; by 1919 Gandhi was referring to Desai as his 'heir'.[11] Desai demurred from undertaking such a public mantle and dedicated himself to his efforts behind-the-scenes of Gandhi's enterprise. In addition to keeping the Mahatma organized, Desai co-edited with Gandhi the latter's publications, *Navajivan* and *Young India*.[12] On Gandhi's request, he also assisted other nationalist leaders in their journalistic endeavours. It was while working on Motilal Nehru's paper *The Independent* that Desai was arrested on 24 December 1921. He was sentenced to thirteen months in prison and served the complete sentence. During that time, his status as a political prisoner enabled him to read extensively – though books of a political nature were prohibited.[13] He immersed himself in a study of the Bible, Glover's *Jesus of History* ('a book of abounding interest'), Tulsidas' *Ramayana*, and Kabir's songs. These last verses served as his 'memory exercises' which would become 'memorised treasure . . . if we are to be put into solitary cells'.[14] Having primed himself to suffer the hardships of prison, Desai was more comfortable than he had expected to be: 'I have had a life quite after my heart, a life of regimen and diet, a life of religious study and meditation.' Prison afforded him a rare opportunity to rest, read and write at length and he made the most of the opportunity. It proved a necessary vacation, for by the time Desai was released the Mahatma was behind bars, and a great deal of the responsibility for running Gandhi's enterprise fell to him. Desai would not have another such enforced vacation for the rest of the decade.

In March 1932, two months after Gandhi had again become a 'guest' of Yeravda Prison – which he called Yeravda *Mandir* (temple) – Desai was transferred from Nasik Prison (where he was serving another jail term himself) to Yeravda in order to join the Mahatma and Sardar Vallabhbhai Patel.[15] During the time these three men spent together, they expanded the practice of solitary study in prison into a collective intellectual practice. Describing this collegiate situation, Rajmohan Gandhi explains that 'Mahadev studied French, Vallabhbhai Sanskrit and Gandhi astronomy'.[16] In addition to studying French and fulfilling his normal secretarial roles for Gandhi, Desai also tutored Patel in Sanskrit. The imprisonment was an enjoyable and fruitful experience for all three men.[17] Soon after being released alongside the Mahatma in 1933, Desai was back in prison serving a nine-month sentence on his own. Desai and Gandhi had not been separated for such a long period in almost a decade. Nevertheless, he managed to pass the time in prison in a manner that rendered service to the Mahatma from a distance. As his cellmate was a common criminal who only spoke Kannada and his jailers did not let him write letters to his wife and son in Gujarati (the only language his family knew), he was totally isolated.[18] The only resources he did not lack were time and books. Given his natural disposition for intellectual work, he turned to reading and writing to occupy himself productively in jail.

During the course of Desai's nine-month stay in Belgaum Central Prison over sixty books in English and a dozen in French were delivered to him.[19] Though it is difficult to determine exactly which parts of these books Desai read, his extensive underlining and annotations in many of them attest to the vast extent of his reading.[20] The subject matter of his reading was eclectic and reflected his wide-ranging interests. The steady arrival of new books brought either from his own personal collection or sent to him by people in India and around the world, illustrates the dynamic nature of the knowledge network on which the Gandhi phenomenon relied.[21] Some of the books, like Eugene O'Neill's play *Strange Interlude*, were sent to Desai from as far away as London; others, such as David Lloyd George's *War Memoirs*, were despatched to Desai from friends within India. The majority of titles that were delivered to Desai during this nine-month incarceration came from his personal collection. Certain volumes were sent to Desai by other political prisoners residing in the Raj's penal institutions, including Belgaum itself.[22] The transmission of knowledge through this dynamic intellectual network was not stifled by prison: in fact the knowledge enterprise supporting Gandhi was often enhanced by the intellectual exchange between associates behind bars, even in different jails.

An intriguing example of this phenomenon survives in the form of a book that was sent to Desai in Belgaum by Patel who was at the time serving a sentence in Nasik Central Prison. In March of 1934, Patel sent Desai a novel called *Durbar* by Dennis Kincaid that had been published in London in 1933. From the confines of his cell, Patel had managed to secure the book months after it was published in England.[23] On the inside cover of the copy of the book delivered to Desai on 23 March 1934, is inscribed the following message:

> Not a very extraordinary performance, but the Author is [two words blotted out here, perhaps by the censor?] serving at present in the Judicial Department in this very District and comes from a family of British Indian Administrators, his father is retired Judge of

his majesty's High Court at Bombay. It is therefore interesting to know what he thinks about conditions in Indian States, especially at a time when it is proposed to [perpetuate?] these conditions by the coming federation. This story is being reproduced in the Times of India chapter by chapter with good number of illustrations at present.

To Mahadev Desai   With love from Vallabhbhai.
12/3/34
N.R.C.P.

Perhaps *Durbar* was not a very extraordinary performance after all, yet the position of its author in colonial India made the book important enough to Patel for him to swiftly share it with Desai.[24] Despite their separate confinement, prison afforded these two men an opportunity for intellectual exchange and development which they seized.

The copy of *Durbar* that Patel and Desai shared demonstrates how the circulation of books within Gandhi's inner circle operated, and how this exchange facilitated their intellectual engagement with the imperial system. Desai was the key node in this book circuit. While Gandhi was otherwise preoccupied with the public duties of being the Mahatma, Desai exercised his voracious appetite for books and passed on useful information from his reading to Gandhi.[25] Since Gandhi had a tendency to focus his reading on specific subjects as they caught his attention, Desai became the resident generalist within Gandhi's inner circle and an intellectual arbiter on Gandhi's behalf. Even when books were sent explicitly to Gandhi, they often ended up in Desai's possession. This is the case with a number of novels by the American writer Upton Sinclair, who sent his books to Gandhi throughout the 1930s. While in Yeravda in 1932, Gandhi requested that several of the copies of the books Sinclair had sent to him (and which he had instructed to be deposited in the Ashram library) be delivered to the prison.[26] He recorded reading one of Sinclair's books, *The Wet Parade* (a novel about prohibition in America), with enjoyment in Yeravda in 1932.[27] After their release from prison, Desai secured his own copy of *The Wet Parade* and later in the decade when Sinclair sent to Gandhi *Co-Op: A Novel of Living Together, Depression Island, Oil: A Novel*, and *World's End* they all came to reside in Desai's collection.[28] Desai augmented the Sinclair collection by acquiring *The Wet Paradise*, a dramatized version of *The Wet Parade*.[29] Since Gandhi had expressed an interest in Sinclair's works, they became Desai's responsibility to study and store.

Another example of the rich fabric of intellectual exchange that occurred out of view within Gandhi's enterprise is preserved in the pages of a book called *The Colonial Policy of British Imperialism* by Ralph Fox.[30] The writing inside the cover of the book indicates that Nehru was given the book in Alipore Central Jail on 1 May 1934 and after reading it, sent it to Desai who received it after he was released from Belgaum Central Prison in late June of the same year.[31] While this exchange follows the distribution pattern discussed above, what is revealing about this volume is the presence of both Nehru and Desai's underlining and markings in the book, side-by-side throughout.[32] Despite sharing a common text, these two men read this book in distinct ways. Any reference to Marx, Engels or other socialist material is consistently marked by Nehru's pencil but ignored by Desai's.[33] Conversely, an early sentence that 'Gandhi has become a popular joke' is greeted by an incredulous exclamation point from Desai but passed over by Nehru.[34] In addition to these discrepancies in assessment, Desai and Nehru's active readings of this common text also converge in places. Desai occasionally finds cause to mark some passages which Nehru has already marked with his pencil.[35] In one instance, Nehru's underlining stops after the first sentence of the paragraph; Desai's underlying picks up exactly where Nehru left off, leaving ambiguity as to whether he saw additional meaning in the rest of the passage that Nehru chose not to mark or thought the second half of the passage crucial while Nehru held the opposite view. Thus, '[l]ike footprints in the sand, these markings allow us to trace the course of the journey but not necessarily the intent, where attention caught and lingered, where it rushed forward and where it ultimately ended'.[36] Given that both Desai and Nehru were avid book collectors and scholars in their attention to details, further consideration is needed to excavate the social life of the books they read: where they came from, when they read them, how they read them, and ultimately how they used them in their public work.

Writing up: putting prison reading to work

The above vignettes demonstrate the nature of the movement of books within Gandhi's enterprise, and Desai's pivotal position in that distribution system. Prison, and the luxury of time that jail provided, gave this network an opportunity to immerse themselves in intellectual affairs. Such close reading served the interests of the freedom movement by keeping the nationalist vanguard fluent in the intellectual idiom of their imperial adversaries and informing their outlook and the decisions they took in politics. It also enabled them to share and repackage information mined from their reading into evidence they wielded, often through the written word, in their intellectual struggle with the imperial system.

Not all such repackaging of information was undertaken for overtly political purposes: Gandhi and his colleagues had deep commitments to social and religious causes which they did not neglect in their intellectual work. Prison was a particularly opportune time to pursue these non-political issues as they were often banned from engaging in political work of any sort – and yet the nature of their knowledge enterprise enabled them to utilize their 'non-political' reading to inform their broader political programme. Desai's 1933–34 prison sentence during which he had no companions inside prison and greatly restricted ability to communicate with the outside world, gave him the opportunity to pursue a major scholarly project in service of Gandhi's knowledge enterprise. Utilizing the books he had at his disposal and drawing on his sharp memory for further source material, Desai undertook a major writing project that consumed him throughout his arrest.[37] The scope and sophistication of the resulting work, *The Gospel of Selfless Action, or The Gita According To Gandhi*, testify to the unique intellect and scholarly abilities that Desai placed in Gandhi's service even when he was separated from the Mahatma.[38]

Throughout his 1932 incarceration with Gandhi and Patel, Desai maintained a full secretarial work-load, but during his isolated confinement in Belgaum Central Prison he was not constrained for time. Not being able to serve Gandhi directly made Desai restless and he took the opportunity to devise an avenue of service to be performed remotely. Three years earlier in 1930 Gandhi had published his own Gujarati translation of the famous Sanskrit work the 'Bhagavad Gita'. The 'Gita' was the most important text in Gandhi's life and therefore in the lives of many of his followers and associates: sections of it were read daily at the Ashram prayer meetings and Gandhi never tired of discussing it or invoking it. The 'Gita' was the intellectual keystone of *satyagraha* (a term invented by Gandhi, meaning 'truth-force') and its importance to Gandhi is difficult to overstate. After Gandhi was arrested in the wake of the Salt March in April 1930, a member of the Ashram complained that his translation of the 'Gita' was difficult to understand. Gandhi responded by writing eighteen letters to the inmates of the Ashram expounding on the meaning of each chapter of the text, one letter per chapter.[39] Given the time Gandhi had devoted to translating the work and assiduously explaining his views on it, Desai thought it necessary that Gandhi's translation of the 'Gita' from Sanskrit into Gujarati be translated into English along with his interpretative commentary, so as to make the material available to a 'larger public'.[40] Translating Gandhi was familiar ground for Desai: in addition to the immense amount of translation he performed in the course of his secretarial duties for the Mahatma, Desai had also undertaken the translation of Gandhi's *Autobiography* into English from Gujarati between 1927–9. His time alone in Belgaum Prison gave him the opportunity he needed to translate Gandhi's translation and commentary into English.

What began as a straightforward translation project, however, quickly mushroomed into a massive intellectual undertaking. Even with a limited collection of reference materials at his disposal, Desai uncovered numerous points of interest in Gandhi's work and the 'Gita' that he felt needed explaining in an introduction to the translation. As the work progressed, Desai had books delivered to him for this undertaking.[41] In addition to many likely titles on the 'Gita' and spiritual matters, Desai also utilized books he received on a wide range of subjects, including books on Islam, Christianity and modern science.[42] Perhaps the most intriguing instance of his fruitful intellectual roaming was his use of the lives and works of western writers. For example, when discussing the last chapter of the 'Gita' and theories of knowledge and human nature, Desai cites Shakespeare (specifically *Julius Caesar* and *Cymbeline*), Plato, Aristotle, Bacon, Spinoza, Herbert Spencer and Henry Drummond. All the while, he continuously weaves the meaning of the 'Gita' into this sustained display of intellectual verve.[43] Only some of the books he mentions and quotes were with him in the prison at the time. Mixing the contents of his exceptional memory with the substance of his immediate reading, Desai produced a work that blended together an impressive number of literary references, especially related to the major religious traditions of the world: '[n]ot that I went out of my way to hunt for those parallels, but I took them just as they came in the course of my quiet reading in my prison cell'.[44]

When he completed his introductory essay to the translation, it was as long as the annotated translation and Gandhi's commentary combined. Thus in *The Gita According To Gandhi* Desai had written a work of formidable scholarship which was a tour de force of his own learning. He had also subliminated the message of humility which *The Gita* advocates, as is evident from the outset of his introduction:

> Let me make it clear that I lay no more claim to scholarship than does Gandhiji, but I am myself a student – as I hope to remain until

my dying day – and it is out of sympathy for the needs of people of my kind that I have presumed to introduce this additional matter . . . as I read Gandhiji's translation over and over again I felt that certain doubts and difficulties that troubled me were likely to trouble other minds too, and that I should offer what explanation I could about them.[45]

In authoring this commentary on Gandhi's philosophy, Desai rendered a remarkable service to the Mahatma that has stood the test of time as one of the most unique and insightful sources of information into Gandhi's personal philosophy.

Conclusion

This chapter illustrates how Gandhi, Desai and their closest associates developed intellectually through reading and writing in prison. These men had active intellects that contributed to the deliberative process informing their social, political and spiritual ideals. Through excavating the intellectual substratum of their 'private' lives in prison, the foundations of their public actions are revealed in their dynamic complexity: their intellectual abilities were conditioned and enhanced by their prison experiences. Books mattered deeply to them and the knowledge they acquired through them was constantly being put to use throughout their lives.[46] Within Gandhi's circle, this was true for Mahadev Desai more than anyone else. His private library, which was dedicated to facilitating his work on behalf of the Mahatma, attests to the scope and quality of Gandhi's knowledge enterprise. If, as Timothy Ryback (following Walter Benjamin) argues, you can 'tell a lot about a man by the books he keeps' and 'a private library serves as a permanent and credible witness to the character of its collector', then Desai's library remains a rare source for insight into an extraordinary man.[47] That Desai was able to continue performing his role as Gandhi's principal intellectual resource even when he was in prison is a testament to the unique contribution he made to Gandhi's enterprise. Desai facilitated the intellectual pursuits of many other members of Gandhi's inner circle and through the practice of common reading they were able to strengthen their mutual bonds even within the confines of prison. The reading and writing practices Gandhi and company developed in prison were essential to building and extending the intellectual arm of their movement. Incarceration created a community around Gandhi that had an enhanced capacity for deep intellectual engagement, a trait that was critical in their struggle with British imperial rule on both ideological and practical levels. Books behind bars were a powerful force in the hands of this unique community of readers.

Notes and references

1. Uma Iyengar, *Oxford India Nehru* (New Delhi: Oxford University Press, 2007), p. 678.
2. Martyn Lyons, *A History of Reading and Writing in the Western World* (London: Palgrave Macmillan, 2010), p. 2.
3. Gandhi seized on the term *inmate* and notions of incarceration to inform his life outside jail. He deliberately called the members of his ashram communities 'inmates' to stress that the type of discipline he expected them to develop should be commensurate with prison life.
4. He published the series in his journal *Indian Opinion*, although when he tried to disseminate versions of the text later in India they were promptly banned by the Government. See Ananda M. Pandiri, *A Comprehensive, Annotated Bibliography on Mahatma Gandhi* (Ahmedabad: Navajivan, 2002), pp. 297, 302.
5. Gandhi to H. S. L. Polak, 26 April 1909, in *The Collected Works of Mahatma Gandhi* [hereafter *CWMG*], Vol. IX (New Delhi: Publications Division, Government of India, 1958–94), p. 213.
6. Gandhi to Leo Tolstoy, 15 August 1910, in *CWMG*, Vol. X, pp. 306–7. See also Pandiri, *A Comprehensive*, p. 306.
7. V. B. Kher, *Stonewalls Do Not A Prison Make* (Ahmedabad: Navajivan, 1964), pp. 102–4.
8. In 1924, Gandhi was released early after undergoing emergency surgery for acute appendicitis. The operation almost cost him his life.
9. Gandhi to Hakim Ajmal Khan, 14 April 1922, in *CWMG*, Vol. XXIII, p. 133; Kher, *Stonewalls*, p. 117.
10. *Everybody's Boswell* was the title of a book Desai had in prison between 1933 and 1934. He was often called Gandhi's Boswell. See volume No. 19 in the Mahadev Desai Library [hereafter MDL], Gandhi Sangrahalaya, Ahmedabad. The European language volumes of this library are listed in the appendices of I. R. B. Desai, 'Producing the Mahatma: Communication, Community, and Political Theatre Behind the Gandhi Phenomenon' (unpublished DPhil thesis, University of Oxford, 2009).
11. Narayan Desai, *The Fire and the Rose* (Ahmedabad: Navajivan, 1995), p. 695. Mahadev Desai is unrelated to the present author.
12. See Narayan Desai, *The Fire and the Rose*, pp. 200ff.
13. Mahadev Desai was a true bibliophile. This is evident from the breadth of his library as well as accounts of his character and his habits: 'I first met him in 1931, when he accompanied Mr. Gandhi to London for the second Round-table Conference, and worked with him for several weeks. His selfless services impressed me deeply, as did his intelligence and reliability – to say nothing of his sense of humour, without which we could not have survived those strenuous days . . . He liked going into English homes and seeing how people lived. *No sooner was he inside than he would gravitate to the bookshelves.*

It could be seen how much he loved books by the way he hand[l]ed them. And one could be quite sure of finding him in some book shop if he had a few minutes to spare.' Letter from a correspondent to the *Manchester Guardian*, 19 August 1942 (Column 3, page 7). Emphasis added.

14. Narayan Desai, *The Fire and the Rose*, pp. 238, 240.

15. At times the Government granted requests to have a member of Gandhi's entourage serving a sentence in another jail transferred to his jail to assist with non-political work.

16. Rajmohan Gandhi, *Patel: A Life* (Ahmedabad: Navajivan, 2005), p. 226.

17. Their imprisonment is well documented in Rajmohan Gandhi, *Patel*; and Judith M. Brown, *Gandhi and Civil Disobedience* (Cambridge: Cambridge University Press, 1977), pp. 311ff.

18. Narayan Desai, *The Fire and the Rose*, p. 593.

19. Approximately half of Desai's personal library remains intact and accessible to researchers at the Gandhi Sangrahalaya in Ahmedabad. The other half of the collection remains in the personal possession of Narayan Desai, Mahadev Desai's son, at his ashram in Veddchi in southern Gujarat. For the purposes of this work, the European language books of the Ahmedabad portion of the collection have been consulted. Analysis of remaining volumes of the collection will likely reveal more volumes that Desai had in Belgaum jail.

20. See I. R. B. Desai, 'Producing the Mahatma', Appendix IV.

21. The prison stamps indicating each volume's date of arrival at the jail provide insight into the sequence of Desai's reading. Transferring books from the outside to prisoners was not always easy. Books were often censored or at times lost by the jail authorities. Book messengers were not always able to perform their duties adequately either. Gandhi's son Devdas managed to lose 'as many as 80 books at the jail gate in 1930. It was the goodness of the stranger that he delivered them to us.' See Gandhi to Devdas Gandhi, *CWMG*, Vol. XLIX, p. 423.

22. See, for example, R. D. Ranade, *A Constructive Survey of Upanishadic Thought*, which was already in the possession of other political prisoners detained at Belgaum in 1932 and subsequently passed on to Desai during the course of his own imprisonment. See I. R. B. Desai, 'Producing the Mahatma', Appendix IV, MDL No. 774.

23. A small stamp on the inside cover of the book reveals that it came from England to India via Taraporevala Booksellers in Bombay.

24. Dennis Kincaid (1905–37) entered the Indian Civil Service (ICS) in Bombay after attending Balliol College, Oxford from 1924–1928 and drowned in 1937. He was the son of C. A. Kincaid, also a Balliol and ICS Bombay man. These details are from the Balliol College registers in Oxford (Judith Brown, personal communication, January 2008).

25. Ironically, this process of information filtering was similar to work Desai did before he met Gandhi when he was employed by the Bombay Government censor to review Indian language books and translate parts of them into English when necessary.

26. Gandhi to Premabehn Kantak, 3 April 1932, in *CWMG*, Vol. XLIX, p. 262.

27. Gandhi to Devdas Gandhi, 24 April and 11 May 1932 and 'Diary, 1932', in *CWMG*, Vol. XLIX, pp. 361, 423, 515, 516; see also Pandiri, *Bibliography*,

p. 301. Gandhi sent the book onto Devdas to read at the Ashram noting that while other books from Sinclair were at the Ashram, 'this new book has probably not arrived there'. Thus, inside prison, Gandhi managed to get reading material unusually quickly. See Gandhi to Devdas Gandhi, 24 April 1932, in *CWMG*, Vol. XLIX, pp. 361ff.

28. Upton Sinclair, *The Wet Parade* (London: T. Werner Laurie, 1931), MDL No. 416; Upton Sinclair, *Co-Op: A Novel of Living Together* (Pasadena, CA: Upton Sinclair, 1936), MDL No. 412, inside front inscribed, 'To M. K. Gandhi / with sincere regards / Upton Sinclair'; Upton Sinclair, *Depression Island* (Pasadena, CA: Upton Sinclair, 1935), MDL No. 413, inside front inscribed, 'To M. K. Gandhi / with best wishes / Upton Sinclair'; Upton Sinclair, *Oil: A Novel* (Pasadena, CA: Upton Sinclair, 1927), MDL No. 413; Upton Sinclair, *World's End* (Pasadena, CA: Upton Sinclair, 1940), MDL No. 417, inside front inscribed, 'To M. K. Gandhi / with best wishes / Upton Sinclair'. See I. R. B. Desai, 'Producing the Mahatma', Appendix III.

29. Upton Sinclair, *The Wet Paradise*, dramatized by Mina Maxfield and Lena Eggleston (Washington DC: Board of Temperance, Prohibition and Public Morals, M.E. Church, 1932), MDL No. 1385.

30. Ralph Fox, *The Colonial Policy of British Imperialism* (London: Martin Lawrence, 1933), MDL No. 1385.

31. Ibid. The inside cover of the book is inscribed to Nehru ['Bhai'] possibly from Amrit Kaur. Nehru has signed it ['J Nehru'] and dated it 1 May 1934. Above Nehru's signature, Desai has written the word 'From' and then signed his own named below Nehru's signature. The top of the page is stamped with the seal of Alipore Central Jail and the word 'PASSED' and an illegible signature is written within the centre of the seal.

32. Nehru's markings are all in gray pencil, whereas Desai's are in the light blue pencil which he used to mark many other volumes in his collection.

33. See, for example, Desai's copy of Fox, pp. 16, 18.

34. Ibid., p. 11.

35. See, for example, ibid., pp. 11, 18.

36. Timothy W. Ryback, *Hitler's Private Library* (New York: Knopf, 2008), p. xvii.

37. See I. R. B. Desai, 'Producing the Mahatma', Appendix IV, for an annotated list of some of the books Desai had in Belgaum jail.

38. Mahadev Desai, *The Gospel of Selfless Action, or The Gita According to Gandhi* (Ahmedabad: Navajivan, 1946).

39. M. K. Gandhi, *Discourses on the Gita*, trans. Valji Govindji Desai (Ahmedabad: Navajivan, 1960), p. 4.

40. Desai, *The Gospel of Selfless Action*, p. 4.

41. Most of the material relevant to his work on the 'Gita' arrived in February, 1934.

42. See I. R. B. Desai, 'Producing the Mahatma', Appendix IV.

43. Desai, *The Gospel of Selfless Action*, pp. 31–3.

44. Ibid., p. 5.

45. Ibid., p. 4.

46. See the quotation from Nehru at the opening of this chapter.

47. Ryback, *Hitler's Private Library*, pp. xiv, xv; Walter Benjamin, *Illuminations* (New York: Schocken, 1968), pp. 60, 69.

12
Remembering Reading: Memory, Books and Reading in South Africa's Apartheid Prisons, 1956–90

Archie L. Dick

Remembering reading is understood here as recalling, and as 're-membering' or putting back together fragments of the evidence of reading. The two meanings provide an opportunity to examine the *evidence of reading*, and to *read the evidence* in the case of political prisoners during South Africa's apartheid era. This chapter evaluates evidence of reading related to state memory, institutional memory and personal memory, and speculates on how together they shape collective memory. It also reads this evidence to show how political prisoners contested and created reading spaces, and explains what kind of reading culture they nurtured to resist the impact of apartheid.

Evidence from a recent case study demonstrates how a community of readers overcame the reading restrictions of political imprisonment.[1] The case study explains how political prisoners undermined censorship in the apartheid jails of South Africa. One source claims that between 1960 and 1990 about 80,000 people were detained without trial, but there were probably many more political prisoners in South Africa.[2] In 1978 alone there were 440 convicted political prisoners, mostly from the African National Congress (ANC) and Pan Africanist Congress (PAC).[3] Of these, 400 were on Robben Island and the rest were in Pretoria Local, Pretoria Central, Kroonstad and other prisons.[4]

To describe the reading practices of apartheid-era political prisoners, I have analysed government documents, institutional records, jail diaries, authorized biographies, autobiographies, prison memoirs, interviews, prison letters and visual material of more than fifty political prisoners and two prison censors. From information fragments the prisoners reconstructed news and life experiences denied to them by prison authorities, until access to reading material gradually improved and prison censorship relaxed in the 1980s. Reading in a way that subverted the intentions of the prison censors, in effect allowed the prisoners to continue their political struggle, although they also read for educational, cultural and recreational reasons.

This chapter is primarily a methodological analysis of the evidence of reading used, and explains how that evidence can be interpreted. The evidence is arranged according to their sources, using as a guide the idea of provenance as understood in archival theory. This is combined with Jonathan Rose's helpful list of sources for the historian of reading to produce three broad categories of evidence for remembering reading by and about apartheid political prisoners, namely state memory, institutional memory and reader's memory.[5] Although these categories are treated separately, there are instances where evidence from one category corroborates or contradicts evidence from another category. This triangulation of data improves accuracy and reliability.

State memory

Rose identifies police records as a source of evidence of reading.[6] There are other records of the criminal justice system that are also potential sources of evidence. There was no ambiguity in the apartheid state's understanding of the political effects of reading. Prosecutors at the first major apartheid-era political trial that lasted from 1956 to 1961, simplistically read the evidence of reading as evidence of treason. Just one year after the adoption of the Freedom Charter by the Congress of the People at Kliptown in Soweto, 156 people representing a complete cross-section of South African society were each charged with, but later acquitted of, high treason.[7] The infamous Treason Trial at which they appeared, produced an impressive archive or library of reading material.

Security police kept meticulous notebooks to record political meetings, and to produce lists of books seized during raids of the homes and offices of political activists. In this way, about 18,000 pages of documents of all kinds were confiscated and presented at the trial as exhibits and evidence of a communist-inspired conspiracy to foment revolution in South Africa.[8] An archives inventory of the Treason Trial reveals some idea of the amount and range of the seized documents.[9] Indiscriminate judgement was passed on this reading material by the state's 'star witness' Andrew Murray, a Professor of Philosophy at the University of Cape Town, and an expert on communist doctrine. He would open a book and condemn it with terse phrases like 'Straight from the shoulder of Communism', or 'Contains Communist matter', or 'Communist Propaganda'.[10]

Even the catering notices 'Soup without meat' and 'Soup with meat' taken from the kitchen of the Congress of the People were submitted as evidence of possibly disguised communist slogans. One of the Treason Trial defendants, Lionel Forman, secretly co-authored an account of proceedings during the trial itself. He recalled that the prosecution spent several weeks of the preparatory examination handing in the thousands of documents as exhibits. Excerpts from the documents were read to the court in the solemn tone normally reserved for 'Show the jury the murder weapon'.[11] But copies of Forman's book, which was banned, were read and autographed by the political prisoners in the holding cells below the Magistrate's court.[12]

Examples of lists of books with the names and signatures of the security policemen and political activists, the titles of the books, dates and times of raids can also be found in the trial records of individuals. The records of the Rivonia Trial of 1963 to 1964 produced Nelson Mandela's booklet *How to be a Good Communist*, by Liú Shàoqí, and *Born of the People* – a first-hand account of the guerrilla uprising in the Philippines ghost-written by William Pomeroy – together with Mandela's study notes.[13] Denis Goldberg, who was sentenced with Mandela but who was held in Pretoria Central Prison because he was classified as white, indicated during a cross-examination in the trial of fellow prisoner Harold Strachan (1965), that even the *Encyclopaedia Britannica* was considered subversive.[14]

These practices continued into the 1980s. At the trial of Carl Niehaus (1982), a list of documents compiled by a security policeman included five placards, a bag of pamphlets, and 'No to Bantustans' stickers found in a refrigerator on the veranda of his home during a raid.[15] Five years into his prison sentence, Niehaus declared in an affidavit that the quality of prison library services was poor and uncertain, in spite of annual reports of the Prisons Department that proudly carried information and photographs of library services and literacy classes.[16] The reports failed to mention discrimination in these services according to race, gender, language and category of prisoner.

The apartheid state's obsession with documenting what its citizens were reading was tied to its obsession with reading this material in very specific ways. The prosecutors in Quentin Jacobsen's trial tried to show links between his political activities and the contents of *The Anarchist's Cookbook* and other banned books seized during his arrest. Jill Ogilvie, an unassuming reference librarian of the Johannesburg Public Library who was subpoenaed to court during the trial, read out a list of titles available in the library similar to those found in Jacobsen's possession.[17] The charges against Jacobsen were subsequently withdrawn.

The catalogues and accession registers of prison libraries was another source of evidence of reading, but as long as they were maintained by prison warders they were unreliable, amusingly so at times. At Pretoria Central Prison, for example, very little could be traced in Chief Warder Du Preez's catalogue of purchased books because most books were filed under the letter 'T' since so many titles started with the definite article 'The'. This catalogue also described William Shakespeare's *The Tempest* as science fiction, and the entry for *Romeo and Juliet* appeared as 'author anonymous'.[18]

Although prison censors' official reports are not easy to trace, a hand-written list of censorship stipulations intended for political prisoner Roland Hunter shows what kinds of reading restrictions were enforced. For example, the police station Commander decided what was and what was not objectionable, and all politics and news from outside was strictly forbidden.[19] The apartheid state's view was that isolation would lead to rehabilitation. These orders and regulations, when not breached through corruption and smuggling, were interpreted and applied more or less rigidly by different officials and censor officers. The Robben Island Prison censor officer James Gregory believed that censorship laws were harsh and wrong; he gradually relaxed the system of censorship of letters and newspapers. Personal accounts of the apartheid-era by prison and censor officials should be treated circumspectly, though, as the recent controversy surrounding the veracity of Gregory's book cautions.[20]

The apartheid state was determined to discover and control what their citizens and opponents were thinking, and produced a large body of evidence of reading. It generated trial records, police notebooks, subpoenas, legal records, prison regulations, library reports, catalogues, and censor guides and reports. All of these can be richly rewarding when read with other evidence. Prisoners' diaries and biographies can colour in these dry state records to provide a more complete and livelier account. The apartheid state's memory reveals its paranoid suspicion of the effects of reading, and of the use of experts and authorities in its criminal justice system to consolidate censorship.

Institutional memory

What Rose identifies as records of educational institutions and sociological surveys, can be understood collectively as the evidence of institutions.[21] This move brings into consideration the records of organizations, associations, and in this case, informal groups with an interest in political prisoner welfare such as the International Committee of the

Red Cross, the United Nations, Amnesty International, the International Defence and Aid Fund, the Lawyers Commission for human rights in South Africa, educational and legal institutions and concerned citizen groups.

Institutional records can be mined for evidence of reading in both straightforward and creative ways. The special *Red Cross Investigation* into South African prisons in 1967 contained the testimony of political prisoners like Dennis Brutus who bluntly contradicted official claims about access to books.[22] In 1964, prison authorities had claimed that there were 4,960 books available in the Robben Island Prison Library, supplemented from Provincial Libraries on a loan scheme.[23] Brutus pointed out that there were only about a thousand books in a large cell in the General Section and that prisoners 'passed and looked longingly at the window but never got any books from this section'.[24] It was only subsequent visits by Red Cross officials and parliamentarians like Helen Suzman that pressured South African prison authorities to make good on their claims.

An empirical survey conducted by concerned academics in 1984 showed that only about half of the 176 respondents held in detention had access to some reading.[25] More detailed information can be obtained through an inventive approach to the records of educational institutions. Prison authorities granted study privileges to political prisoners after sustained pressure from concerned human rights bodies and from prisoners themselves. Many took the opportunity to enrol for correspondence courses at colleges and universities to start or carry on their education.

For those who enrolled at the correspondence University of South Africa (UNISA) there are available records of the degrees, the required subjects, the study guides, and the reading lists of required and recommended titles, and sometimes even the written assignments of the prisoners. The mini-dissertation on libraries and information written by Denis Goldberg reveals his wide-ranging and meticulous reading, as well as his political interpretation of the topic.[26] Some political prisoners used university studies as a way of obtaining books for their own political, cultural and recreational interests. In their autobiographies, political prisoners confirm this, and point out that those who already had university degrees used the subject registrations of enrolled fellow prisoners to order a wide range of books for personal use.[27]

There was evidence of reading in the records of legal applications brought on behalf of political prisoners to challenge the prohibition of reading and to protest poor library services. In the case of Rossouw *v.* Albie Sachs in 1964, a court decision to allow reading and writing material to political prisoners held in detention was cynically reversed. Sachs's own jail diary fills in some of the details. At first, he was only given a Bible and he carefully rationed his reading so that he could stretch its use as far as possible.[28] Before the court decision was overturned, he had read widely and considered anything less than 500 pages to be a short story.

Sachs enjoyed such 'long books' as Miguel de Cervantes's *Don Quixote*, Thomas Mann's *Buddenbrooks*, Irving Stone's *The Agony and the Ecstasy* and James Michener's *Hawaii*. He also wanted to read 'books alive with people' instead of abstract books of philosophy, or politics or criticism.[29] In a case brought against the Minister of Prisons, Police and Justice in 1977 by Denis Goldberg and seven others to get access to newspapers at Pretoria Central Prison, Goldberg prepared a list that included women's magazines (*Fair Lady*) and sports journals (*Sports Illustrated*) that were 'politically censored'. He was forbidden from giving this list to the lawyer who would argue their case, and because tape recorders were also forbidden he had to communicate everything orally for the lawyer to write down during visits. In the end, the case was successful and the court record listed several magazine titles that were censored. After sixteen years in the Pretoria prison, political prisoners finally got access to newspapers.[30]

The work of informal groups of concerned citizens that supplied reading material to political prisoners can also be a valuable source of evidence. How these groups operated is still mostly unknown, and evidence is sparse. When Albie Sachs was allowed to read and write, for example, he explained how a police constable would take his list of books to the local library. The assistance of the librarian helped to save him from a breakdown during his first spell of detention. Sachs's reference to this 'unknown' librarian led me to consult the Cape Town City Library Annual Reports, and after a few telephone calls I confirmed that the librarian in question was the late J. P. Nowlan. The search for this 'unknown' librarian also revealed that he was a fellow librarianship student of retired librarian Colette Thorne, who had written letters to Albie Sachs and Denis Goldberg while they were in prison. In an interview, she mentioned that there were informal letter-writing campaigns by politically sympathetic citizens to ease the isolation of political prisoners, and slip news from outside past the prison censors.[31]

Some librarians used their institution's infrastructure to supply subversive reading to political prisoners. Records of such actions could have invited state sanction on institutions during the apartheid period, but they are now available materially and personally. One of Robben Island's qualified prison librarians, Sedick Isaacs, told me in an interview that a librarian (Mrs Haslam) whom he knew at the University of Cape Town Library sent boxes of books after he had made a written request for material for the prison library. The books included Karl Marx's *Das Kapital*, which the prison censor vetting the books considered to be acceptable because it was a book 'about money'. A balanced supply of communist and anti-communist literature from Mrs Haslam allowed Isaacs to develop the library collection.[32]

The evidence of reading produced by institutions in the shape of records of special investigations, scientific surveys, educational reading lists of required and recommended books and journal articles, written assignments, legal records, the testimony of members of concerned citizen groups, and of librarians secretly using institutional facilities can be appreciated in interesting ways. Institutional memory of political prisoners' reading shows that apartheid was an unstable system that changed over time, and that its prison censorship and rehabilitation policies were undermined by elements of civil society.

Reader's memory

I have collected Rose's sources of memoirs, diaries, commonplace books, oral history and iconography under the category of the reader's memory.[33] Many publications about and by ex-political prisoners have appeared since 1990; they contain brief and sometimes lengthy sections on reading. Each type of source presents its own challenges for the historian of reading, but it is possible to assess their credibility through cross-checking with other sources because they cover the same period, and they deal with similar experiences.

Autobiographies and biographies published before and after 1990, make up the largest group of evidence. The autobiographies yield evidence of the personal impact of specific reading material on prisoners during emotionally low periods, and in solitary confinement. Some ex-prisoners said that this is often what prevented them from psychological breakdowns. Tim Jenkin's account of the successful and daring breakout from Pretoria Central Prison, on the other hand, is vivid evidence of reading and high drama. He says that Henri Charrière's *Papillon* – a story about a prison escape – taught him a number of valuable lessons that guided his thinking and actions.[34]

Jail diaries and private correspondence provide insights into the prisoners' day-to-day reading lives. The sudden tightening or relaxation of prison censorship and the suspension of study privileges were unpredictable and frustrating to serious readers. Although it is unclear if this was his motive, it is possible to pinpoint the exact day when Raymond Suttner wrote that he read a passage from Antonio Gramsci's *Letters from Prison* saying that a political prisoner must squeeze blood even from a stone, and that every book can be useful to read. (As it happens, it is possible also to trace the exact day when Gramsci wrote these lines.[35]) The dates from Fatima Meer's jail diary, on the other hand, reveals how long prison authorities delayed before giving her the academic books she had requested to prepare for sociology lectures she would present after her release. Her diary also confirms that the book *Is South Africa a Police State?* was held back.[36]

Personal files, archives and reading records can link titles with specific prisoners, describe general reading interests, and identify actions on censored books. The personal files of political prisoners list the titles of books purchased by prisoners while serving their sentences, although many prisoners chose to donate them to the prison library when released. A popularity poll taken by Sedick Isaacs identified that *National Geographic* was the most popular magazine among Robben Island political prisoners in the 1970s.[37] A borrowers' register kept by another qualified prisoner-librarian, Ahmed Kathrada, indicated that at Pollsmoor Maximum Security Prison Library, Sergeant Brand had 'taken away' *Transvaal Episode* by H. Bloom on 28 May 1984, and André Brink's *Looking on Darkness* on 12 November 1984. It shows also that Menán Du Plessis's *A State of Fear*, which deals with the states of emergency in South Africa, was returned to the library by a prison censor on 21 May 1985.[38]

Archival records include the scrapbooks and copybooks containing extracts from selected sources that were used secretly for political education among political prisoners on Robben Island. Ahmed Kathrada's own commonplace book reveals the most detailed accounts and records of the private reading of a single South African political prisoner. They are a kind of intellectual biography, and they demonstrate what some political prisoners could and did eventually read.[39]

Visual material is especially helpful in recalling and recreating the atmosphere and circumstances in which reading occurred. Fatima Meer's colour painting of her prison cell shows self-constructed book shelves with a few books, newspapers and magazines. It depicts not so much the cramped segregation cell provided by prison authorities as her determination to create a personal reading space for herself in a forbidding locale.[40] The attempt to portray a similar reading space in a photograph of Nelson Mandela's cell is however a piece of apartheid state propaganda for a special visit by inspectors and journalists to Robben Island in 1977.[41] The neat rows of books on bookshelves belie the chaos of unannounced raids and suspension of reading privileges that characterized everyday prison life.

Films and documentaries about prison censorship can provide more vivid evidence, and reach a wider audience. A short documentary film called *Hidden Books* includes a segment on ex-political prisoner Hugh Lewin in an interview about his banned book on prison life, *Bandiet*.[42] This kind of oral evidence introduces the voice of the ex-political prisoner as reader and writer, but for all its media advantages as evidence it still prevents direct interaction between the source and the historian of reading.

Such engagement becomes possible in interviews. I conducted interviews with ex-political prisoners, three of which are discussed here. It was not easy to obtain or conduct these interviews. Access was not always easy, and only personal recommendations and introductions, as well as sheer persistence made the interviews possible. The interviews brought back haunting memories for the interviewees, and bothered me for having been the cause of them. One ex-prisoner was hesitant to speak in too much detail while another was unusually specific, but all were helpful.

The interviews added new evidence, substantiated the print record, and explained partial evidence found elsewhere. Methodological challenges included the consequences of not sticking to a uniform set of questions; poor or inaccurate memory; unsuitable interview locations that often led to interruptions; and technical difficulties with recording equipment.

Sedick Isaacs was on Robben Island from 1964 to 1977. I learned from him about a form of censorship by political prisoners themselves when anti-communists stole the communist books and communists stole the anti-communist books from the Robben Island prison library. Ironically, unexpected cell raids by prison guards restored all these books to the library, which Isaacs used as an open space for debate and discussion.

Isaacs also taught vertical or speed-reading, which explains accounts by other prisoners of how they rapidly extracted information from smuggled newspapers, and transcribed and circulated the contents throughout the Robben Island political prison community.[43] This explained Isaacs' claim that he had read about a thousand library books per year.[44] Isaacs taught reading in Robben Island's 'primary school', where he taught South African President Jacob Zuma how to read.[45]

I was able to interview Denis Goldberg after I discovered his librarianship mini-dissertation, which he had written more than twenty years earlier, and offered to return it to him. Goldberg was arrested in 1963, and served twenty-two years in Pretoria Local and Central Prisons. In the interview, I learned about his deep love of books and voracious reading appetite, which later led to his work with a charity organization after his release, work that still brings thousands of books to children in South Africa's informal settlements today. This charity had also supplied books to the libraries of universities that were financially disadvantaged during the apartheid era, such as the Medical University of South Africa, the former University of Transkei and Fort Hare University.

Goldberg was able to write UNISA examination answers with footnotes that identified authors, titles and publishers of books. He numbered the pages of examination answer books and then made cross-references back and forth across pages, and across examination questions. One of the explanations for these intellectual feats was that he had constructed a sophisticated index in the form of a make-shift filing cabinet, based on the bibliographies and reading lists in the UNISA study guides as sources for index entries. The files consisted of little cards on which the entries were written, and then punched in the middle. These cards were held together by wires that used the tops of toothpaste tubes as screws on each end. Even during security raids by prison guards the cards remained intact. For Goldberg, the UNISA library service was a 'sanity saver'. During his studies, he also wrote an essay on censorship but this has not yet been located.[46]

Marcus Solomons was detained in 1985 and held at the Victor Verster Prison before going to Robben Island. His interest in books and reading was shaped by the example of his father who was an Indian waiter, and an avid reader. His early reading was the common fare that circulated in the working-class townships of Grahamstown in the Eastern Cape, where he grew up. These included Westerns, James Hadley Chase thrillers, newspapers and comics. At Trafalgar High School in Cape Town, he met the influential teacher Cosmo Pieterse who was also a well-known actor. Pieterse introduced books to Solomons and his fellow learners through theatre, cinema and other visual means. The themes were always about the great working-class struggles, such as the Russian and Chinese revolutions.

This approach rekindled his reading appetite. Solomons recalled how he read novels as a way to understand history. These included Charles Dickens's *A Tale of Two Cities* as a way of getting to grips with the French Revolution. He read also Émile Zola's work in order to understand the revolutions of 1848, as well as other works of Dickens. While in detention, he borrowed and read a book that belonged to a fellow detainee, Llewellyn MacMaster, and which influenced his political work. Written by Gustavo

Gutierrez, it dealt with Christian communities of common people in Latin America, and explained how to raise levels of political awareness.

On Robben Island he also registered at UNISA, so that access to books would give him access to the outside world. During his first year studies in history he ordered and read Isaac Deutscher's three-volume history of the life of Trotsky, even though it was recommended only for third-year students. He had to fabricate a story for the prison warder in charge of studies in order to obtain these volumes. The other book that had a huge impact on him in prison was Tolstoy's *War and Peace*. He said that the culture of reading nurtured on Robben Island was integrated into other cultural activities. Political prisoners were encouraged to read the history of sports personalities, about ballet, and many other subjects outside of politics.[47]

The documented memories of political prison readers disclose the interior aspects of their reading experiences, and the interview evidence offers glimpses into even more private spaces that reading filled during traumatic times in their lives.

Reading the evidence

Rose argues that historians of reading have drawn on all the sources of evidence he listed to test theories of reading.[48] Another direction in which to proceed is to show how the evidence 'intersects with historical issues of broad social or cultural significance', as Martyn Lyons has argued, following the examples of Robert Darnton and Roger Chartier.[49] Evidence of the reading practices of apartheid-era political prisoners offers an opportunity to introduce a reading response to apartheid and censorship. The culture of reading nurtured in apartheid jails reveals hidden aspects of the South African liberation struggle, and shows that empirical analyses of intellectual resistance to apartheid should draw also on the evidence of reading. An outline of how this can proceed is presented here, although the details will have to be added by others.

In difficult circumstances, and with minimal state and institutional support, political prisoners nurtured a reading culture, in which their reading practices might be summarized as having been *survivalist, substitutive* and *subversive*.

Survivalist

Political prisoners mixed silent reading, reading aloud, intensive reading, extensive reading, self-rationed reading and speed reading to survive a bleak and oppressive reading environment. At the same time, they tried to maintain and consolidate their political identities through their books and reading. There were numerous examples of cooperation between rival groups, and in some prisons ANC and PAC members shared newspapers.[50] Sedick Isaacs pointed out that in the early 1960s there was a tolerant attitude on Robben Island, and talks on communism and anti-communism were attended by all. There were times, however, when tensions and intolerance surfaced, as for example when the PAC said that no foreign ideology can be allowed in Africa. As a result, each political organization started its own political education meetings, but cultural activities such as sport, art, music and the prison library were shared by all.[51] The library collection was itself the target of propaganda campaigns by rival groups that stole books, indicating some of the reading complexities of the liberation struggle.

Substitutive

Immaterial texts and ideas could be separated from and substitute for the material book, and circulate undetected by prison authorities. Political and secular educational activities on Robben Island could proceed with and without actual teaching materials. There are extant copies of notebooks in the Robben Island archives that were used for political education and that required clandestine reading.[52] News and instruction were also shared orally. At one point, crude but inventive literacy and communication tools included the brown paper of cement bags for writing paper, sticks for pens, and milk for ink. The milk would dry almost immediately and the paper would look blank. Disinfectant to clean prison cells was sprayed on the dried milk and made the writing reappear. Nelson Mandela remembers that they did not receive milk regularly and had to wait until someone was diagnosed with an ulcer.[53] Reading also substituted for an abnormal social life. As Raymond Suttner explains: 'Psychologically, we have needs that can't be fulfilled in real life, and . . . reading had to substitute for a normal social life.'[54] 'Prison', Jean Middleton contends more strongly, 'creates a social and emotional, even a sensory, desert . . . There was no real life worth speaking of; I had only reading, nothing else, to fulfil the need for new experience, and I have never read with such relish and delight.'[55]

Subversive

Reading both banned books and officially approved books in unusual ways subverted the aims of censors and political authorities. Underqualified censors let in many books unknowingly while many actually needed were stopped. Neville Alexander admits that he read books in prison that he would never have had the time or chance to read outside.

He read classics of European literature, Gibbon, Shakespeare, Dickens, African history, international law, economics, languages and lots of German literature, and adds: 'I had more banned books inside prison than I ever had outside.'[56] Forbidden and 'approved' journals and magazines were read in interesting ways. Most of the apartheid propaganda organs such as *SA Panorama*, *Lantern*, *Archimedes*, *Bantu Inkubela* (Homelands), *Fiat Lux* (Indian Affairs) and *Alpha* (Coloured Affairs) were found in prison libraries. Political prisoners read them 'critically' by simply standing 'the news on its head', so that if an article in a government journal argued that Bantu Education was being accepted, they concluded that it was in fact being resisted.

The combined qualities of this survivalist, substitutive and subversive reading culture come together in examples like that of Robert Harold Strachan who was randomly given a history book with some of its pages already torn out to roll cigarettes, and smoked away by fellow prisoners. He simply read these gaps imaginatively, creating alternative narratives and outcomes because, as he said, 'most history seems to be such prostheses anyway'.[57] Without too much difficulty, a fairly accurate indication of all the significant titles and numbers of books and magazines read by political prisoners, as well as those that were censored by prison authorities can be ascertained from available sources. In this way, it is possible also to identify surprising key texts used in some political organizations.

Fikile Bam noted that the *Yu Chi Chan* Club, which was started to study guerrilla warfare, used Deneys Reitz's *Commando: A Boer Journal of the Boer War*. At his trial, state prosecutors ignored this book and focused their attention instead on the books of Mao Zedong and Che Guevara.[58] Omar Badsha, who was detained several times, recalled in an interview that as a young man in the 1960s he was told to read chapter fourteen of John Steinbeck's *Grapes of Wrath*, just as his political mentors had done at Congress Party Schools in the 1930s.[59] The chapter deals with organizing the poor, and the voice of the grassroots. This kind of empirical evidence can help to consolidate a list of the key texts that shaped the ideas and strategies of smaller and larger political organizations involved in South Africa's liberation struggle.

Conclusion

What we remember collectively about the reading practices of apartheid-era political prisoners is shaped by the evidence we trace, and how we read that evidence. State memory identifies official efforts to align reading and censorship with a belief in separation and isolation as a way to rehabilitate political prisoners. This was compatible with the apartheid government's policy of racial segregation, international isolation and separate development as a way to solve the problems of South Africa's population diversity. Institutional and readers' memory, on the other hand, affirm efforts by civil society and political prisoners to read in order to develop and connect with each other and with the outside world in ways that resisted separation and isolation, and that continued the liberation struggle. Through their reading, political prisoners resumed their personal and social lives, and re-assessed their political convictions and those of others. The evidence of reading can improve the historiography of intellectual resistance to apartheid and censorship.

Notes and references

1. Archie Dick, '"Blood from stones": censorship and the reading practices of South African political prisoners, 1960–1990', *Library History*, 24 (2008), 1–22.
2. 'Human Rights Commission, Violence in Detention', in *People and Violence in South Africa*, ed. Brian McKendrick and Wilma Hoffmann (Cape Town: Oxford University Press, 1990), pp. 410–3; *A Crime against Humanity: Analyzing the Repression of the Apartheid State*, ed. Max Coleman (Cape Town: David Philip, 1998), pp. 43–67.
3. The African National Congress (ANC) was founded in 1912 as the South African Native National Congress. It started as a moderate even conservative organization, but opted for an armed struggle against the National Party regime after being banned in 1960. Its military wing was called *umKhonto we Sizwe* (Spear of the nation); see *Reader's Digest Illustrated History of South Africa: The Real Story*, ed. Christopher Saunders (Cape Town: Reader's Digest Association, 1989), p. 486. The Pan-Africanist Congress (PAC) was established in 1959 by breakaway Africanist members of the ANC under the Presidency of Robert Sobukwe. Its military wing was called *Poqo* (alone or pure); see *Reader's Digest Illustrated History*, p. 490.
4. Jürgen Schadeberg, *Voices From Robben Island* (Randburg: Ravan Press, 1994), p. 48.
5. Jonathan Rose, 'The history of education as the history of reading', *History of Education*, 36 (2007), 595–605.
6. Ibid., p. 596.
7. The Congress of the People was organized by the Congress Alliance, led by the African National Congress, and adopted the *Freedom Charter* at Kliptown on 26 and 27 June 1955; see *The Penguin Concise Dictionary of Historical and Political Terms*, ed. Jacob P. Brits (London: Penguin Books, 1995), p. 55.
8. '18,000 pages of documents in treason trial', in *Treason Trial, 1957–1961: Newspaper Clippings; Scrapbook ex libris the Presiding Judge, F. L. H. Rumpf* (PLACE: Body & Mind Foundation, 1997), unnumbered.

9. Records relating to the 'Treason Trial', File AD1812, Historical Papers, University of the Witwatersrand Library, Johannesburg. For a detailed record, see Thomas Karis, *The Treason Trial in South Africa: A Guide to the Microfilm Record of the Trial* (Stanford, CA: Hoover Institute, Stanford University, 1965).

10. Helen Joseph, *If this be Treason: Helen Joseph's Dramatic Account of the Treason Trial, 1956–1961* (Johannesburg: Contra, 1998), p. 47.

11. Lionel Forman, *A Trumpet from the Housetops: The Selected Writings of Lionel Forman*, ed. Sadie Forman and André Odendaal (London: Zed Books, 1992), p. 108.

12. Joseph, *If this be Treason*, p. 17.

13. Rusty Bernstein, *Memory Against Forgetting: Memoirs from a Life in South African Politics, 1938–1964* (London: Viking, 1999), p. 229.

14. Prison trials: State *versus* Strachan, 1965, File A643, Historical Papers, p. 2848.

15. Carl Niehaus (re: possession of banned publications, 1982), File AK2532, Historical papers, p. 1.

16. Carl Niehaus and four others (re: conditions in Pretoria Maximum Security Prison, 1987), File AK2532, Historical Papers.

17. Quentin Jacobsen, *Solitary in Johannesburg* (London: Michael Joseph, 1973), p. 244.

18. Baruch Hirson, *Revolutions in My Life* (Johannesburg: Witwatersrand University Press, 1995), p. 207.

19. Censorship Provisions contained in Rules handed to Roland Hunter on 17-2-1987, File AK2532, Historical Papers (handwritten in Afrikaans).

20. James Gregory, with Bob Graham, *Goodbye Bafana: Nelson Mandela, My Prisoner, My Friend* (London: Headline, 1995), pp. 126–7, 239.

21. Rose, 'The history of education as the history of reading', pp. 596–7.

22. *South African Prisons and The Red Cross Investigation: An Examination by International Defence and Aid Fund, With Prisoners' Testimony* (London: Christian Action Publications, 1967), p. 27.

23. Before that, a prison psychologist had supplied books for a library in a specially converted cell in the Zinktronk. The books, which included some political works (English biographies) and classical novels (including Dickens), were heavily censored. See Moses Dlamini, *Hell-Hole Robben Island: Reminiscences of a Political Prisoner in South Africa* (Trenton, NJ: Africa World Press, 1984), p. 171.

24. *South African Prisons and The Red Cross Investigation*, p. 27.

25. Don Foster, *Detention and Torture in South Africa: Psychological, Legal & Historical Studies* (Cape Town: David Philip, 1987), pp. 98, 201.

26. The author has a copy of this mini-dissertation.

27. Timothy Jenkin, *Inside Out: Escape from Pretoria Prison* (Bellevue: Jacana, 2003), pp. 182–3; Hirson, *Revolutions in My Life*, pp. 208–9.

28. Foster, *Detention and Torture*, p. 98.

29. Albie Sachs, *The Jail Diary of Albie Sachs* (Cape Town: David Philip, 1990), pp. 165, 250.

30. E-mail to the author from Denis Goldberg, 14 April 2006.

31. Interview with Colette Thorne, 14 November 2007.

32. Interview with Sedick Isaacs, 9 April 2008.

33. Rose, 'The history of education as the history of reading', pp. 597–9.

34. Jenkin, *Inside Out*, pp. 77–8, 259.

35. Raymond Suttner, *Inside Apartheid's Prison: Notes and Letters of Struggle* (Pietermaritzburg: University of Natal Press, 2001), pp. 177–8. For Gramsci's original quotation, see *Letters from Prison: Antonio Gramsci*, ed. Frank Rosengarten, 2 vols, trans. Raymond Rosenthal (New York: Columbia University Press, 1994), I, 262–3.

36. Fatima Meer, *Prison Diary: One Hundred and Thirteen Days, 1976* (Cape Town: Kwela Books, 2001), pp. 104, 127.

37. Sedick Isaacs Collection, Box 48, Robben Island Archives, Mayibuye Centre, University of the Western Cape, Bellville.

38. Ahmed Kathrada Collection, File 13.4 (fiction books), Robben Island Archives.

39. *A Free Mind: Ahmed Kathrada's Notebook From Robben Island*, ed. Sahm Venter, (Johannesburg: Jacana Media, 2005); Ahmed Kathrada, *A Simple Freedom: The Strong Mind of Robben Island Prisoner, no. 468/64* (Highlands North: Wild Dog Press, 2008).

40. Meer, *Prison Diary*, painting no. 3 between pp. 64 and 65.

41. 'Nelson Mandela's cell', *South African Panorama*, 22 (July 1977), p. 2.

42. Hugh Lewin, *Bandiet: Seven Years in a South African Prison* (London: Heinemann, 1974). The documentary film *Hidden Books* was screened by the South African Broadcasting Corporation. A copy of the DVD version is available from the author.

43. *Island in Chains: Prisoner 885/63: Ten Years on Robben Island as told by Indres Naidoo to Albie Sachs* (London: Penguin Books, 1982), pp. 155–6.

44. Alan Wieder, *Voices from Cape Town Classrooms: Oral Histories of Teachers who Fought Apartheid* (New York: Peter Lang, 2003), p. 69.

45. Interview with Sedick Isaacs, 9 April 2008.

46. Interview with Denis Goldberg, 5 March 2003.

47. Interview with Marcus Solomons, 12 November 2007.

48. Rose, 'The history of education as the history of reading', pp. 599–605.

49. Martyn Lyons, *Reading and Writing Practices in Nineteenth-Century France* (Toronto: University of Toronto Press, 2008), p. 11.

50. Letlapa Mphahlele, *Child of this Soil: My Life as a Freedom Fighter* (Cape Town: Kwela Books, 2002), p. 123.

51. Interview with Sedick Isaacs, 9 April 2008.

52. Govan Mbeki, *Learning from Robben Island: The Prison writings of Govan Mbeki* (London: James Currey, 1991).

53. Stanley Mogoba, *Stone, Steel, Sjambok: Faith on Robben Island*, ed. Theo Coggin (Johannesburg: Ziningweni Communications, 2003), p. 41; Nelson Mandela, *Long Walk to Freedom: The Autobiography of Nelson Mandela* (London: Abacus, 1994), p. 500.

54. Suttner, *Inside Apartheid's Prison*, pp. 92, 94.

55. Jean Middleton, *Convictions: A Woman Political Prisoner Remembers* (Randburg: Ravan Press, 1998), pp. 99, 87.

56. Neville Alexander, in Barbara Hutton, *Robben Island: Symbol of Resistance* (Johannesburg and Bellville: Sached Books and Mayibuye Books, 1994), p. 69.

57. Harold Strachan, *Make a Skyf Man!* (Johannesburg: Jacana, 2004), pp. 141–2.

58. Tom Lodge and Bill Nasson, *All Here, And Now: Black Politics in South Africa in the 1980s* (Cape Town: Ford Foundation; David Philip, 1991), p. 307.

59. Interview with Omar Badsha, 11 October 2008.

Further Reading and Weblinks

Selected books

Allan, David., *A Nation of Readers: The Lending Library in Georgian England* (London: The British Library, 2008)

Andersen, Jennifer and Elizabeth Sauer (eds), *Books and Readers in Early Modern England: Material Studies* (Philadelphia: University of Pennsylvania Press, 2002)

Badia, Janet and Jennifer Phegley (eds), *Reading Women: Literary Figures and Cultural Icons from the Victorian Age to the Present* (Toronto: University of Toronto Press, 2006)

Boyarin, Jonathan (ed.), *Ethnography of Reading* (Berkeley: University of California Press, 1993)

Brokaw, Cynthia J. and Kai-wing Chow (eds), *Printing and Book Culture in Late Imperial China* (Berkeley: University of California Press, 2005)

Brooks, Jeffrey, *When Russia Learned to Read: Literacy and Popular Literature, 1861–1917* (Evanston: Northwestern University Press, 2003)

Brown, Matthew P., *The Pilgrim and the Bee: Reading Rituals and Book Culture in Early New England* (Philadelphia: University of Pennsylvania Press, 2007)

Chartier, Roger, *The Order of Books: Readers, Authors, and Libraries in Europe between the Fourteenth and Eighteenth Centuries*, trans. by Lydia G. Cochrane (Stanford: Stanford University Press, 1994)

Clanchy, Michael T., *From Memory to Written Record: England 1066–1307* (London: Edward Arnold, 1979)

Gamsa, Mark, *The Reading of Russian Literature in China: A Moral Example and Manual of Practice* (Basingstoke: Palgrave Macmillan, 2010)

Ghosh, Anindita, *Power in Print: Popular Publishing and the Politics of Language and Culture in a Colonial Society, 1778–1905* (New Delhi: Oxford University Press, 2006)

Gilmore, William J., *Reading Becomes a Necessity of Life: Material and Cultural Life in Rural New England, 1780–1835* (Knoxville: University of Tennessee Press, 1989)

Griswold, Wendy, *Bearing Witness: Readers, Writers, and the Novel in Nigeria* (Princeton: Princeton University Press, 2000)

Hackel, Heidi Brayman and Catherine E. Kelly (eds), *Reading Women: Literacy, Authorship, and Culture in the Atlantic World, 1500–1800* (Philadelphia: University of Pennsylvania Press, 2008)

Jackson, H. J., *Marginalia: Readers Writing in Books* (New Haven: Yale University Press, 2001)

Johnson, William A. and Holt N. Parker (eds), *Ancient Literacies: The Culture of Reading in Greece and Rome* (Oxford: Oxford University Press, 2009)

Joshi, Priya, *In Another Country: Colonialism, Culture and the English Novel in India* (New York: Columbia University Press 2002)

Kaufman, Paul, *Borrowings from the Bristol Library, 1773–1784: A Unique Record of Reading Vogues* (Charlottesville: Bibliographical Society of the University of Virginia, 1960)

Lyons, Martyn, *Reading and Writing Practices in Nineteenth-Century France* (Toronto: University of Toronto Press, 2008)

Lyons, Martyn, *A History of Reading and Writing in the Western World* (Basingstoke: Palgrave Macmillan, 2010)

Lyons, Martyn with Lucy Taksa, *Australian Readers Remember: An Oral History of Reading 1890–1930* (Melbourne: Oxford University Press, 1992)

Manguel, Alberto, *A History of Reading* (London: Harper Collins, 1996)

Newell, Stephanie, *Literary Culture in Colonial Ghana: 'How to play the game of life'* (Bloomington: Indiana University Press, 2002)

Ramsay, David, *The History of South Carolina, from its first settlement in 1670 to the year 1808, in two volumes* (Charleston: privately printed, 1808)

Raven, James, Helen Small and Naomi Tadmor (eds), *The Practice and Representation of Reading in England* (Cambridge: Cambridge University Press, 1996)

Reuveni, Gideon, *Reading Germany: Literature and Consumer Culture in Germany before 1933*, trans. Ruth Morris (New York: Berghahn, 2006)

Ryback, Timothy W., *Hitler's Private Library* (New York: Knopf, 2008)

Sharpe, Kevin and Steven N. Zwicker (eds), *Reading, Society and Politics in Early Modern England* (Cambridge: Cambridge University Press, 2003)

Zboray, Ronald J. and Mary Saracino Zboray, *Everyday Ideas: Socioliterary Experience Among Antebellum New Englanders* (Knoxville: Tennessee University Press, 2006)

Selected articles

Bell, Bill, 'Bound for Botany Bay; or, what did the nineteenth-century convict read?' in Robin Myers, Michael Harris and Giles Mandelbrote (eds), *Against the Law: Crime, Sharp Practice and the Control of Print* (New Castle: Oak Knoll Press, 2004), 151–75

Cambers, Andrew and Michelle Wolfe, 'Reading, family religion, and evangelical identity in late Stuart England', *The Historical Journal*, 47 (2004), 875–96

Dick, Archie L., '"To make the people of South Africa proud of their membership of the great British Empire": home reading unions in South Africa, 1900–1914', *Libraries and Culture*, 40:1 (2005), 1–24

Gross, Robert A. 'Much instruction from little reading: books and libraries in Thoreau's Concord', *Proceedings of the American Antiquarian Society*, 97 (1987), 129–88

Higman, Francis, '"Without great effort, and with pleasure": sixteenth-century Genevan Bibles and reading practices', in *The Bible as Book: The Reformation*, ed. Orlaith O'Sullivan (London and New Castle: British Library and Oak Knoll Press, 2000), 115–22

Holt, Elizabeth M., 'Narrative and the reading public in 1870s Beirut', *Journal of Arabic Literature*, 40 (2009): 37–70

Johanningsmeier, Charles, 'Welcome guests or representatives of the "malodorous class": periodicals and their readers in American public libraries, 1876–1914', *Libraries and Culture*, 39:3 (2004): 260–92

Kloek, Joost, 'Reconsidering the reading revolution: the thesis of the "reading revolution" and a Dutch bookseller's clientele around 1800', *Poetics*, 26:6 (1999): 289–307

McDowell, Kate. 'Toward a history of children as readers', *Book History*, 12 (2009), 240–65

McHenry, Elizabeth, '"An association of kindred spirits": black readers and their reading rooms', Thomas Augst and Kenneth Carpenter (eds), *Institutions of Reading: The Social Life of Libraries in the United States* (Amherst: University of Massachusetts Press, 2007)

Molekamp, Femke, 'Using a collection to discover reading practices: the British Library Geneva Bibles and a history of their early modern readers', *Electronic British Library Journal*, article 10 (2006), 1–13

Murphy, Sharon, 'Imperial reading? The East India Company's lending libraries for soldiers, *c.*1819–1834', *Book History*, 12 (2009): 74–99

Naimark-Goldberg, Natalie, 'Reading and modernization: the experience of Jewish women in Berlin around 1800', *Nashim: A Journal of Jewish Women's Studies and Gender Issues*, 15 (2008): 58–87

Price, Leah, 'Reading: the state of the discipline', *Book History*, 7 (2004), 303–20

Radway, Janice, 'Reading is not eating: mass produced literature and the theoretical, methodological and political consequences of a metaphor', *Book Research Quarterly*, 2 (1986), 7–29

Todd, Emily B., 'Walter Scott and the nineteenth-century American literary marketplace: antebellum Richmond readers and the collected editions of the Waverley novels', *Papers of the Bibliographical Society of America*, 34 (1999), 495–517

Topham, Jonathan R., 'Scientific publishing and the reading of science in nineteenth-century Britain: a historiographical survey and guide to sources', *Studies in History and Philosophy of Science*, 31 (2000), 559–612

Selected weblinks

Bibliotheca Eruditionis: http://www.eruditio.hu/index_eng.html

British Fiction, 1800–1829: A Database of Production, Circulation & Reception: http://www.british-fiction.cf.ac.uk/

History of the Book Online: http://www.english.ox.ac.uk/hobo/

Labyrinth: Resources for Medieval Studies: http://labyrinth.georgetown.edu

The Library History Database: http://www.r-alston.co.uk/content/libraryhistory/

Making Books, Shaping Readers: http://www.ucc.ie/en/mbsr/

North American Women's Letters and Diaries, Colonial to 1950: http://solomon.nwld.alexanderstreet.com/

Oxford Dictionary of National Biography: http://www.oxforddnb.com/

The Reading Experience Database, 1450–1945: www.open.ac.uk/Arts/reading/UK/

Society for the History of Authorship, Reading and Publishing: http://www.sharpweb.org/

What Middletown Read: http://cms.bsu.edu/Academics/CentersandInstitutes/Middletown/Research/MiddletownRead.aspx

Women Writers and their Audiences: http://neww.huygens.knaw.nl/

Index

Page numbers for illustrations are given in bold. References to tables are indicated in brackets.